W9-DAK-319

"QUESTIONS OF SPECIAL URGENCY"

The Church in the Modern World
Two Decades after Vatican II

"QUESTIONS OF SPECIAL URGENCY"

The Church in the Modern World
Two Decades after Vatican II

JUDITH A. DWYER, S.S.J.
Editor

GEORGETOWN UNIVERSITY PRESS
WASHINGTON, D.C.

Library of Congress Cataloging-in-Publication Data
Main entry under title:

Questions of special urgency.

    1. Catholic Church—Doctrines—Addresses, essays, lectures. 2. Church and the world—Addresses, essays, lectures. 3. Vatican Council (2nd : 1962–1965) Constitutio pastoralis de ecclesia in mundo huius temporis—Addresses, essays, lectures. I. Dwyer, Judith A.
BX1751.2.Q48 1986   282'.09'048   86-218
ISBN 0-87840-434-1
ISBN 0-87840-425-2 (pbk.)

222214

CONTENTS

Part IV
Socioeconomic Life

Part V
War

Introduction

Vatican II's most forward-looking document, *The Pastoral Constitution on the Church in the Modern World*, frequently referred to by its Latin title, *Gaudium et Spes*, marks its twentieth anniversary today, December 7, 1985. This volume celebrates Vatican II's achievements by assessing, from the perspective of the two decades which have transpired since *Gaudium et Spes'* promulgation, that document's treatment of certain "questions of special urgency": marriage, culture, socioeconomics, politics, and peace. This volume also updates analysis of these questions by investigating, frequently from the viewpoint of the American Roman Catholic experience, the current state of these questions.

No issue is perhaps more controversial in the church today than that of marriage and the sexual, biomedical, and canonical problems related to it. I therefore deliberately tried to "situate the debate" on this particular issue by inviting Professor James Gaffney of Loyola University and Professor William E. May of The Catholic University of America to address this topic. It is no secret, among those who follow the current methodological debate within Roman Catholic moral theology, that Professors Gaffney and May approach marriage and its related problems from very different perspectives. It is my hope that in presenting both viewpoints, the reader will be able to assess for herself/himself the varying positions and their methodological underpinnings. This juxtapositioning of different approaches, a method which I used in my *The Catholic Bishops and Nuclear War* (Georgetown University Press), respects, in the spirit of Vatican II, one of the "signs of the times" of this era: debate, and sharp differences of opinion regarding marriage, generally, and sexual morality, specifically.

Professor James Gaffney cites "real progress" in the approach of *Gaudium et Spes* insofar as the document refused to subordinate the mutual love of spouses to their reproductive functioning. Equally important for Gaffney is the Council's tendency to view marriage in relation to family as a social achievement, to see the family not only as domestic community but as a vital component of larger society, and in general, to avoid "moral sexology" —the whole traditional array of

ostensibly rational norms that Roman Catholic officialdom has applied
to sexual behavior. He criticizes the document, however, for its failure
to examine adequately such issues as widowhood, the plight of orphans,
and overpopulation. Professor William E. May, noting that the church's
teaching on human dignity provides the context for its teaching on
marriage, inspects how Vatican II summarized, deepened, and developed the church's position on marriage and how subsequent
development occurs with Pope Paul VI's pronouncements and, in
particular, with those of Pope John Paul II. May presents marriage as a
person-affirming, love-enabling, and life-giving reality, one that has
God as its author from whom it has received its specifying goods or
ends.

In addition to the insights of Gaffney and May, Kathleen and James
McGinnis present some practical ways in which a Christian family can
incorporate the social teachings of the Catholic church. They concentrate heavily on the issues of materialism, individualism, racism,
sexism, militarism and violence and, in light of these problems, propose
a four-part strategy for overcoming them.

Professors Richard A. McCormick, S.J., and Anne E. Patrick,
S.N.J.M. investigate the question of culture and specifically, bioethical
and feminist issues dominant in the American culture. McCormick, of
the Kennedy Institute of Ethics at Georgetown University, presents the
framework for an approach to bioethical problems which *Gaudium et
Spes* establishes: the mandate that human activity be judged insofar as it
refers to the human person integrally and adequately considered, and
the emphasis on the church's duty to scrutinize the "signs of the times."
McCormick then goes on to inspect such current bioethical issues as the
role of the physician, the increasing depersonalization of health care,
the question of eugenics, and care of the dying. Anne E. Patrick,
assistant professor of religion at Carleton College, sees *Gaudium et Spes*
as a catalyst for Catholic feminist theology, since the changes which
have occurred since 1965 are, at least in part, a result of Vatican II.
Patrick, after citing the Council's key theological affirmations for this
topic, the essential equality of all persons and the recognition of a more
dynamic, historically conscious understanding of God's will for humanity, traces the women's movement into professional theological
circles. She then renders a "feminist reading" of *Gaudium et Spes*.

Professor John Langan, S.J. of Woodstock Theological Center and
Senator Patrick Leahy, United States Senator from the state of Vermont,
analyze and update the Council's treatment of the political sphere.
Langan contrasts *Gaudium et Spes'* vision with the pessimistic outlook of
Alasdair MacIntyre in his recent work, *After Virtue*. For Langan, the
Council's contributions are fourfold since it offers the human com-

munity a theological anthropology whose keystone is the dignity of the human person, Christian ideals, moral norms, and policy directions and recommendations. It is the task of Langan's chapter to investigate and develop that fourfold conciliar contribution. Leahy's chapter, an interview with the Senator conducted by John B. Breslin, S.J., Director of Georgetown University Press, assesses the impact of Vatican II on political life in general and on the United States political scene in particular. Leahy criticizes American individualism and the American citizen's failure to have a sense of history. Dominant throughout the interview are such topics as separation of church and state, the level of specificity appropriate for ecclesial pronouncements, and the notion of the "common good," as it applies to both the international and national community.

The impact of the Council's teaching on socioeconomics is the topic of chapters by Professors Manuel Velasquez and Daniel Finn. Velasquez, associate professor of philosophy at the University of Santa Clara, claims that the socioeconomic doctrine in *Gaudium et Spes* contains "a distillation of the best of the prior seventy-five years of the traditional church teaching on economic issues as well as, in embryo, the foundational ideas that emerged as major new themes during the two decades following Vatican II." Velasquez summarizes the Council's teaching on socioeconomic issues, investigates the roots of that teaching, and assesses conciliar impact on subsequent papal, liberationist, and North American episcopal documents. Finn, Dean of the School of Theology at Saint John's University, provides an overview of *Gaudium et Spes'* vision of socioeconomic life in the context of Catholic social teaching prior to Vatican II, and reviews subsequent developments in the church and the world which are pertinent to the topic. He then considers the influence of economic science on public moral discourse and concludes with four critical questions which remain on the Catholic social agenda: the relative autonomy of economic life, competing economic ideologies, consequentialism and moral public policy, and the defense of social justice.

The final question of special urgency taken up by *Gaudium et Spes* centers on the problem of peace in the modern world. My essay, after briefly summarizing conciliar teaching on war and peace, indicates how the American Roman Catholic bishops both draw from and press beyond Vatican II in their recent pastoral letter, *The Challenge of Peace: God's Promise and Our Response.* Professor Gordon C. Zahn, national director of Pax Christi USA's Center for Conscience and War, focuses on the question of nonviolence as developed in Pope John XXIII's encyclical, *Pacem in Terris*, Vatican II, and the American Roman Catholic episcopal letter, *The Challenge of Peace.* He chides the American bishops for not having been sufficiently prophetic regarding both nonviolence as a national stance and the question of nuclear deterrence.

All the contributors to this volume are Roman Catholic, a decision not meant to offend the ecumenical spirit of Vatican II. Undoubtedly, a volume gathering the insights of Protestant and Jewish scholars, as well as those of Roman Catholics, would be quite interesting and indeed, a contribution to analysis of *Gaudium et Spes'* impact. My intent with this volume, however, is more limited in scope; I am interested in determining how Roman Catholics, writing from the American experience and culture, perceive, through the lens of twenty years, the achievement of Vatican II. It is not surprising, for instance, that several contributors to this volume see fit to relate either their *personal* involvement in or reaction to the Council. *Gaudium et Spes* not only intrigued the Catholic mind; it touched, deeply at times, the joys and hopes, the griefs and anxieties which the Roman Catholic living in that era felt about the Catholic church.

I want to thank John B. Breslin, S.J., Director of Georgetown University Press, and his quite competent staff for their invaluable assistance with this volume. I have enjoyed working with them on this project as well as on my previous book, *The Catholic Bishops and Nuclear War*. Frances Hart, S.S.J. also assisted me with proofreading the manuscripts, and I am grateful for her help.

Finally, this volume would not exist if the participants at the Council has not experienced the need, in the early sessions of Vatican II, to have the Catholic church take the modern world, its joys and hopes, griefs and anxieties, seriously. The questions of special urgency, which the Council eventually took up, remain crucial problems today. The same vision and courage which prompted the initial analysis of these issues is essential to the necessary, ongoing investigation of these problems as well. May this volume both celebrate the achievement of Vatican II and contribute to the church's continuing concern for the serious questions facing humanity today.

December 7, 1985   Judith A. Dwyer, S.S.J.
                                    Weston School of Theology
                                    Cambridge, Massachusetts

PART I

Marriage

Marriage and Family: Between Traditions
and Trends

Marriage and Human Dignity

The Social Mission of the Christian Family

James Gaffney

Marriage and Family: Between Traditions and Trends

The Second Vatican Council in its *Pastoral Constitution on the Church in the Modern World*[1] interpreted marriage by a curious combination of old formulations and new sympathies, thereby producing an account of marriage that was cryptically conservative and blatantly progressive. Its progressive aspect, originally so vivid to Catholic perceptions, grew dimmer during two subsequent decades, and is all but imperceptible to most young adults of the present. Today's average college or high school student, informed by a teacher that the Catholic church no longer insists on making all other marital purposes subordinate to that of procreation, and even regards marriage primarily as a personal relationship established on the mutual love of spouses, responds with a sense of banality, modified, if at all, by some faint curiosity as to how views contrary to these could ever have been seriously entertained. The questions about marriage to which *Gaudium et Spes* gave its most welcomed answers are, for a new generation of Catholics, no longer vital questions, any more than they were twenty years ago for those who owned no special fealty to Catholic ecclesiastical authority. For indeed, to most Catholics of that time, what *Gaudium et Spes* said about marriage came not as a revelation but as a relief, enabling them to profess without inhibition views that the modern word had long taken for granted and incorporated into respectable mores. In certain important respects, Catholics could now think, talk, and behave about marriage as their decent, conscientious neighbors thought, talked, and behaved about it. The modern world, or at least the better elements of it, had been right after all, the church had the wisdom to perceive it and the decency to admit it, and Catholics could maintain their places in that world with less cognitive dissonance and moral anxiety.

Not everyone, of course, was relieved. There was resentment among those, mostly of a certain age, who felt either personally betrayed by or ideologically committed to previous trends in doctrine and discipline. There was also suspicion among those who attended to some rather different things *Gaudium et Spes* seemed to be saying about marriage in less publicized passages, but even more, to things in-disputably germane about which *Gaudium et Spes* maintained a silence the more disquieting because enforced.[2] The fact that such silence was enforceable was a reminder that in practice, even though not in theory, Vatican II was subordinate to higher authority. And the fact of its being enforced peculiarly in this matter of marriage was plainly ominous. The omens were fulfilled two and a half years later, with the publication of *Humanae Vitae*.[3]

CONTRACEPTION AND DIVORCE

Between *Gaudium et Spes* and *Humanae Vitae* there was, strictly speaking, no contradiction. Yet readers of the two documents typically experienced a strong sense of contrariety. Although *Gaudium et Spes* had refrained from answering the question to which *Humanae Vitae* re-sponded, its general treatment of marriage and the family had established a perspective in which *Humanae Vitae's* answer was not readily anticipated, and with which a different sort of answer seemed plainly congruous. Not only was Pope Paul's conclusion not delivered by the Council, the premises on which he based that conclusion were not expounded by it. Those premises pertained to elements of Catholic tradition that the Council had not dwelt upon, and by judicious inattention to which it had been enabled to construct a statement about marriage that impressed the generality of modern Catholics as reason-able and wholesome. For two and a half years, such was the practical understanding of marriage assumed by the majority of conscientious Catholic wives and husbands. Marriage was a covenant of mutual love between spouses, faithful, companionable, and erotic, sustained and enriched by the spontaneous behavior of friends who have become lovers, meaningful and fulfilling—and demanding—in itself. As such, under usual circumstances it invited and disposed to parenthood, which must, however, be undertaken responsibly, and postponed when it would be clearly imprudent.

It all seemed sufficiently sensible and sufficiently idealistic. The human values of marriage, personal and social, were respected and preserved. And those values were illuminated and enhanced by characteristically Christian insights, especially into the moral pre-eminence and quickening power of generous love. No wonder *Humanae Vitae* proved so disappointing. No wonder, either, that it proved so ineffectual. And no wonder that it engendered a tide of diffidence concerning church authority that shows no signs of turning and many signs of spreading. Why, it continues to be asked, could not the Pope have left well enough alone? Why could he not have left the whole matter to the Council? Or why, at least, could he not have deferred to the advice given by most of those experts he himself had chosen to be his consultors?[4]

To those questions the answer, however uncongenial, is not mysterious. The Pope knew that the issue of birth control had already been addressed, explicitly, directly, and officially by the church. He knew that the most explicit and direct church teaching on this subject had been given, not in some bygone age when thoughts or problems were simpler, but by men who had been his predecessors within the present generation.[5] He knew that artificial contraception had been denounced consistently, although with varying rationales, by church authorities since antiquity. He knew that the modern church was not insensitive to the plight of married couples, and even tried to provide new assistance, compatible with tradition, by offering guidelines for exploiting "natural infertility." All these things the Pope knew. And one thing he believed, that church teaching in moral matters, if it was genuinely traditional and unmistakably official, must be true, and most not be contradicted or countermanded. Given that knowledge and that belief, and the courage of his convictions, the teaching of Paul VI in *Humanae Vitae* was, if not quite a foregone conclusion, at least a perfectly understandable one. It was, indeed, heartily applauded by confirmed traditionalists and infallibilists, and the muted quality of the resultant noise revealed them to be even scarcer than many of us might have supposed—at least when traditionalism and infallibilism interfere with such cherished homely goods as connubial lovemaking.

As things turned out, Paul VI's reassertion of traditional strictures against artificial contraception appears to have had remarkably little effect on the relevant behavior of Catholic couples. It has had, of course, a profound effect on their confidence in and docility toward Vatican guidance in such matters, even when it is put forth with the rhetorical power and relentless persistence of John Paul II. At the same time, for a broad appreciation of marital values, what *Gaudium et Spes* had to say on the subject continues to reflect—I do not say shape or determine—the views of most conscientious Catholics more closely than any other official statement.

No doubt the other issue on which prevailing views of Catholics would seem hardest to reconcile with their church's tradition is that of divorce. *Gaudium et Spes* mentions "the plague of divorce" among factors having an "obscuring effect" on marriage, links divorce with adultery as factors by which marriage is "profaned," and refers to "indissolubility" based on an "unbreakable compact" of "irrevocable personal consent."[6] Yet, since these scattered phrases constitute its whole treatment of marital dissolution, and since this was not, like contraception, a matter left to the Pope for separate handling, the Council conveys no sense of urgency about divorce. It takes no special cognizance of the prodigious increase of civil divorce among Catholics. It does not even allude to the unprecedented facility with which supposed sacramental marriages are annulled by ecclesiastical courts, or betray any sense of irony at this juridical panacea. How different history might have been had one of our acquiescent modern marriage tribunals been available to Henry VIII! *Gaudium et Spes*, having duly registered both its disapproval of divorce and its belief in the indissolubility of marriage, lets it go at that. And this way of proceeding seems to typify an important aspect of this approach. It is not greatly preoccupied with problems, abuses, or actual and imminent crises, even in dealing with matters in which all of these notoriously abound, and despite the fact that this whole section of *Gaudium et Spes* is entitled "Some Questions of Special Urgency."

This absence of any very urgent tone was in keeping with the basic approach deliberately adopted, against considerable resistance, by the formulators of *Gaudium et Spes*.[7] They were determined from the outset not to confront modernity with expressions of dismay and salvos of denunciation, and as far as possible to cultivate a positive appreciation of those aspects of the modern world that could be harmonized with enlightened Christian values. Hence, insofar as typically modern ideals of marriage and family expressed or upheld such values, *Gaudium et Spes* proclaimed its approval. This was true especially with regard to its explicit emphasis on a covenant of mutual love and its implicit assumption of the equality of spouses. As suggested earlier, these appear to be the elements, and often the only ones, popularly retained as representing the substance of the Council's teaching on this topic. Actually, of course, there was more to it than that.

MARRIAGE AND FAMILY

No less important, though much less attended to, is the insistence of *Gaudium et Spes* on closely linking the notions of marriage and family. Once again, a modern reader's initial sense of banality needs to be modified by appreciation of the fact that, in the history of church pronouncements, this linkage was by no means habitual—any more than was the linkage of marriage with love as an essential constituent. The emphasis on family represents the Council's very wholesome tendency to envisage marriage primarily in social, rather than biological or legal, terms. The same tendency is suggested by how relatively little direct attention is paid to sex, as such, or to a contractual bond—even the word "contract" being regularly replaced by the connotatively quite different term, "covenant." In adopting this approach, the Council seems significantly comfortable with the common secular view that, for what we normally mean by marriage, mere mating is less than sufficient, whereas an actual contract exceeds what is necessary. The former point may have bearing on particularly radical new views about marriage. The latter point, however, is of immediate importance as detaching the Council, practically speaking, from that Catholic theological tradition which identifies the very essence of marriage with contract. It is noteworthy that it was precisely the biological and the juridical that came together in producing a canonical definition of marriage which, although modern persons find it abhorrent, has had, and still has vast practical consequences for the dealings of Catholic couples with their church: a contract conveying perpetual and exclusive right over the body in respect of acts intrinsically apt for the generating of off-spring.[8]

Wisely, the Council did not impose on its discussion this or any other precise definition of marriage. It seems to presuppose the sort of understanding of marriage that finds expression in what a modern secular reference work takes to be "ordinary usage", which "includes two distinct ideas: (a) that a man and a woman cohabit, generally with the intention of founding a family; (b) that some distinction can be drawn between marriage and other forms of sexual union, qualifiable as pre-marital, extra-marital, adulterous, etc."[9] The same article notes, however, that although "in the analysis of advanced modern societies usage in general follows the above, . . . mating arrangements in societies studied by social anthropologists display so much diversity that it is impossible to find a comprehensive definition that is not tautologous." To be reminded of this cultural diversity is also to recall that, in dealing with marriage, as with some other matters, the Council's "modern world" is in effect largely confined to Western industrialized society—a limitation scarcely avoidable but by no means inconsequential.

FAMILY AND SOCIETY

The social perspective adopted by *Gaudium et Spes* is brought out immediately by its opening sentence: "The well-being of the individual person and of human and Christian society is intimately linked with the healthy condition of that community produced by marriage and family."[10] This is not, strictly speaking, either a religious or a moral statement, but a sociological one. It is concerned with a certain state of human affairs called community, which results from marriage and family. It recognizes that such community may exist in a more or less wholesome condition, and asserts that its state of health is closely related to the welfare not only of individuals but of society as a whole. Like the definition previously cited, *Gaudium et Spes* both makes a distinction and supposes a normally close relationship between marriage and family. It then clearly rejects the notion that they constitute an essentially private good, whose values are exhausted within domestic confines. Trite as it might have seemed in other times and cultures, this position is an important one for the Council to take in an era when the assumption is rapidly gaining ground that marriage is an entirely private arrangement, perhaps best conceived as a peculiarly erotic variety of personal friendship.[11] Because this position is important, it is surprising and disappointing that *Gaudium et Spes* fails almost entirely to defend, explain, or apply it. It reappears briefly at the end, when it is stated that "the family is the foundation of society. In it the various generations come together and help one another to grow wiser and to harmonize personal rights with the other requirements of social life."[12] Even here, however, the scope of the family's influence is envisaged only longitudinally, as relating past to future within a lineage, while nothing is said about how the family's contemporaneous influence affects the society that contains it, or other elements within that society. Indeed, what follows in the document conceives only a passive role for the family vis-à-vis the larger society, which is accordingly exhorted to take good care of families.

Another aspect of this omission is the apparent failure of *Gaudium et Spes* to recognize the family's potential influence on surrounding society as constituting a formidable political factor. One need only allow one's historical sense to be focused by such modern parables as Huxley's *Brave New World* and Orwell's *1984* to be reminded of the critical tension that exists between vigorous family solidarity and the prospects of totalitarianism. Regrettably, the kind of problem that vigorous families pose for the advancement of tyranny seems always to be better appreciated by tyrants than by their victims. Regrettably also, in our own society this appreciation has been virtually monopolized by the "Moral Majority", who immerse it indiscriminately in a morass of reactionary ideology.

It is worth recalling in this connection the interestingly different ways in which those two novels just mentioned imagined the dissolution of strong family ties in the interests of a tyrannical statism. In the earlier book by Huxley, couples were "liberated" from fidelity and parenthood by combining a culture of promiscuous eroticism with a technology of genetic engineering. In the later one by Orwell, they were "liberated" from intimacy and social agency by a culture of dispassionate copulation as surrogate breeders for the parental State. Despite the differences in procedure, in both cases family, as a potent sociopolitical force, is destroyed; the sexual partners are socially sterilized. Oddly, and I believe quite accidentally, those two satirical designs respectively caricature the most extreme tendencies of traditional Catholic teaching about sexuality—emphasis on reproduction and nervousness about everything else—and of its modern secular antithesis—emphasis on orgasm and cynicism about everything else. Whether or not the two extremes are equally bad, the satirical parity may suggest that they are, at least, equally absurd.

Gaudium et Spes has not, of course, expunged all traces of those numerous elements in Catholic tradition which contributed to such absurdity. Sometimes the traces are so obscure that one readily gives them the benefit of doubt. Yet what, for example, prompted someone to insert that isolated and enigmatic pronouncement, "Widowhood, accepted bravely as a continuation of the marriage vocation, will be esteemed by all"?[13] The reader's perplexity is only increased by the footnote reference to Ephesians 5:3, "Honor widows who are real widows", which is commonly interpreted as pertaining to an early institutional arrangement for providing needy widows with church support while devoting themselves to pious offices—an anticipation of later forms of nunhood. It seems unlikely that *Gaudium et Spes* is thus cryptically urging a revival of that institution which, anyway, was scarcely thought of as "a continuation of the marriage vocation." Much more important than a suspicion that the Council may have admitted here a rather fatuous obiter dictum about widows is the document's failure to say something sensible about them, including at least some praise for their frequently very constructive enterprise, and some forthright counteraction of the dismal Pauline legacy of grudgingly condescending to their remarriage. Widows nowadays are numerous, important, and often very impressive. Tradition has been narrow-minded in their regard, and masculinely narrow-minded at that, while modern pastoral trendiness seldom gives them a glance. *Gaudium et Spes* did not rise to the occasion.

For anyone with biblical habits of association, thinking about widows leads spontaneously to thinking about orphans. And if such thoughts arose in the context of deliberations about "that community produced by marriage and family" and its importance to larger society, it would seem difficult not to reflect on the peculiar poignancy of its importance to orphans. Family community is, after all, what orphans most pathetically need, and providing for that need must rank among the noblest services families can render to larger society. The adoption and fostering of parentless, rejected, or displaced children is among the plainest social needs and purest social opportunities of our time and, generally speaking, no agency is likely to do it better than a married couple or a natural family. It is likewise by far the most wholesomely helpful of all available responses to that epidemic recourse to abortion which *Gaudium et Spes* is content merely to denounce, along with infanticide, as "unspeakable crimes." The Council's disregard of this topic in the present context suggests a certain blindness. Probably that blindness is rooted in an unconscious bias: that strong, old Catholic bias against detaching one's thoughts about marriage and family from reproduction, so that families constituted by means other than reproduction simply do not come into the picture. Yet, is it not odd that the New Testament's one reference to marriage as a metaphor for God's saving union with his people has shed so much ethereal luster upon matrimony, while its several references to adoption as a metaphor for precisely the same thing has had no comparable effect in Christian imagination?[14] Surely, this too "is a great mystery."

One significant issue linking marriage and the family to society at large that *Gaudium et Spes* approaches differently from earlier modern church teachings is that of overpopulation. That issue has two primary aspects, the demographic and the economic: sheer growth of population, and limited access to consumer goods. One looks accordingly in two directions for the ingredients of a solution: the direction of controlled reproduction, and the direction of improved production and distribution. Somewhat surprisingly, these matters are entirely ignored in the chapter on socioeconomic life and merely mentioned in the chapter on marriage and the family, being discussed instead in the chapter on the fostering of peace and the promotion of a community of nations.[15] The main originality of the discussion is its straightforward assertion that "government officials" (an unfortunate phrasing!) have rights and duties, including the enactment of social legislation affecting families, to deal with population problems.[16] The important qualification is added that such government action must not impose "solutions contradicting the moral law" and that the "question of how many children should be born belongs to the honest judgment of parents" and "can in no way be committed to the decision of government."

It seems regrettable that this topic was not more closely and explicitly related to the appeal for procreative responsibility in the chapter on marriage and the family. The Council appears to take the view that governments may use their powers to influence decisions about reproduction, but must leave the actual decisions to parents. This is an uneasy formula in that it guarantees certain rights to couples, yet acknowledges the legitimacy of governments' powerfully discouraging the exercise of those rights. The prospective conflict is a serious one that requires moral guidance. On the one hand, sexual partners need to be persuaded of the moral relevance of public interests to their private reproductive choices, awkward though it may be for the church to undertake such persuasion while narrowly restricting its approval of available means of birth control. On the other hand, moral limits of governmental intervention, while not susceptible of detailed pre-scription, need greater clarification, as do such pertinent political considerations as economic and immigration policies. It should also be noted that there are obvious practical connections between this topic of overpopulation and the one previously introduced concerning the adoption or fostering of parentless children by married couples, especially when such practices extend across national boundaries.

Such considerations also have bearing on another topic whose practical importance, now obvious, was not commonly appreciated at the time of Vatican II, namely, the possibility of technologically replacing various functions of natural reproduction. Most of the demand for reproductive technologies is occasioned by the desire of married couples to have families despite physical impediments to ordinary reproduction. Hence the development of such procedures as artificial insemination, gamete donation, and fertilization and gestation outside the maternal uterus. These technologies raise several kinds of moral questions, the most basic of which have to do with the decision itself to employ technological alternatives in order to have "a child of one's own." That such decisions may be perfectly innocent and even admirable cannot reasonably be doubted, although particular tech-nologies present special ethical problems. Yet, antecedent to those issues is the moral importance of weighing the values entailed in any such decision against those of practical alternatives. Above all, it should never be overlooked or understressed that every childless couple who desire a family represent, to that extent, a potential opportunity for some parentless child who needs one. At a time when overpopulation and abortion are problems of the first magnitude, that consideration takes on special urgency. To be considered also is the extreme cost of some of these reproductive technologies, and the effect of their cultivation on the distribution of available medical resources. Clearly, this is not a matter to be dealt with by simple moral imperatives. It is a matter that calls for sensitive moral reflection over a whole range of competing values, predicated on recognition that what one does about one's family matters, for good or ill, not to its members only, but to society at large.

MARRIAGE AND ETHICS

It will be clear by now that what I chiefly value as real progress in the approach taken by *Gaudium et Spes* to marriage and the family is not simply its refusal to subordinate the mutual love of spouses to their reproductive functioning. No less important, I believe, is the Council's tendency to view marriage in relation to family as a social achievement, and to view family not only as domestic community but as a vital component of larger society. Seen in that light, family morality must be conceived as a public as well as a private and personal value. Accordingly, the moral disvalues of individualistic ideology and egoistic choice must be recognized as vices not only of individuals but also of families. Although *Gaudium et Spes* did not pursue this line of thought systematically, it both introduced it and cleared a way for it. The most important contribution it made to that clearing of the way was by its general avoidance of what, for lack of a better phrase, I shall call "moral sexology."

What I intend by that phrase is the whole traditional array of ostensibly rational norms that Roman Catholic officialdom, as "custodian and interpreter of the natural law," has applied so peculiarly to sexual behavior. Most of these norms are said to be based on certain knowledge of the "true nature" or "intrinsic purpose" of various relevant components of sexual behavior. Recently, one often hears reference to their "meaning" instead of to their "nature", but the difference is usually more rhetorical than philosophical.[17] A frequent influence on such norms is a persistent assumption that there is something inherently wrong with sexual desire and sexual pleasure, such that deliberate entertainment of the one or enjoyment of the other needs to be justified or "excused" on the basis of ulterior purposes. Although I cannot here defend, neither do I wish to conceal my opinion that these norms are to a great extent ill-founded and unreasonable. In any case, it is evident that scarcely any ethical thinkers about sex who do not have Roman Catholic commitments either build on the same foundations or arrive at the same conclusions. It is also evident that, among Roman Catholic moralists themselves, the kind of argumentation commonly employed in sexual matters tends to be strangely different from that brought to other departments of life. To approach the subject of marriage by way of this kind of moralizing is nowadays to arouse almost immediately a degree of perplexity, skepticism, and defensiveness that paralyzes serious discussion. I am personally convinced that Catholic moralists would do well to impose a protracted moratorium on the "special ethics" of sex, that is, on reprobating certain kinds of sexual behavior on the basis of principles not applied to other kinds of behavior. *Gaudium et Spes* did not, of course, go so far as that, but it did, I think, go far enough in that direction to suggest a better way of proceeding.

The chapter on which this discussion is focused was given the significant title, "Fostering the Nobility of Marriage and the Family."

And in fact, what the chapter emphasizes is the fulfillment of potentialities for good through marriage and family in which the fostering of their nobility precisely consists. Such an approach enables one to advance general commendations of marital and familial values without condemning whatever falls short of them or dismissing the relevance of circumstantial variables. One can thus reasonably urge that, other things being equal, a marriage that generates offspring is a fuller realization of relevant values than one that does not. And one can also reasonably insist that, insofar as other things are not equal, this may simply not be the case. One can likewise urge that a marriage which provides reciprocal sexual satisfaction is, to that extent, more adequate than one that does not. The same is true of a marriage that encompasses deep personal friendship between the spouses, or one that extends its love and protection to the forlorn and the handicapped. And one can do all this in a spirit of encouragement and exhortation, without at the same time doing what Catholic moralizing has so often done, making the better the enemy of the good. The marital and familial lives of human beings can be lived better or worse in all sorts of ways, just as can their intellectual lives, their social lives, and their professional lives. In all these and other vital aspects of human existence, nobody achieves even the relative perfection of realizing their own potentialities, and most people fall enormously short of it.

We do not know, in any absolute sense, "the purpose" or "the meaning" of marriage. The purposes and meanings of things people do derive entirely from the intentions, usages, and expectations that people entertain, whether these be good or bad, wise or foolish.[18] What we do know are some of the good things that can result from marriage. It is reasonable to hope and urge that as many as possible of these good results be sought in any given marriage. But it is simply not reasonable to insist that whenever certain of these good results are not sought, the seeking of others is thereby rendered corrupt. If the reason certain of these good things are not sought is selfishness, or cowardice, or laziness, or if the reason they are not achieved is dishonesty, or unfairness, or cruelty, it is these vices that should be morally condemned, not the imperfect achievements they prevent a marriage from exceeding. A marriage that aspires to no more than mutual pleasure, or security, or companionship is a disappointing thing because it is so much less than a marriage can be. But that does not make its actual achievements of companionship or security or pleasure into moral evil. If there is moral evil, it lies in the wrongfulness of decisions and dispositions that inhibit richer accomplishments of good. A family that educates its children poorly is to that extent worse than one that educates them well. But it is only morally worse if its educational shortcomings are the result of some culpable negligence, and the moral evil lies not in the education but in the wrongfulness of the neglect. What marital moralizing needs primarily is a rich comprehension of the manifold goods that marriage and family can ideally achieve. What it needs secondarily is experienced understanding of what, in given cases, prevents marriages and families from encompassing those ideals. And what it needs finally is wise discrimination between limiting factors that arise from vice or malice and those that do not. In other words, the imperfect human achievements of human marriages and families need to be assessed in the ways sensible people normally assess imperfect human achievements in other important areas of life. *Gaudium et Spes* seems to me to come closer to adopting that approach to marriage and the family than any comparable teaching of official Catholicism. It certainly comes closer to it than subsequent teachings by Catholic popes.

Many years ago in Africa, a student who had become Christian told me of the decision of his father, a highly respected tribal chief, not to follow his son's example even though he was strongly attracted by what he had learned of the life and teachings of Jesus. Like all chiefs in his tribe, the father had a number of wives of various ages. He loved these women and they loved him; they cared deeply for their many children and maintained an exemplary family. But this missionary had told him that, for a Christian, the relations he had with all but one of the wives would be sinful, and must therefore be renounced before baptism. The chief did not pretend to know whether or not, in some ideal sense, monogamy would be better than polygamy. He did know that to abandon the duties of a devoted husband and father to most of his family would be disgraceful. And he thought that doing so in the interest of embracing what he had come to admire as a gospel of love would be strangely ironic. Surely he was right. And surely the kind of morality that would defame and destroy such goodness as he and his family had achieved, in the name of an ideal definition of marriage, is wrong. That kind of wrongness is, I believe, the besetting folly of traditional Catholic moralizing about marriage and the family.

Recently, in a West German university town, I noticed some students of both sexes displaying the arresting slogan, "*Weiblichkeit, Ja; Frauenrechtlertum, Nein!*" On inquiring, I found that what these people were opposing as "feminism" and contrasting with "femininity" was, in their view, a compulsive competition with men for power. They claimed that people who constantly contend for power became personally repulsive and socially destructive; that, in Germany anyway, men had been demonstrating that thesis from time immemorial; and that women should be dissuaded from imitating them. They noted in particular the destructiveness—and repulsiveness—of marriages between power-seeking contestants.

These students were, no doubt, reactionaries, emphasizing in the manner of reactionaries certain authentic values, without bestowing equal attention on others. Nevertheless, their point, as far as it goes, is sound, inasmuch as families often do suffer from power struggles between spouses and such power struggles are often generated or exacerbated by particular interpretations of feminism. This is an area of controversy which *Gaudium et Spes* touched upon in its chapter on marriage and the family by asserting the "equal dignity of spouses" and insisting that a mother's "domestic role ... must be safely preserved, though the legitimate social progress of women should not be underrated on that account."[19]

From what I have already said about marital moralizing, it must be clear that I could not begin to justify any general moral disapproval of women who marry, enjoy normal social and sexual relations with their husbands, while preventing conception in order to cultivate a career humanly valuable in itself, even though incompatible with the responsibilities of motherhood. If they arrived at such a course through deceiving their husbands, or out of motives no better than arrogance or greed, that would be, of course, another matter. But the Council's insistence that a mother's domestic role "must be ... preserved" for mothers does not imply that any such role must be imposed on women simply because they marry. Women should be allowed and encouraged to do whatever genuinely worthwhile things they can do, and to enjoy the normal rewards of doing them well. To that end, the church should obviously practice what it preaches, by hastening to dissolve its clerical androcracy and to repudiate the theological sophistries that support it.

Within marriage, affirming the "equal dignity of spouses" should not be equated with assigning identical prerogatives to spouses. What equal dignity demands, in families as in larger societies, is not that prerogatives be distributed identically, but that they be distributed fairly. A family polity based on nothing subtler than a principle of "one spouse, one vote" is simply foolish. Because monogamous marriage would constitute a democracy of two, no majority is achievable, and every disagreement must be a stalemate. Once the conventional subordination of wives to husbands is done away with, spouses have to learn the social arts of partnership, how to cultivate practical agreements through clarification and compromise, and how to cope with disagreement by mutually acceptable procedures. Equal dignity does not exclude the pragmatic subordination of one spouse to the other as long as that subordination is not simply imposed by one spouse upon the other, but freely endorsed by both for their common good. If, on the other hand, every practical disagreement between husband and wife is interpreted as a skirmish in ideological warfare, the prospects are grim indeed.

Fostering the nobility of marriage and the family has never, perhaps, been quite so difficult or quite so urgent as it is now. Marriage and the family have suffered from some very unwholesome traditions, and are now suffering from some very unwholesome opposite trends. A principal merit of *Gaudium et Spes* was its disciplined ability to neither canonize the traditions nor anathematize the trends, but to approach both sympathetically and to examine both critically. The hope of appropriating that precedent is probably the best of all reasons for returning to that document after twenty years, to rediscover the wisdom it exhibited both by what it said and by what it left unsaid—and to go on from there.

NOTES

1. Quotations of this document are from the translation of Walter M. Abbott, ed., *The Documents of Vatican II* (New York: America Press, 1966). References to *Gaudium et Spes* are indicated as GS followed by the appropriate paragraph numbers.

2. Pope Paul VI effectively appropriated the issue of birth control by his address on June 23, 1964 to a group of cardinals. AAS (*Acta Apostolicae Sedis*) 56 (1964), 581–89.

3. Both the encyclical *Humanae Vitae* and an exceptionally thorough ethical critique of it by Carl Cohen are published together in Robert Baker and Frederick Elliston, eds., *Philosophy and Sex* (Buffalo, N.Y.: Prometheus Books, 1975), 131–65.

4. The circumstances surrounding and influencing the Pope's deliberations, and early reactions to his decision, are described with unusual vividness by Robert Blair Kaiser, *The Politics of Sex and Religion* (Kansas City, Mo.: Leaven Press, 1985).

5. In particular, Pope Pius XI's encyclical, *Casti Connubii*, AAS 22 (1930), 559–61, and Pope Pius XII's allocution to a meeting of Italian Obstetrical Nurses, AAS 43 (1951), 835–54.

6. GS, nos. 47, 48, 49, 50.

7. The contrasting approach the Council ultimately rejected is represented by the "Schema Proposed by the Theological Commission on Chastity, Virginity, Marriage, and Family," *Acta et Documenta Concilio Oecumenico Vaticano II Apparando*; series II, volumen II, pars III (Vatican: Typis Polyglottis, 1968), 893-937. The discussion which followed this proposal is recorded, idem, 937-85.

8. Compare the definition of matrimonial consent in the "old" (1917) *Codex Iuris Canonici,* 1081 #2, with its modified counterpart in the "new" (1983) code, 1057 #2.

9. Julius Gould and William L. Kolb, eds., *Dictionary of the Social Sciences* (New York: The Free Press, 1964), 409-410.

10. *GS,* no. 47.

11. For a plausible analysis of factors conducing to such an understanding of marriage, see Edward Shorter, *The Making of the Modern Family* (New York: Basic Books, 1975), esp. 255-68. For a valuable sociological critique of family relations withdrawn from larger society, see Richard Sennett, "Destructive Gemeinschaft," *Partisan Review* 43 (1976), 341-61.

12. *GS,* no. 52.

13. *GS,* no. 51.

14. See Eph. 5:52, and compare Rom. 8:15, 23; 9:4, Gal. 4:5, and Eph. 1:5. In the latter texts, the literal sense of *huiothesia* is sometimes obscured by modern English translations.

15. *GS,* no. 87.

16. This view is a notable departure from that of Pope John XXIII's *Mater et Magistra,* nos. 186-192, issued three years earlier; it is adopted less than two years later by Pope Paul VI's *Populorum Progressio,* no. 37.

17. A useful summary of recent literature in this vein is provided by James P. Hanigan, *What Are They Saying About Sexual Morality?* (New York: Paulist Press, 1982). A good example of "advanced" traditional teaching current at the time of *Gaudium et Spes* is Joseph Fuchs, *De Castitate et Ordine Sexuali* (Rome: Gregorian, 1963).

18. Traditional determinations of such absolute purposes typically claim to be based on natural law, as expressing divine intentions. Justifications of such claims are often plain instances of question-begging or circular argumentation. Probably the most sophisticated approach is that of Germain Grisez and Russell Shaw, *Beyond the New Morality: The Responsibilities of Freedom* (Notre Dame, Ind.: University of Notre Dame Press, 1974) which, in my opinion, confuses normative ethics with perfectionist idealism, and does some question-begging of its own in its determination of perfectionist ideals. It is, nevertheless, an illuminating work, which has been further developed in subsequent writings of Grisez and his disciples.

19. *GS,* nos. 49, 52.

William E. May

Marriage and Human Dignity

The dignity of the human person is a cardinal doctrine of Catholic faith and is the cornerstone of Vatican Council II's *Pastoral Constitution on the Church in the Modern World* (*Gaudium et Spes*).[1] The church's teaching on human dignity provides the context for its teaching on marriage, which Vatican Council II summarized, deepened, and developed, and which has been subsequently further developed by Pope Paul VI and, in particular, by Pope John Paul II.[2] A profound reverence for human dignity shapes the church's teaching on marriage and does so precisely because marriage, *as understood by the Church*, is willed by God as an indispensable means for respecting and protecting the dignity of human beings. Thus some brief observations on human dignity will help to set the stage for an examination of marriage.

HUMAN DIGNITY

According to the church's understanding of divine revelation, there is a twofold dignity proper to human beings. The first is an intrinsic and inalienable dignity, one that is ours as members of the human species, the species that God called into being when, in the beginning, he "created man in his image . . . male and female he created them" (Gn 1:27). Every living human body, the body that comes into existence when new human life is conceived, is a living image of the all-holy God. Moreover, in creating man, male and female, God created a being inwardly receptive of his own life, the kind of being that the all-holy God could become should he choose to "other" himself in what is not divine.[3] God cannot become incarnate in a dog or a chimpanzee because these animals are not inwardly capable of divinization, but he can become incarnate in the human animal, for he made this bodily being the sort of being able to receive his very own life. And we know that God in fact did choose to become truly one of us. Thus every human being, every living member of the human species, can rightly be said to be a "created word" of God, the created word that the Uncreated

Word became (Jn 1:4, 14) precisely to show us how deeply we are loved by the God who fashions us in our mother's womb (cf. Ps 139:13-15). Thus every human life is to be revered and respected from its very beginning.[4]

By virtue of this inherent, inalienable, and inviolable dignity, every human being, of whatever age or sex or condition, is a being of moral worth, irreplaceable and nonsubstitutable, a being that *ought to be loved*.[5]

But in addition to this inherent dignity, there is another human dignity of which the church speaks, namely, the dignity to which we are called as intelligent beings capable of determining our own lives by our own free choices. This is the dignity we give to ourselves when, with the help of God's grace, we freely choose to conform our lives to what Vatican Council II called "the highest norm of human life," namely, the "divine law itself—eternal, objective, and universal, by which God orders, directs and governs the whole world and the ways of the human community according to a plan conceived in his wisdom and love." God has so made us that we are able, through the mediation of our conscience, to "recognize the demands of this divine law."[6] Indeed, as Vatican Council II insists,

> deep within his conscience man discovers a law which he has not laid upon himself but which he must obey. *Its voice, ever calling him to love and to do what is good and to avoid evil*, tells him inwardly at the right moment, do this, shun that. For man has in his heart a law written by God. *His dignity lies in observing this law*.[7]

Fidelity to conscience, the Council likewise insists, means a "search for truth" and for the true solutions to moral problems; conscience can, of course, err "through invincible ignorance without losing its dignity" (so long as sufficient care is taken "for the search for the true and the good"), but "to the extent that a correct conscience holds sway, persons and groups turn away from blind choice and seek to conform to the *objective* norms of morality."[8]

Thus human beings, who *are* beings of incalculable dignity by virtue of their being human to begin with, are called and obliged to give to themselves, with the help of God's grace, the added dignity of persons who freely choose to shape their lives in accordance with the truth, to say "yes" to God's invitation to choose life. In short, human beings are not only beings who *ought to be loved*, but they are also beings who *are obliged to love* so that they can be fully themselves, fully the beings that God wills them to be.[9]

MARRIAGE: A PERSON-AFFIRMING, LOVE-ENABLING, LIFE-GIVING REALITY

If human beings are to be wanted and loved as they ought to be, and if they are to succeed in shaping their lives in accordance with the truth and thereby carry out their vocation to love even as they have been and are loved by God in Christ, then God's plan for marriage must be recognized and put into practice.

This is the constant teaching of the church, which insists that marriage is a specific sort of human reality. It is a specific kind of reality because it has God, not man, as its author,[10] and from him it has received its specifying "goods and ends," as Vatican Council II affirmed.[11] From God, not man, marriage has received, as Edward Schillebeeckx put it, "its intrinsic conditions of existence, its defined limits."[12]

Just as only one specific kind of animal is inwardly capable of receiving God's life, namely, the human animal, so only a specific kind of male-female interpersonal relationship counts as the human reality that merits the name *marriage*, as understood by the church, and is thus intrinsically capable of being integrated into God's salvific act and of serving as a sacrament of the new law. This is the sort of reality described in the opening chapters of Genesis, in the Priestly and Yahwist accounts of "creation" or, as Pope John Paul II describes them, the accounts of our "beatifying beginnings."[13] It is the reality to which our Lord referred when, in responding to a question on divorce, he pointed to these Genesis narratives in order to affirm the inherent indissolubility of the marital union (cf. Mk 10:2-12, Mt 19:3-12).[14] And it is this specific sort of reality that a man and a woman freely bring into being when, forswearing all others, they give themselves to one another irrevocably and unconditionally and by so doing capacitate themselves to do something that nonmarried men and women cannot do, namely, to give to one another marital love and to give life procreatively, as cooperators with God's loving design for human existence. Marriage, as a specific kind of human reality, is the union of one man and one woman, brought into being by their own free and irrevocable choice, one through which they define themselves as spouses and commit and capacitate themselves to foster a unique form of love and to honor the good of human procreation in its fullness.

These specifying goods of marriage have, since the time of St. Augustine to the present, been identified as the good of indissoluble unity (the *bonum sacramenti*),[15] the good of steadfast fidelity (*bonum fidei*), and the good of progeny (*bonum prolis*), and Vatican II made these goods its own in its presentation of marriage.[16] I will consider the good of indissoluble unity under the heading of marriage as a person-affirming reality, the good of fidelity under that of marriage as a love-enabling reality, and the good of progeny under that of marriage as a life-giving reality. In considering each, my focus will be on the way in which these specifying goods of marriage enable human persons both to respect the intrinsic dignity of human beings and to give to themselves the added dignity of persons who choose in accordance with the truth.

1. Marriage as a Person-Affirming Reality. "Not uniqueness establishes the marriage, but marriage establishes the uniqueness."[17] These perceptive words of the German Protestant theologian Helmut Thielicke express the Catholic (and catholic) truth that marriage comes into being only as a result of a free, self-determining choice of a man and a woman, and that this choice not only effects marriage but also effects a radical change in the *being* of the man and the woman. Prior to the choice, freely made, whereby they give themselves to one another in marriage, the man and the woman are separate individuals, at liberty to go their own ways. But in and through their consent to marriage, which Vatican Council II rightly designates as an "act of irrevocable personal consent,"[18] the man and the woman freely give to themselves a new identity: the man becomes this particular woman's *husband*, the woman becomes this particular man's *wife*, and together they become *spouses*. In and through this act the man and the woman show their respect for the intrinsic and inalienable dignity of each other, for in and through this act they constitute each other as irreplaceable and nonsubstitutable spouses. Each freely gives his or her "word," that is, his or her person, to the other, and each freely receives the "word" of the other.[19]

The cardinal significance of the act of marital consent is beautifully expressed in the Yahwist creation narrative. There we read that the male-man, Adam, on seeing the being equal to himself that the Lord Yahweh had fashioned for him, the being whose body expressed a priceless person,[20] exclaimed: "Here at last is bone of my bone and flesh of my flesh. . . . For this reason a man shall leave father and mother and cleave to his wife, and the two shall become one flesh" (Gn 2:23-24).[21] Commenting on this passage, of transcendent significance for human existence, Pope John Paul II has noted:

The very formulation of Gn 2.24 indicates not only that human beings, created as man and woman, were created for unity, but also that precisely *this unity, through which they become "one flesh," has right from the beginning a character of union derived from choice.* We read, in fact, "a man leaves his father and mother and cleaves to his wife." If the man belongs "by nature" to his father and mother by virtue of procreation, he, on the other hand, "cleaves" by choice to his wife (and she to her husband).[22]

The choice that establishes marriage at the same time establishes the uniqueness, as spouses, of the man and woman who freely consent to marriage. The change that this choice effects in their being is lasting, and is so because of its irrevocable character. I simply cannot, by an act of my will or by anything that I can do, un-husband myself, nor can my wife un-wife herself. We cannot undo what we have irrevocably done, and we have irrevocably made ourselves to be, by our own free and self-determining choice, spouses. I can no more be an ex-spouse than I can be an ex-father, for I have freely determined myself *to be* a particular woman's husband until death[23] do us part. I have irrevocably given myself to her alone and she to me, and she has irrevocably chosen to receive me and me alone and I have so received her, so that I simply cannot "give" myself to someone else.[24]

This truth, although today regarded by some as unrealistic and harsh, is rooted in a profound respect for the dignity of human persons and the dignity of marriage as a person-affirming reality. It recognizes that a man and a woman, by freely choosing to give themselves to each other irrevocably in marriage, have chosen to respect each other's intrinsic dignity by establishing each other as unique, irreplaceable, and nonsubstitutable spouses. Moreover, by choosing in this way a man and a woman give to themselves capacities that nonmarried men and women do not have. For now they are able to give to each other "a singular kind of love,"[25] married love, and they can cooperate with God in giving life lovingly to new human persons (these points will be pursued in subsequent sections).

The truth that marriage brings about a change in the *being* of the man and woman who consent to marriage is at the heart of the church's understanding of the good of indissoluble unity (*bonum sacramenti*), the good that marriage is. By giving to themselves the identity of *spouses*, a man and a woman bring into being marriage itself, which the church dares to call a holy or sacred bond.[26] While this good, this holy bond that marriage itself is,[27] is dependent on human choice for its coming-into-being, its continuance-in-being is not conditioned by subsequent human choices.[28] To the contrary, this holy bond, the marriage itself, precisely because it is rooted in the inner being of the spouses, conditions their lives and actions. It *enables* them to live and act as spouses, that is, as persons who are now capable, precisely because of the holy bond of marriage that indissolubly unites them, of vicariously imaging forth in this world the love, spousal and life-giving, of God himself. For marriage is not only a holy bond (a *sacrum* or *sacramentum vinculum*), it is also a holy symbol (a *sacramentum signum*) inwardly capacitating the spouses to mediate the love-giving and life-giving grace that God wills to give us through the spousal love of his only begotten Son, Jesus Christ. Here a remarkable passage from Pope Leo XIII's 1880 encyclical on marriage is instructive:

> Since marriage has God for its author, and since it has been even from the beginning a shadowing forth of the incarnation of the Word of God, therefore there is in it something sacred and religious, not adventitious but innate, not received from man but implanted by nature. Wherefore, Innocent III and Honorius III, our predecessors,[29] were enabled to say, not unjustly nor rashly, that the sacrament of marriage exists both among the faithful and among the infidels.[30]

What Leo meant in saying this was that the human reality of marriage as a holy or sacred bond rooted in the being of the spouses is itself a fitting sign of the union that God wills to exist between himself and his people, of the grace-filled mystery of Christ's indissoluble union with his bride, the church.[31] As such, the human reality of marriage is inwardly receptive of the covenant of God's grace, and through the will of God and the redemptive death-resurrection of Jesus Christ it has actually been integrated into the economy of salvation. The marriages of non-Christians are indeed, in a very real sense, open to integration into the mystery of salvation and are thus in an implicit and veiled sense "sacraments" of grace.[32] But when baptized men and women give themselves to one another in marriage, the mystery of Christ's grace-filled, sanctifying, and redemptive spousal union with his church is explicitly manifested and efficaciously made present in the world so long as the spouses themselves place no obstacles in the way.[33]

Thus, when Christian men and women marry, they do so as persons who are already, through baptism, inseparably united with Christ and with his body, the church (cf. 1 Cor 6:15-20). By means of their baptism, "man and woman are definitively placed within the new and eternal covenant, in the spousal covenant of Christ with the Church. And it is because of this indestructible insertion that the intimate community of conjugal life and love, founded by the creator, is elevated and assumed into the spousal charity of Christ, sustained and enriched by his redeeming power."[34]

Marriage, therefore, is a person-affirming reality, a holy bond rooted in the being of the husband and wife, a being they give to each other through their free and irrevocable choice of each other as irreplaceable and nonsubstitutable spouses. It is, moreover, a holy sacrament enabling husband and wife to mediate to the world the spousal love of Christ, the love that redeems and sanctifies human persons. It is, therefore, not true to say that marriages (and in particular the marriages of Christians, of the baptized, of those who "marry in the Lord") can "die" or become "irretrievably lost." For the holy and sacramental bond uniting husband and wife is by its inner dynamism and nature capable of being caught up into God's saving and redemptive love, and we know that God has actualized this capacity in the marriages of those who have become indissolubly united to Christ's body through baptism. Just as nothing will "be able to separate us from the love of God that comes to us in Christ Jesus, our Lord" (Rom 8:39), so nothing can tear asunder the holy union of husband and wife. It is always possible for them to affirm, with God, the irreplaceable and non-substitutable person of their freely chosen spouse, for marriage, this great gift of God, makes it so.

2. Marriage as a Love-Enabling Reality. Indissoluble unity (the *bonum sacramenti*), since it is the good that marriage is, is inseparable from marriage, so that no marriage can exist without this good. The goods of steadfast fidelity (the *bonum fidei*) and of progeny (the *bonum prolis*), on the other hand, are not goods that marriage is, so that a marriage can exist without these goods. However, these are goods to which the spouses commit themselves when they give themselves to one another irrevocably in marriage. They are goods which they are to honor and respect throughout their lives, and *they are above all goods for which they are inwardly capacitated by their marriage itself*.

First, let us consider the good of steadfast fidelity, with the spousal love that is this very good of steadfast fidelity viewed from the perspective of its inner dynamism. For, as Pope Pius XI noted in 1930 in his encyclical on Christian marriage,

> This conjugal faith, which is most aptly called by St. Augustine the "faith of chastity," blooms more freely, more beautifully, and more nobly, when it is rooted in that more excellent soil, the love of husband and wife which pervades all the duties of married life and holds pride of place in Christian marriage. For matrimonial faith demands that husband and wife be joined in an especially holy and pure love.[35]

Vatican Council II spoke at length on the specific nature of marital love,[36] and the teaching of the Council on marital love was ably summarized by Pope Paul VI, who identified its characteristics by describing it as a love that is *human, total, faithful, exclusive,* and *fruitful.* As a fully human love, it is a love "of the senses and spirit . . . and mainly, an act of free will, intended to endure and to grow . . . in such a way that husband and wife become one heart and one soul and together reach their human perfection." As a love that is total, marital love is "a unique form of personal friendship, in which husband and wife generously share everything, without undue reservation or selfish calculations." It is, moreover, "faithful and exclusive until death." And finally, it is a fruitful love, "not exhausted by the communion between husband and wife but destined to continue by raising up new lives."[37] This love, it ought also to be noted, is fittingly, properly, and uniquely expressed in marital acts, "the acts proper to marriage."[38]

What I want to stress, first and foremost, about this beautiful good of marriage, this unique form of human friendship love, is that it is a love made possible only by marriage itself. Men and women who are unmarried, while they may aspire to this love, are simply not capable of giving it to each other. But a man and a woman who have given themselves to one another in marriage have, by their consent to marriage, acquired the capacity to give to each other this unique and special form of love.

Why is this? This is so because marital or spousal or betrothed love differs from every other form of human love in that it is an exclusive, not inclusive, kind of love. We are called upon to love everyone with the redeeming, saving love of Christian charity or agape; we need to have several close friends of both sexes to cherish and love us for ourselves, who seek to help us overcome our faults and grow to full maturity as persons; and parents are obliged to love all their children with a deep, filial kind of love. But the love of which we are now speaking is an exclusive kind of love precisely because it is the sort of love that aspires to a full and total communion. But "its decisive character," the character that makes it spousal or marital or betrothed love and not some other kind of love, is, as Karol Wojtyla put it, "the giving of one's own person to another. The essence of betrothed love is self-giving, the surrender of one's 'I'."[39] But it is the giving of this "I" that constitutes, as we have seen, marriage itself. It is in the mutual donation of their very persons to one another that a man and a woman "establish their uniqueness" and give to themselves the identity of husband and wife, the identity of spouses. And by this gift of self the man and the woman give themselves the ability, which other men and women do not have, to give to each other this unique form of love. Spousal love may indeed arise as an *aspiration* or desire in unmarried persons who *desire* to give themselves to one another and to unite their lives intimately and fully. Yet as an *actuality* spousal love is possible only for the man and the woman who have irrevocably *chosen* each other as irreplaceable and nonsubstitutable spouses. There is indeed a true sort of *pre*marital love between a man and woman who aspire to marriage and to spousal love, but this love remains *pre*marital and *non*marital until the uniqueness and exclusiveness that this love foreshadows and toward which it tends is realized in the act that brings marriage into being, the act of irrevocable personal consent that gives to the man the identity of *husband* and to the woman the identity of *wife*.[40]

Moreover, precisely because spousal love is grounded in and made possible by the marriage itself, the holy and sacramental union of husband and wife, the love of spouses merges, as Vatican Council II taught, the human with the divine.[41] The spousal love made possible by marriage is the kind of love that God wills to merge with his own spousal love for mankind. Thus the love of spouses is a sanctifying and redeeming kind of love which has as its ultimate goal the sanctification of the spouses and, through them, of their families.[42] Indeed, because their love is grounded in their marriage itself, the family of Christian spouses can rightly be regarded as a domestic church,[43] summoned to participate in the life and mission of the church.[44]

Spousal love, moreover, aspires to full communion, which includes bodily, sexual union of the spouses. Although a man and a woman are truly husband and wife by virtue of their free consent to marriage and not by virtue of their union in the "spousal act,"[45] and although they can freely choose, should they mutually agree, to lead a virginal marriage, in consenting to marriage they implicitly consent to the marital act. This act, moreover, uniquely expresses their marital union. Consequently, as Vatican Council II taught, "the acts in marriage by which the intimate and chaste union of spouses takes place are noble and honorable; the truly human performance of these acts fosters the self-giving they signify and enriches the spouses in joy and gratitude."[46] But note that what inwardly expresses and uniquely signifies the holy union of husband and wife are *marital* acts, i.e., acts that are chaste and self-giving, acts that participate in the holiness and sanctity of the marriage itself.

In and through the marital act—which is not simply a sexual, genital act that happens to take place between persons who are married, but which is itself an inward participation in their marital union— husband and wife become "one flesh" and show their openness to the goods of marriage, to the goods of exclusive marital love and to the good of their procreative sexuality. When spouses choose to unite in the marital act, they choose to come to "know" one another in an intimate and unforgettable way; and they choose to do so as nonsubstitutable and irreplaceable spouses precisely because they have *already* made one another nonsubstitutable and irreplaceable by their act of marital consent. Their choice, therefore, is the choice to unite in an act that is truly "the sign and fruit of a total personal self-giving."[47] Sexual union, as a *marital act*, thus unites two persons who indeed want each other and who can be secure in the knowledge that they are wanted and will be wanted "for better or for worse, in sickness and in health, until death." Their choice to unite in the marital act is guided not by blind passion or mindless sentiment but by truth, by the certain knowledge that they are indeed recognized by one another as persons toward whom the only adequate and proper response is love.

I said that the marital act must not be confused with a simple genital act between persons who happen to be married. The marital act, as Vatican Council II insisted, is a *chaste* act, one that respects the goods of marriage and the personhood of the spouses. If one of the spouses should force himself or herself upon the other, against the other's reasonable desires, the act in question would not be a marital act, an expression of marital love and of the marriage itself. Similarly, I submit (although there is not space to pursue this matter here), a married couple are not choosing the marital act when they choose deliberately to set aside its openness to the transmission of human life, to make it to be the kind of act that is opposed to the good of human life in its transmission.[48]

Spousal love, and the chaste one-flesh unity that inwardly expresses this love, are great and wonderful goods. But the point is that these goods are made possible by marriage itself. Contrast, for example, the beautiful act of oblative, betrothed love between spouses in the marital act and sexual coition between unmarried individuals. In the marital act, husband and wife "give" love to one another, and they can give love because they have made themselves able to do so. When nonmarried individuals copulate, they attempt to "make love," but love is something one does not make. It is only something that one can give. And the nonmarried copulators cannot "give" love because they have not made themselves irreplaceable and nonsubstitutable persons. Their copulation does not, therefore, unite two irreplaceable persons but rather joins two individuals who are *in principle* replaceable and substitutable. Although there may be, in the genital union of non-married individuals, some genuine affection, tenderness, and even concern,[49] there is not present authentic marital love. Something is missing in their union that *ought to be* present, namely, the gift of self, the gift one makes in getting married. And this gift is the necessary precondition for genital union if it is to respect the irreplaceable *dignity* of human persons and express a choice inwardly shaped by love.

3. Marriage as a Life-Giving Reality. God is the author of human life. But he chooses to give life to us not immediately from himself as exclusive cause, but through the causality of human persons, one a female, the other a male. Whenever human life is given, it is a splendid gift of God and as such is of incalculable value.[50] Not for nothing did Augustine the Manichee call the son born to him and his unnamed mistress *Adeodatus*, "given by God"—a child, be it noted, who was unwanted when conceived against the will of its parents but whose personhood, once visible, compelled love.[51] Yet in God's plan children are not meant to be given life in the random copulation of unwed males and females. They are meant to be "begotten" in the loving embrace of husband and wife. The reason, as Augustine the Catholic so beautifully put it centuries ago when meditating on the "creation accounts" of Genesis, is that children "are to be begotten lovingly, nourished humanely, and educated religiously," i.e., in the knowledge and love of the one true God.[52] When unmarried couples generate new human life, they do not "procreate" in the true sense, for they do not rightly participate in God's loving design for human life. They do not do so because they are not capable of caring properly for the person to whom they give life—they have not capacitated themselves to give life lovingly, to nourish it humanely, and to educate it religiously. History and human experience give eloquent yet tragic witness to this. Of all living creatures the human child, both unborn and newly born, is the most vulnerable and helpless. Unborn, it requires a mother's womb where it can develop and grow, and its mother requires the support and help of the man by whom she conceived. Once born, the human child needs a home where it can take root and continue its growth. Unmarried individuals, alas, are simply not equipped to meet these needs adequately.[53]

As a human reality that has God as its author, marriage has as one of its principal goods, indeed in one sense its *raison d'être*,[54] the generation and education of children. This is the constant and firm teaching of the church, a point emphasized time and time again by Vatican Council II, Paul VI, and most recently by John Paul II.[55] Marriage and children go together. Not only are children the "crowning glory" of marriage, as Vatican Council II stressed,[56] marriage actually *capacitates* a man and a woman to give life lovingly and procreatively. Husband and wife, precisely because they are spouses and thus able to give to one another what nonspouses cannot give—namely, spousal love—are led by their love for one another to the "reciprocal 'knowledge' which makes them 'one flesh'." They are led to a union upon which the blessing of fertility can descend. Their love, precisely because it is, as marital love, both exclusive and open to the giving of human life, "makes them *capable* of the greatest possible gift, the gift by which they become cooperators with God for giving life to a new human person. Thus the couple, while giving themselves to one another, give not just themselves but also the reality of children, who are a living reflection of their love, a permanent sign of conjugal unity and a living and inseparable synthesis of their being a father and a mother."[57]

Parenting, moreover, is not limited to the loving begetting of human life. The life begotten, as I have already noted, needs a home where it can be nurtured and educated, where it can be received as a priceless gift from God, a person of incalculable value, and a person who needs loving discipline in order to grow to full dignity. And marriage is the abiding reality that enables husbands and wives to meet their parental responsibilities and allows their spousal love "to become for their children the visible sign of the very love of God, 'from whom every family in heaven and earth' (Eph 3.15) is named."[58]

Marriage, thus, respects the intrinsic dignity of children, both born and unborn, whether male or female, "normal" or handicapped. It does so because a man and woman united in marriage are equipped to welcome new human life, to look upon pregnancy as something good and not as a disease. It does so because such men and women are able, by virtue of their marriage, to provide an environment suffused by spousal love, a home where the child will be recognized not as a pet or toy or "product" subservient to its producers' desires, but as a person equal in dignity and sanctity to its parents. Moreover, because spousal love, the love made possible by marriage, enables children to grow in the knowledge and love of God and thus acquire the dignity of persons ready and willing to shape their lives and actions in accord with the truth, marriage respects the dignity to which children are called.

CONCLUSION

Today many, in particular advocates of contraception and abortion, insist that "no unwanted baby ought ever to be born." The church, drawing on divine revelation and the holy Word of God, insists that "no human being ought ever to be unwanted." This truth—that no human being ought ever to be unwanted—is central to the teaching of Vatican Council II, and it is the guiding motif of the pontificate of John Paul II. What we want is a society in which every human being, male or female, young or old, intelligent or incompetent, healthy or handicapped, will be recognized as a living image of God. What we want is a society in which these precious icons of the all-holy God will be *enabled* to give themselves the added dignity to which they are called, the dignity of persons earnestly seeking for "true solutions" to moral problems, endeavoring to shape their choices and actions by conforming them to the objective norms of God's holy and liberating law.

Marriage, as understood by the church, has an indispensable role to play if persons are to be wanted and loved and if persons are to love, even as they have been and are loved by God in Christ. For marriage is a person-affirming, love-enabling, and life-giving reality, one that has God as its author, from whom it has received its specifying goods or ends. Marriage, moreover, is a reality inwardly receptive of God's grace, healing and redemptive. The result of a free, self-determining act, it gives to husbands and wives new capabilities, merging their love with God's love, and empowering the families founded by them to participate in the saving work of Christ himself.

NOTES

1. Thus the very first chapter of Part One of *Gaudium et Spes* is called "The Dignity of the Human Person," while the whole of Part Two is devoted to showing how the dignity of persons is to be respected through a proper regard for marriage, the right development of cultures, rightly ordered economic, social, and political life, the establishment of peace and harmony among nations, and respect for the universally binding principles of the natural and evangelical law in waging war justly.

2. Paul VI developed the thought of *Gaudium et Spes* on marriage in his encyclical *Humanae Vitae*. John Paul II, even before his election as pope, had thought deeply and written extensively on human dignity, love and marriage. Of particular importance is his 1960 work, translated into English under the title *Love and Responsibility*, trans. H.T. Willetts (New York: Farrar, Straus, Giroux, 1981). Since his election as pope, he has devoted much of his considerable energy to thought and writing on human dignity and marriage. Of particular importance are his Apostolic Exhortation on the Role of the Christian Family in the Modern World of November, 1981 (*Familiaris Consortio*) and the series of Wednesday conferences devoted to articulating a "theology of the body." These talks have been collected into three volumes: *The Original Unity of Man and Woman* (Boston: St. Paul Editions, 1981), *Blessed Are the Pure of Heart* (Boston: St. Paul Editions, 1983), and *Reflections on Humanae Vitae* (Boston: St. Paul Editions, 1984). A fine summary of his thought is provided by Richard M. Hogan and John LeVoir, *Covenant of Love: Pope John Paul II on Sexuality, Marriage, and Family in the Modern World* (New York: Doubleday, 1985).

3. On this, see Karl Rahner, "Incarnation," in *Sacramentum Mundi*, 3.110-17, especially 113-15.

4. Thus Vatican Council II insisted, in *Gaudium et Spes*, that "all offenses against life itself, such as murder, genocide, abortion, euthanasia and wilful self-

destruction . . . all these and their like are criminal: They poison civilization, and they debase their perpetrators more than their victims and militate against the honor of the Creator" (no. 27). In no. 51, *Gaudium et Spes* also insisted that "life must be protected with the utmost care from the moment of conception; abortion and infanticide are abominable crimes."

5. It is precisely because human beings are beings of moral worth that Karol Wojtyla (Pope John Paul II) formulated his "personalistic norm." "This norm," he writes, "in its negative aspect states that the person is the kind of good which does not admit of use and cannot be treated as an object of use and as such the means to an end. In its positive form the personalist norm confirms this: the person is a good towards which the only proper and adequate attitude is love"(*Love and Responsibility*, 41). On this, see also *Gaudium et Spes*, no. 35: "Here then is the norm for human activity: that it harmonize with the authentic interests of the human race, in accordance with God's will and design, and enable men as individuals and as members of society to pursue and fulfill their total vocation."

6. Vatican Council II, *Dignitatis Humanae* (*Declaration on Religious Liberty*), no. 2.

7. Vatican Council II, *Gaudium et Spes*, no. 16. Italics mine.

8. Ibid. Italics mine. On this whole matter, it is worth consulting the excellent essay by John M. Finnis, "The Natural Law, Objective Morality, and Vatican II," in *Principles of Catholic Moral Life*, ed. William E. May (Chicago: Franciscan Herald Press, 1981), 113-49, in particular 118-19.

9. Thus John Paul II writes: "God is love and in himself he lives a mystery of personal loving communion. Creating the human race in his own image and continually keeping it in being, God inscribed in the humanity of man and woman the vocation, and thus the capacity and responsibility of love and communion. Love is therefore the fundamental and innate vocation of every human being" (*Familiaris Consortio*, no. 11).

10. That God is the author of marriage is the constant teaching of the church. On this, see the following: Council of Trent, in *Enchiridion symbolorum definitionum et declarationum*, ed. Henricus Denzinger and Adolphus Schönmetzer (hereafter DS) (Barcelona: Herder, 1963, 33rd ed.), no. 1797; Leo XIII, *Arcanum Divinae Sapientiae*, in *Official Catholic Teachings: Love and Sexuality*, ed. Odile Liebard (hereafter Liebard) (Wilmington, N.C.: McGrath Publications, 1978), 9, no. 9; Pius XI, *Casti Connubii*, in Liebard, 24-25, No. 31 (a particularly powerful paragraph); Vatican Council II, *Gaudium et Spes*, no. 48; Paul VI, *Humanae Vitae*, no. 8; John Paul II, *Familiaris Consortio*, no. 11. This teaching is also supported by sound scholarship. See in particular the fine book by Edward Schillebeeckx, *Marriage: Human Reality and Saving Mystery* (New York: Sheed and Ward, 1965), 11-26.

11. *Gaudium et Spes*, no. 48: "For God himself is the author of marriage and has endowed it with various benefits and ends in view" (*Ipse vero Deus est auctor matrimonii, variis bonis et finibus praediti*). At this point, the official note to *Gaudium et Spes* refers readers to the *loci classici* for the "goods" of marriage, namely, to St. Augustine's *De bono conjugii*, PL 40.375-76, 394; St. Thomas Aquinas's *Summa theologiae*, Supplementum, q. 49, a. 3, ad 1; the Decree for the

Armenians issued by the Council of Florence in 1439, DS, no. 1327; and Pius XI's *Casti Connubii*, DS 3703-14.

12. Schillebeeckx, *Marriage*, 20.

13. John Paul II, *Original Unity of Man and Woman*, 109.

14. On the teaching of our Lord in these gospel pericopes, see Schille-beeckx, *Marriage*, 142-55. Schillebeeckx insists (as do the majority of contemporary exegetes) that our Lord taught the absolute indissolubility of marriage. On the so-called Matthean "exception," see Joseph Fitzmyer, "The Matthean Divorce Texts and Some New Palestinian Evidence," *Theological Studies* 37 (1976): 197-226. Fitzmyer, developing an interpretation defended by Joseph Bonsirven, argues persuasively that the *porneia* in Matthew which would "permit" and indeed require separation (with a right to remarry) referred to an incestuous type of sexual relationship, the kind that would invalidate marital union. A different interpretation of these Matthean texts is provided by A.L. Descamps in his essay, "The New Testament Doctrine on Marriage," in *Contemporary Perspectives on Christian Marriage: Propositions and Papers from the International Theological Commission*, ed. Richard Malone and John Connery, S.J. (Chicago: Loyola University Press, 1984), 217-74. Still, Descamps agrees that our Lord taught the absolute indissolubility of marriage, and the interpretation of Fitzmyer seems to be the one most favored by Catholic exegetes today.

15. For the multiple significance of the *bonum sacramenti* and the development of the understanding of this "good" of marriage within Catholic thought, see Schillebeeckx, *Marriage*, 280-338.

16. *Gaudium et Spes*, no. 48. See note 11 above.

17. Helmut Thielicke, *The Ethics of Sex* (New York: Harper and Row, 1963), 108.

18. *Gaudium et Spes*, no. 48.

19. On the significance of "word," see John L. McKenzie, "Toward a Biblical Theology of the Word," in his *Myths and Realities* (Milwaukee: Bruce Publishing Co., 1963).

20. "When the first man exclaims, at the sight of the woman: 'This is bone of my bones, and flesh of my flesh' (Gn 2.23), he merely affirms the human identity of both. Exclaiming in this way, he seems to say: *here is a body that expresses the 'person'!*" John Paul II, *Original Unity of Man and Woman*, 109.

21. In addition to the perceptive comments of John Paul II on this matter in his *Original Unity of Man and Woman*, see also the excellent essay by Walter Brueggemann, "Of the Same Flesh and Bone (Gn2.23a)," *Catholic Biblical Quarterly* 32 (1970):532-42.

22. John Paul II, *Original Unity of Man and Woman*, 81-82. Italics mine.

23. Here it is necessary to say that the *death* to which a man and a woman refer when they give themselves to one another in marriage "until death do us part" is the real, bodily death that humans suffer, after which they can be buried. It is necessary to say this because some contemporary theologians speak of a "moral" and "spiritual" death of a marriage, after which the marriage is no longer in being. Joseph Ratzinger, commenting on this view (expressed by, among others, Bernard Häring), notes that it is predicated upon an uncritical acceptance of a particular type of contemporary philosophy that ignores the

34   *William E. May*

deeper dimensions of human life and experience, *limiting the real and important simply to what may be occupying conscious thinking and living at the present moment* (cf. Ratzinger, "Zur Frage nach der Unauflöslichkeit der Ehe," in *Ehe und Ehescheidung,* heraus. von F. Heinrich und E. Eid (Munich, 1972), 49-50). I believe that Ratzinger has correctly identified the mindset.

24. On this matter, see the fine essay by the Anglican lay and married theologian, J.R. Lucas, "The *Vinculum Conjugale:* A Moral Reality," *Theology* 78 (1975): 225-30.

25. This expressing designation of marital love is provided by St. Bonaventure. See his *In IV sententiarum,* d. 33, a. 1, q. 2 (Opera Omnia. Ad Claras Aquas: Ex Typis Collegii S. Bonaventurae, 1889, Tom. iv, 750). The medieval scholastics had a fine sense of the beauty of marital love and the goodness of the marital act as an expression of this love. On this matter, see Fabian Parmisano, "Love and Marriage in the Middle Ages I and II," *New Blackfriars* 50 (1969): 599-606, 649-60. See also the discussion of medieval thought on love and marriage in Ronald Lawler, Joseph M. Boyle, Jr., and William E. May, *Catholic Sexual Ethics: A Summary, Explanation and Defense* (Huntington, Ind.: Our Sunday Visitor Press, 1985), 42-51.

26. *Gaudium et Spes,* no. 48: "Marriage is an institution confirmed by the divine law and receiving its stability, even in the eyes of society, from the human act by which the partners mutually surrender themselves to each other: for the good of the partners, of the children, and of society, this sacred bond (*hoc vinculum sacrum*) no longer depends on human decision alone."

27. For a further development of the thought that the good of the sacrament is the good that marriage is, and for references to pertinent theological texts, see Parmisano, "Love and Marriage in the Middle Ages," and William E. May, *Sex, Marriage, and Chastity* (Chicago: Franciscan Herald Press, 1981), 35-39.

28 *Gaudium et Spes,* no. 48, text cited in note 26 above.

29. Innocent III, 1198-1210; Honorius III, 1216-1227.

30. Leo XIII, *Arcanum Divinae Sapientiae,* in Liebard, 9, no. 9.

31. On marriage as a sacrament, see Schillebeeckx, *Marriage,* 280-338; May, *Sex, Marriage, and Chastity,* 49-57. On the fact that the marriages of non-Christians, insofar as they are truly marriages and open to its goods, "share, in an inchoate way, in the marital love which unites Christ with his Church," see the "Propositions on the Doctrine of Christian Marriage" formulated by the International Theological Commission in December, 1977, Proposition 3.4. The text of these propositions is found in Malone and Connery, eds., *Contemporary Perspectives on Christian Marriage,* with the text of the pertinent proposition given on p. 22. Note also the comment on this proposition by the chairman of the Commission, Monsignor Philippe Delhaye, on pp. 23-26.

32. On this, in addition to the sources listed in the previous note, see Schillebeeckx, *Marriage,* 157-70.

33. For a further development of this very important matter, see the scholarly essay by Carlo Caffarra, "Marriage as a Reality in the Order of Creation and Marriage as a Sacrament," an essay prepared for the International Theological Commission and found in Malone and Connery, eds., *Contemporary Perspectives on Christian Marriage,* 117-80.

34. John Paul II, *Familiaris Consortio*, no. 13.

35. Pius XI, *Casti Connubii*, in Liebard, 30, no. 47.

36. *Gaudium et Spes*, no. 49.

37. Paul VI, *Humanae Vitae*, no. 9.

38. *Gaudium et Spes*, no. 49; *Humanae Vitae*, no. 9.

39. Karol Wojtyla (Pope John Paul II), *Love and Responsibility*, 96. For a more complete development of this thought, see May, *Sex, Marriage, and Chastity*, 69-79.

40. The subject of premarital love as preparing for marriage has not, unfortunately, been the subject of much recent discussion. An interesting and thoughtful presentation is provided, however, in the S.T.D. dissertation of Michael F. McAuliffe, *Catholic Moral Teaching on the Nature and Object of Conjugal Love* (Studies in Sacred Theology, Series 3, no. 79; Washington, D.C.: The Catholic University of America Press, 1954), 1-27.

41. *Gaudium et Spes*, no. 49.

42. On this, see Pius XI, *Casti Connubii*, in Liebard, 31, no. 50; Schillebeeckx, *Marriage*, 161 ff.

43. *Lumen Gentium* (*Dogmatic Constitution on the Church*), no. 11; *Apostolicam Actuositatem* (*The Decree on the Apostolate of the Laity*), no. 11.

44. This point is developed at length by John Paul II in *Familiaris Consortio*, nos. 49-64. See a commentary on this section of *Familiaris Consortio* by William E. May in *Pope John Paul II and the Family*, ed. Michael Wrenn (Chicago: Franciscan Herald Press, 1983), 167-92.

45. On this, see the discussion of the "consensus-copula" controversy in Schillebeeckx, *Marriage*, 287-302.

46. *Gaudium et Spes*, no. 49.

47. John Paul II, *Familiaris Consortio*, no. 11.

48. The point succinctly made here is developed at some length in my *Sex, Marriage, and Chastity*, 80-89 and also by Lawler, Boyle, and May in *Catholic Sexual Ethics*, 151-67.

49. A fine analysis of the difference between sentimental love, tenderness, and authentic marital love is provided by Karol Wojtyla (Pope John Paul II) in *Love and Responsibility*, 109-18, 200-10.

50. "Human life, even if weak and suffering, is always a splendid gift of God's goodness." Pope John Paul II, *Familiaris Consortio*, no. 30.

51. St. Augustine, *Confessions*, Book 4, chap. 2, no. 2: "In those days I had a woman companion, not one joined to me in what is named lawful wedlock, but one whom my wandering passion, empty of prudence, had picked up.... With her I learned at first hand how great a distance lies between the restraint of a conjugal covenant, mutually made for the sake of begetting children, and the bargain of a lustful love, *where a child is born against our will*, although once born he forces himself upon our love." Italics mine.

52. St. Augustine, *De genesi ad literam*, 9.7.

53. I recognize that unmarried individuals can at times care for their children, and parents who become single because of widowhood or abandonment or other causes seek heroically in many instances to provide properly for their children. Yet nothing can supply the home that loving spouses are capable of giving.

54. Which of the "goods" of marriage is primary depends on the perspective from which one is examining those goods. St. Thomas clearly recognized this when he discussed the goods of marriage in *Summa theologiae*, Supplement, q. 49, a. 3. But as a wise plan of God for the loving generation of children, marriage does have as its end, even in a primordial sense, the generation and education of new human life. Thus *Gaudium et Spes* teaches that "marriage and married love are by nature ordered to the procreation and education of children. Indeed children are the supreme gift of marriage (*praestantissimum matrimonii donum*). . . . God himself said, 'it is not good that man should be alone' (Gn 2.18) and 'from the beginning he made them male and female' (Mt 19.4); wishing to associate them in a special way with his own creative work, God blessed man and woman with the words, 'be fruitful and multiply' (Gn 1.28). Without intending to underestimate the other ends of marriage (*non posthabitis ceteris matrimonii finibus*), it must be said that true married love and the whole structure of family life which results from it is directed to disposing the spouses to cooperate valiantly with the love of the Creator and Savior, who through them will increase and enrich his family from day to day (*unde verus amoris coniugalis cultus totaque vita familiaris ratio inde oriens . . . eo tendunt ut coniuges forti animo dispositi sint ad cooperandum cum amore Creatoris atque Salvatoris, qui per eos Suam familiam in dies dilatat et ditat*). In the *Acta* of the Council, the Commission on the *modi* (or suggested changes in the text of proposed documents) said that "it must be noted that one can consider the hierarchy of goods under different aspects. . . . But in any case the primordial importance (*momentum primordiale*) of procreation and education is mentioned at least 10 times in the text" (*Acta Synodalia Sacrosancti Concilii Oecumenici Vaticani Secundi*, vol. IV, pars VII (Rome: Typis polyglottis Vaticanis, 1978), 477).

55. *Gaudium et Spes*, nos. 48, 50; Paul VI, *Humanae Vitae*, no. 1, 8, 9; John Paul II, *Familiaris Consortio*, nos. 28-35.

56. *Gaudium et Spes*, no. 48.

57. *Familiaris Consortio*, no. 14. Italics mine.

58. Ibid.

JAMES AND KATHLEEN MCGINNIS

The Social Mission of the
Christian Family

1. INTRODUCTION

Vatican II's *Church in the Modern World* defined the family as "a kind of school of deeper humanity."[1] Participation in the social mission of the church, as a family, is one way in which to fulfill clearly the conciliar definition. In order to show that such participation is both possible and enriching, this chapter combines ecclesial principles with practical suggestions as to how a family might go about incorporating the social teaching of the Catholic church into daily family life. The ideas found in this chapter are the fruits of 25 years of social action, 20 years of teaching, 18 years of marriage, and 15 years of parenting. They also include the insights and experiences of a dozen other families who have attempted, as we have, to integrate family life and social ministry. We are grateful that the Council called for dialogue with the modern world; this chapter updates an assessment of contemporary issues which currently exist within the human community and which, in a special way, affect family life.

2. THE FAMILY AS CELL OF SOCIETY AND
TEACHER OF SOCIAL VIRTUES

The well-being of marriage and family life has a substantial influence on the well-being of the individual and of society as a whole. Nowhere is this influence more essential than in the educational task of parents, a responsibility clearly mandated in *Gaudium et Spes* and in other documents of the Second Vatican Council.[2] *The Declaration on Christian Education*, for example, notes that "the family is the first school of those social virtues which every society needs ... it is through the family that they [children] are gradually introduced into civic partnership with their fellow human beings, and into the People of God."[3] Parents ultimately educate for nothing less than the transformation of the world and the building of the Kingdom of God.

Hierarchical teaching also clearly indicates how parents are to fulfill this duty to teach social virtues. The Council's *Decree on the Apostolate of the Laity* embraces a developmental approach. Parents are to prepare their children from an early age, within the family circle, to discern God's love for all persons; parents are to teach their children little by little—and above all, by their example—to have concern for their neighbors' needs, material and spiritual.[4]

The example which parents must give is nct just a matter of what parents do in front of their children, but also a matter of what they do *with* their children. The whole family needs to be involved in concern for the neighbors' needs. When children, as well as parents, experience Christian service and action for justice *as a regular part of family life*, then justice can truly become a "constitutive dimension" of their preaching the gospel.[5] This integrated approach to justice and family life is clearly preferable to the method by which children participate in Christian service and action for justice only in a special elementary school Lenten program or a special high school religion course. Such fragmented attempts tend to have children perceive the social mission of the church as something "extra."

3. HOW THE SOCIETY/CULTURE AFFECTS THE FAMILY

Before considering how the Christian family can affect society, however, it is necessary to examine the various ways in which the larger society affects family life and values. As *Gaudium et Spes* and subsequent papal teaching have indicated, manifold problems confront the modern world and affect the quality of family life. In the spirit of *The Church in the Modern World*, this section examines five problems particularly prevalent in the United States today, questions which influence families in a special way. Significantly, family life also plays a special role in challenging these issues.

Materialism. While modern capitalist and socialist economies have provided a more decent life in material terms for hundreds of millions of people, they have also created a very real problem for Christian families, especially in capitalist societies. Pope Paul VI's warning that superfluous goods may be enslaving modern men and women[6] points to a tendency in affluent societies: objects are becoming more important than persons. Objects are personified and persons are commodified. Even a cursory study of modern-day advertising reveals that objects are presented as providing us with identity, companionship, joy, intimacy—all values traditionally associated with people. Persons, on the other hand, are often treated as objects—sex objects, sales targets, units of labor. The effects of materialism and the commodification of the person devastate families in three distinct ways.

The first effect which materialism can have on family life is to encourage a "more is better; happiness is having" mentality. This drive takes a terrible toll on both adults and children as recognition and affirmation come to center on what we have rather than on who we are. The more we seek security in money, goods, and huge insurance policies, the less we find our security in the Lord and in one another. Fearing economic consequences, we become afraid to take risks for the gospel. Material novelties, constantly dangled before us, threaten fidelity to our spouse, our children and our work. This constant message to possess more and to enjoy the good life tantalizes children as well as adults, poor as well as rich, and threatens to shortchange the spiritual dimension of life, if not to jeopardize it altogether.[7]

A second effect of materialism, flowing directly from the first, is the tendency to look down upon the "have-nots." These people, the economically poor, the elderly, the disabled, the unborn, the not-so-beautiful people of our society, are disregarded, disdained, and in some cases even destroyed.

A third effect centers on the exploitation of the earth. The prevailing "more is better" attitude threatens the earth itself, since the needs of future generations can easily be ignored in the face of pressing contemporary needs and desires.

Individualism. Not surprisingly, materialism fosters individualism. Generated by a mentality which exalts possessions,[8] individualism separates personal freedom from its social context and manifests itself in such forms as a private property ethic which entitles one to use private resources at whim. Such a use of private property is very different from the Catholic church's teaching which reminds us that God intended the earth and all that it contains for the use of every human being; the right to property, therefore, must never be exercised to the detriment of the common good.[9]

This individualism weighs heavily on families in a particular fashion. The highly competitive nature of our economic system and society, combined with the image of rugged individuals raising themselves up by their own bootstraps, high levels of mobility, and the ascendancy of nuclear families over extended families, have isolated many families. This isolation has increased the need for material security and fosters competition for grades, jobs, affection, positions, prestige, power. Supportive, noncompetitive relationships, even within families, become much more difficult in such an atmosphere.

Governments and economic systems also place great burdens on the family when they do not guarantee the basic necessities of life for each person. Often, both parents are forced to work long hours; frequently, unemployed fathers are forced to leave their homes in order to secure minimal assistance for other family members. Unemployment, whether caused by automation, multinational corporations closing factories for cheaper labor elsewhere, government budget cuts, or the failure to plan and direct more capital to job-creating industries, affects workers and their families in many dimensions—spiritual, psychological, physical, and economic, as noted in the recent second draft of the American Catholic bishops' pastoral letter on economic life.[10]

Racism.   The connection between economic problems which families face in our society and the problem of racism is clearly pointed out in the pastoral letter on racism, *Brothers and Sisters to Us*:

> Racism and economic oppression are distinct but interrelated forces which dehumanize our society. Movement toward authentic justice demands a simultaneous attack on both evils. Our economic structures are undergoing fundamental changes which threaten to intensify social inequalities in our nation . . . the poor and racial minorities are being asked to bear the heaviest burden of the new economic pressures . . . [11]

The letter also discusses the hard facts of racism and its effect on families—disproportionate unemployment, the stereotyping of minorities in the media and even in school textbooks, the low self-image of minority people, and the growing housing crisis which plagues minority families. It remains clear that racial discrimination "has only exacerbated the harmful relationship between poverty and family instability."[12]

Sexism.   Sexism, that is, discrimination based on sex, is similar to racism in\ its intensity and consequences. The economic effects, for instance, are becoming clearly evident as more women, due to financial need, join the workforce. Problems such as unequal pay and unequal opportunity often create serious crises for a family, especially if the family depends solely on the woman's income for support. For minority women, a double burden of discrimination exists.

The cultural consequences of sexism are perhaps less blatant but no less serious for families, and thus for society as a whole. Stereotypes regarding what it means to be a "man" and a "woman" limit the emotional, physical, and spiritual development of men and women, boys and girls. To view nurturing and service solely as "the woman's role" is to imprison women and inhibit men in the development of the nurturing/service dimension of their person. As with racial stereotypes, sex role stereotypes infect the books children and adults read, the toys with which children play, advertising, television, and films.

Similarly, to present women and men as mere sex objects threatens both friendships between men and women and marital fidelity. This presentation finds blatant expression in pornography and more subtle but equally pervasive expression in advertising, television, and film.

Militarism and Violence. Violence as a means of resolving conflict—from the interpersonal to the international level—constitutes a fifth problem for family life in particular and for society in general. Military budgets throughout the world continue to increase; the pursuit of security through bigger and better locks, police forces, prisons, armies, and nuclear warheads accelerates. Terrorism and repression threaten families, especially socially active ones, in many countries. Competition among countries to secure scarce resources, favorable overseas investments, and other acquisitions of "vital interest," leads to greater preparation for war rather than to less.

Growing militarism and violence hold a number of frightening consequences for family life and society. When school children in Michigan are recruited in a contest to design an insignia for the new Trident submarine, a first-strike weapon with 408 warheads and the destructive capacity of 2,040 Hiroshimas, then we fear that militarism has become part of a national mentality. The economic impact is equally pervasive. Military budgets which absorb billions of dollars are a major reason why families cannot find adequate food, shelter, medical care and education.[13]

4. FAMILY PARTICIPATION IN THE CHURCH'S SOCIAL MISSION

The social teaching of the Catholic church, especially since *Gaudium et Spes*, makes it clear that to confront the oppressive situations and structures described above is integral to the church's mission. The 1971 synodal document, *Justice in the World*, explicitly notes that to love our neighbor involves working for justice.[14] It is not sufficient to care for the victims of injustice through corporal works of mercy; it is also necessary to change the situations and structures (economic, political, cultural) which create the victims in the first place—a task of justice. In other words, the structural dimension or level of reality needs our loving activity. It is nothing less than social sin itself which families must address—a task clearly indicated in Catholic social thought:

> The family must also see to it that the virtues of which it is the teacher and guardian should be enshrined in laws and institutions. It is of the highest importance that families should together devote themselves directly and by common agreement to transforming the very structure of society. Otherwise, families will become the first victims of the evils that they will have watched idly and with indifference.[15]

Before specifically elaborating how families can be part of this mission, however, it is important to investigate certain of the obstacles which prevent families from participating in this call of the church and to present a general strategy for overcoming these obstacles.

Obstacles Limiting Family Participation.   In addition to the five problems cited in Part Three of this chapter, three other issues present obstacles to a family's full participation in the social mission of the church: lack of inspiration, lack of imagination, and lack of integration.

Many families, faced with so many pressing problems of their own, are not inspired to work with and for others. Economic insecurity and other fears keep them from taking the risks involved in social action. Often isolated from the victims of injustice, from people working for change, and from a supportive community, many families have not been touched or moved to want to act on behalf of justice.

Frequently, families who *are* inspired to act do not know how to go about becoming involved in the social aspects of the church's mission. Lack of imagination and insight keep them from acting, especially when the problems seem so complex and overwhelming. Some may limit peace and justice activity to demonstrations, of which they are afraid, or hunger relief programs, to which they already contribute. The "what more can we do?" question frequently occurs when families lack the imagination and courage to get in touch with actual victims of injustice and to network with people currently working for social change.

Lack of integration, closely related to a lack of imagination, centers especially on the obstacle of time. Active Christian parents are among the most beleaguered of peoples—raising children, building their own relationship, participating in school, parish, and neighborhood life, trying to survive financially. Unless parents can imaginatively integrate family life and apostolic life, family ministry and social ministry, they will never have time for both forms of services.

In addition to time, lack of integration also reflects itself in the dichotomy which many people experience between their personal spirituality and social action. Some Christians do not participate in the church's social mission because they neither see such participation as an essential expression of their faith nor do they understand the call to transform the world as a call from Jesus. This group, therefore, tends to regard action on behalf of peace and justice as a realm solely for "activists" or secular humanists.

A Four-Part Strategy for Overcoming These Obstacles. To secure the inspiration, imagination, and integration necessary for the church's mission, and to have these components take root in one's heart, calls for a conversion process composed of four major steps.[16]

Experiencing Social Ministry as a Call from Jesus. A Christian is more likely to respond to the call to social ministry if she/he understands that call as part of the mission of Jesus which Christians now carry out in the world. Fostering a personal relationship with Jesus, especially through prayer and thoughtful reflection on the Scriptures, is essential to hearing the voice of God. Parents must do this with their children, as should teachers with their students and parish ministers with their parishioners.

The liturgical year, embodying the life of Jesus, also highlights his social mission. Advent/Christmas reminds us that God takes the world so seriously as to come among us as a human being, in simplicity, to serve rather than to be served. Lent marks the call to repentance for social sin as well as personal sin; this rich liturgical season also calls us to respond to Jesus as he suffers today—in the hungry, the elderly, those victimized by racism or repression. Easter/Pentecost are liturgical sources of hope and action, since the power of the Spirit who raised Jesus from the dead is continuously at work in the world.[17] The Eucharist itself calls us to build the unity of the Body of Christ which we symbolize and celebrate in that sacrament. This deep, inexhaustible richness of the church's liturgical life, and its significance for the social mission of the community, merit continual reflection in the conversion process.

Experiencing Advocates for Justice. People working hard for justice provide us with both inspiration and imagination. The witness of people who give of themselves generously, often at some risk, can dispel fears regarding involvement in justice issues; their witness, whose motivation is not financial, also offers an important countermodel to the materialism which surrounds us. These people teach us what a living faith means as they translate religious ideals such as peace and justice into practice. This life of service and social activity brings joy and satisfaction but also, at times, pain and discouragement; yet, people committed to action on behalf of the gospel realize the truth of God's word: "Give and you shall receive."

The activities, stories, and ideas of those who advocate justice can spark an imaginative spirit. A wide range of channels for social involvement exists; people already engaged in justice and peace issues can help us to see them.

Experiencing the Victims of Injustice. Statistics about hungry people or victims of racism often do not touch our hearts and move us to action. Direct experience of those who suffer from injustice can and frequently does. Encountering such victims helps us to sense the urgency which surrounds questions of justice, dispelling complacent attitudes. Direct encounter with victims of injustice, furthermore, dispels such myths as "the poor are lazy" or victims of injustice "are incapable of helping themselves." On the contrary, the poor and those who suffer from injustice are often gifted people from whom we can learn much. Direct experience, therefore, helps to break down dangerous stereotypes.

Experiencing Support in Community. Participation in the church's social mission often involves some risk—a factor which the support of others helps to overcome. Working with other families not only increases the effectiveness of social action but also provides accountability, challenge, and the necessary ingredient of enjoyment. This need to enjoy social involvement, especially prevalent in children, helps to integrate peace and justice work into the larger fabric of life.

Prayer communities, families that come together regularly to celebrate the Eucharist, and other bondings of families often evolve into groups who share economic resources and involve themselves more fully in the church's social mission.

5. SPECIFIC WAYS FOR FAMILIES TO PARTICIPATE IN THE CHURCH'S SOCIAL MISSION

The suggestions that follow relate specifically to the five social problems identified in Part Three of this chapter. Although these problems do not exhaust the areas for social action, they nevertheless constitute key issues which plague today's world—a world with which

Gaudium et Spes invited dialogue. We neither wish to suggest that a family should be doing everything listed below, nor do we want to limit other imaginative possibilities which may emerge. The suggestions simply come from our own experience, prayer, reading, and reflection, as well as the insights and experiences of a dozen other families who have been trying, as we have, to integrate family life and social ministry. Three categories emerge—life-style changes, works of mercy, and works of justice.

Materialism and Individualism.   A life-style which seeks to offset the materialism and rugged individualism so prevalent in today's culture must emphasize fidelity, simplicity/stewardship, and a critical awareness of the pervasiveness of these problems.

Vatican II's *Church in the Modern World* attests to the powerful witness of fidelity within family life:

> The Christian family, which springs from marriage as a reflection of the loving covenant between Christ and the Church and as a participation in that covenant, will manifest to all the Savior's living presence in the world, and the genuine nature of the Church. This, the family will do by the mutual love of the spouses, by their generous fruitfulness, their solidarity and faithfulness, and by the loving way in which all members of the family work together.[18]

To fulfill this conciliar mandate is a daily challenge for the Christian family. Spouses face many assaults on their covenant to each other. The culture promises instant gratification, problem-free relationships, quick fixes, escape when things get rough. Covenantal love, on the other hand, demands sacrifice, "hanging-in," forgiveness, vulnerability, and efforts to keep a freshness in the relationship.

Parents face an even greater challenge in their fidelity to their children. Homework, sick and sleepless nights, frustrating interruptions, resolution of difficulties—all require daily parental sacrifice, time, and patience. Fidelity in family life means listening to children share personal crises, as well as insignificant happenings; it also means empowering children to resolve their own conflicts, nonviolently, rather than intervening and solving problems for them. Encouraging older children to become more independent also tests parental fidelity. The teenage years entail watching children make mistakes, renegotiating limits, promoting self-esteem, deciding which behaviors or problems to ignore and which to confront.

By practicing the solidarity and faithfulness about which the Council speaks, parents teach covenantal love not only to their children, but also to the world around them. The sacrificial demands of this covenantal love, moreover, prepare parents and children for the sacrificial demands of discipleship in the larger world. Parents, who foster a healthy self-esteem within their children and who provide a harbor of love to which children can always return, empower their children to hold personal convictions in a skeptical public arena and to be other-centered. Parents, whose fidelity over the years purifies their love, are better prepared to face the risks and "deaths" of following Jesus to the cross as they confront the political, economic, and cultural institutions of their society.

In addition to fidelity, simplicity/stewardship also mark the life-style of the family confronting the materialism/individualism of these times. Recycling materials is a basic way to care for the earth's resources. Some families now share economically, by exchanging tools or outgrown clothes or, in a community of families, by pooling incomes and dividing according to need.

To prove that it is not necessary to own in order to enjoy, many families turn to libraries, parks, and other public facilities. Teaching children to use and care for library books and records, because others equally deserve the use of these goods, is a simple yet profound way to practice stewardship.

Alternative gift-giving presents another opportunity to simplify the family life-style. Replacing costly and generally less personal gifts with home-made presents, providing the gift of one's time and talent, or purchasing the handicrafts of the economically poor, all promote a sense of simplicity.

Stewardship itself flows from a deep reverence for the earth. Certain activities—a family or community garden, hiking, camping trips, a contemplative walk through the park with a child—put us in touch with creation and the Creator. They provide regular opportunities to experience beauty and to learn to care for it.

Finally, families need to foster a consciousness of and a critical attitude toward the prevalent cultural values of materialism and individualism. Advertising, packaging, television, and film frequently foster these values, and both children and adults need to be sensitive to manipulative techniques found in the media and in marketing.

Engaging in works of mercy provides a second channel to offset the problems of materialism and individualism. Treating one's home, the family's most precious possession, as a gift from the Lord meant for service and sharing is a major way to concretize stewardship. To open the family home to a person in need of temporary or long-term housing—a teenager who cannot make it home, an overnight traveler, an elderly relative, a foster child—is to welcome the Lord. The sharing of the family home, if emotionally and financially feasible, also has profound impact on the children of the host family, since this action affects the daily life of the family.

Opportunities for sharing other goods with the economically poor abound. Poor parishes or neighborhood centers frequently need food, clothing, and toys. Houses of hospitality, such as those operated by the Catholic Worker, often seek families to prepare and serve meals as well as to donate goods.

Whenever possible, such sharing should be reciprocal. Serving the poor means "doing with" more than "doing for," and efforts on behalf of justice should recognize, affirm, and call forth all peoples' giftedness. Helping the elderly, for instance, entails more than just running errands for them; it means inviting them to share their wisdom, insights, and skills.

Works of social justice must also accompany these works of mercy. Attempts at structural change could include efforts to enhance the quality of the media and to encourage more social responsibility on the part of large corporations. Christian families, in order to counteract the dehumanizing values of consumerism and materialism, should work to promote the human and aesthetic quality of network and local programming and policies. They should also dedicate energies to the limitation of programs depicting excessive violence and irresponsible sex.[19]

Similarly, Christian families can challenge corporations that pursue maximization of profit at the expense of people. Participation in boycotts of certain products, made at the expense of third world peoples or first world minority groups, is an action in which the entire family can participate. On the more positive side, Christian families can also support businesses which do not exploit people or the earth. Buying fruits and vegetables directly from small farmers or from local food cooperatives is one way to offset the giant agribusiness corporations which exert a growing control over North American food production. Parish or neighborhood credit unions also offer an alternative to large commercial banks which frequently choose to ignore poorer neighborhoods.

Racism. Family life-style challenges racism when it helps the children experience and desire a more multicultural and multiracial world. Is the home environment multicultural or monocultural? Do the visuals in the home—the art work, magazines, toys, books—portray a variety of peoples and cultures? Are visitors to the family home always of one race?

Parents should ask these same questions of other locales—the neighborhood, school, church, the local shopping center. Similarly, children who see only white middle-class professionals—teachers, dentists, physicians—come away with certain impressions regarding which racial group is really important. When the wider environment is monocultural, however, it is more difficult to provide children and adults with the multiracial experiences, friendships, and contacts which promote respect of and appreciation for people of different races and cultures. Therefore, consciously to pursue a multicultural environment by deliberately searching for such educational, worship, entertainment, and professional opportunities enriches the family as it helps to shape attitudes which are essential to building the Kingdom of God.[20]

In addition to a life-style which fosters an appreciation of the rich diversity of ethnic, racial, and cultural groups in our society, families should also challenge institutions and institutional practices which encourage racism. Children, as well as adults, can write to publishers to protest books which portray racial stereotypes; likewise, advocates for justice ought to commend those publishers whose books seek to eliminate racial or cultural stereotyping. Similar pressure or commendation can be directed at toy store managers and developers of school curricula.

The media, whose impact is vast, have a special obligation regarding the elimination of racism. Christian families should give careful scrutiny to television and radio programs; a call to a station in protest of a racially offensive joke, for instance, can be one tiny prophetic voice on behalf of justice. Amusement parks and other entertainment centers should be held accountable for their portrayal of diverse racial and cultural groups.

Sexism. Family life provides many opportunities to challenge sexism. Parents, who most effectively teach their children through their example, should distribute more equitably and especially in some nontraditional ways such household tasks as cleaning, laundry, cooking, child care, transportation, and repairs. Children themselves, furthermore, need to learn these basic human survival skills. Rotating household chores, regardless of sex, and promoting a diversity of physical, intellectual, and artistic capabilities are ways in which parents can resist the limitations which society often imposes on boys and girls, but especially on girls. Besides fostering the development of a variety of skills and interests in children, parents also need to encourage their children to cultivate internal qualities; caring, nurturing and sensitivity are important for *both* sexes, as are assertive, independent, decisive, inventive qualities.

Parents can also help their children to become more critical of the media and the way in which television, radio, and so forth portray women and men. Watching television as a family, for instance, presents frequent opportunities for parents to invite children to question why men or women are depicted in certain stereotypical roles. Conversely, parents should encourage children to read stories or to watch television shows which provide role models that are different from prevalent mores.

On a wider scale, parents must critically evaluate institutions, such as the school, which are in a position to shape children's attitudes regarding sex roles. Instructional materials which present nonsexist images and the contributions of women, as well as men, are essential. Extracurricular opportunities in athletics, student government, music programs, or science clubs should be open to all, without discrimination; guidance programs, likewise, should eliminate biases when promoting career choices. The school's own careful use of role models, such as male elementary teachers and female administrators, imparts a quiet but important message to students.

Pressure placed on toy manufacturers, publishers, and the media in regard to racism is equally applicable to the problem of sexism. Similarly, families must also direct social action to the economic sector in an attempt to eradicate discriminatory wages, lack of affirmative action in hiring and promotion, sexist expectations regarding appearance and sexual availability, and discriminatory credit practices.

Militarism/Violence.   The development of nonviolent, cooperative attitudes and skills in children is an important responsibility which parents can exercise in a variety of ways. The home environment itself influences children immeasurably, since a cooperative, accepting climate nurtures nonviolent attitudes and skills within the family. Affirmation and affection, rather than criticism and coldness, should dominate family life as parents check homework, attend children's musical or athletic events, and generally encourage self-esteem and community involvement. Cooperative chores and games can balance a competitive spirit; family prayer and vacations enforce a spirit of unity rather than division.

To offset the violence of today's world, the home environment must be one which forgives as well as accepts. Such a climate reduces tensions, diffuses resentment, and promotes nonviolent means of conflict resolution. Parental example is especially crucial here; a wife and husband who feel secure about their own relationship and who work for marital harmony provide irreplaceable role models.

The development of basic communication skills is also essential to a family seeking to promote an alternative to war and violence. Learning to express one's ideas, feelings, and desires clearly is as important as learning to listen carefully. Nonviolent conflict resolution, which builds upon communication skills, includes the ability to generate alternative solutions in conflict situations and to evaluate these alternatives in light of the needs/wants of the parties involved. Regular family meetings or councils provide a structure for nonviolent conflict resolution and mutual problem-solving. Regarding the question of discipline, parents should seek alternatives to physical or psychological forms of punishment, since children who experience violence tend to use it themselves.

In addition to challenging the violence which saturates the media, families can also engage the political/military establishment. Letters to political representatives which call for a reversal of the arms race, and participation in public demonstrations giving prophetic witness to gospel values are channels of action which are legal and which can involve the entire family. The question of tax resistance is a bit more risky; illegal, and therefore beyond most of us, it nevertheless is an option which families must address.

6. CONCLUSION

Is this too much to expect of families? Yes, if this call remains only a general one. Families need to see that specific possibilities for action, such as we have suggested here, do exist and that such activity enriches the entire family.

Family participation in the church's social mission provides children with a hope which is rooted in reality; they come to know through experience that change, although difficult to effect, is none-theless possible and that they themselves have the power to bring it about. While we do not recommend overloading children with social problems, we believe, nonetheless, that helping them to deal more creatively with the problems which already surround them, and combining that endeavor with other dimensions of childhood and family life encourages children to be creative and alive, rather than warped and cynical.

Gaudium et Spes asked the church to take the world and its problems seriously. The activities described in this chapter attempt to do just that.[21] They testify to our belief that if this world is to become a more peaceful, just, human community, then such a process must start with the cell of society, the family.

NOTES

1. *Pastoral Constitution on the Church in the Modern World*, no. 52, in Walter M. Abbott, S.J., general ed., *The Documents of Vatican II* (New York: Guild Press, 1966). All conciliar documentation in this chapter uses the Abbott edition and indicates the appropriate section number(s) for reference.

2. *Pastoral Constitution on the Church in the Modern World*, nos. 47-52. See also, for instance, *Decree on the Apostolate of the Laity*, no. 11.

3. *Declaration on Christian Education*, no. 3.

4. *Decree on the Apostolate of the Laity*, no. 30.

5. Synod of Bishops, *Justice in the World* (Washington, D.C.: United States Catholic Conference, 1972), introduction.

6. Paul VI, *A Call to Action: Apostolic Letter on the Eightieth Anniversary of Rerum Novarum* (Washington, D.C.: United States Catholic Conference, 1971), no. 9.

7. For an elaboration of this point, see Bishops of Appalachia, *This Land Is Home to Me*, in David J. O'Brien and Thomas A. Shannon, eds., *Renewing the Earth: Catholic Documents on Peace, Justice, and Liberation* (New York: Image Books, 1977), 472-515.

8. *Justice in the World*, Part Three.

9. Paul VI, *On the Development of Peoples* (Washington, D.C.: United States Catholic Conference, 1967), nos. 22-23.

10. National Conference of Catholic Bishops, *Pastoral Letter on Catholic Social Teaching and the U.S. Economy*, second draft, October 7, 1985 (Washington, D.C.: United States Catholic Conference, 1985), chap. III, 135-68.

11. National Conference of Catholic Bishops, *Brothers and Sisters to Us* (Washington, D.C.: United States Catholic Conference, 1979), 1-2.

12. Ibid., 4.

13. See Ruth Leger Sivard, *World Military and Social Expenditures, 1984* (Washington, D.C.: World Priorities, 1984), for an account of current military spending. The criticism that families, especially the poor, suffer when resources, monies, and energies are directed to the military instead of to resolving pressing human needs such as hunger and housing is a constant theme in Catholic social teaching.

14. *Justice in the World*, Part Two.

15. "Lineamenta," *The Role of the Christian Family in the Modern World* (Washington, D.C.: United States Catholic Conference, 1979), 44.

16. Section Five of this chapter indicates specific ways in which to inspire action, foster imagination, and integrate the experience into daily family life.

17. *Justice in the World*, 47.

18. *The Church in the Modern World*, no. 48.

19. Paul VI, *A Call to Action*, no. 20.

2222/4

20. In this regard, it is better to understand our society as one composed of diverse ethnic, racial, and cultural groups rather than as the traditional "melting pot."

21. These suggestions are expanded in *Parenting for Peace and Justice* (Maryknoll, N.Y.: Orbis Books, 1981) and in a variety of leadership materials for adult and family education, including *Christian Parenting for Peace and Justice Program Guide*, the *Partners in Peacemaking* guidebook for leaders. These are all updated regularly through the quarterly newsletter and other mailings of the Parenting for Peace and Justice Network, of which we are the national co-coordinators. For these resources and/or further information, contact us at the Institute for Peace and Justice, 4144 Lindell Blvd., #400, St. Louis, Mo. 63108.

PART II

Culture

Toward Renewing "The Life and Culture of
Fallen Man": "Gaudium et Spes" as Catalyst
for Catholic Feminist Theology

"Gaudium et Spes" and the Bioethical
Signs of the Times

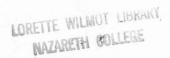

Anne E. Patrick, S.N.J.M.

Toward Renewing "The Life and Culture of Fallen Man": "Gaudium et Spes" as Catalyst for Catholic Feminist Theology[1]

In discussing "The Proper Development of Culture," *Gaudium et Spes* (hereafter cited as *GS*) ranges widely over theological, ethical, and educational matters pertaining to "the cultivation of the goods and values of nature" (no. 53). The tone of this section of the conciliar document is largely positive, conveying an openness to new possibilities and a hope that proper development of culture will lead to "a world that is more human" (no. 57). Twenty years later, the church continues to grapple with the items this text identified as sufficiently novel to warrant our times being called "a new age of human history" (no. 54), items which include cultural and religious pluralism, new developments in the physical and human sciences and in technology, and increasing aspirations toward autonomy and responsibility on the part of women and men across the globe. But when one surveys the section, "The Proper Development of Culture," in light of the entire document of *GS*, and in light of subsequent developments in the church, there is a change in the scene since 1965 that stands out for its significance and impact, a change which seems not to have been anticipated by the document and yet is arguably, at least in part, a result of *GS*. This development is the enhanced sense of full personhood and moral and social responsibility now articulated by Catholic women, a number of whom are solidly established as professional theologians.

How did it happen that women, once presumed to be silent and acquiescent, docile and supportive of male ecclesiastical authority, came to take positions in opposition to "official" Catholic teachings on questions ranging from God-language and women's ordination to conception control, homosexuality, and even abortion?[2] An extraordinary development has taken place in Roman Catholicism since the appearance of *GS*, and this chapter indicates the connection I see between the words of this document and the emerging feminist critique of the tradition by Catholics who regard themselves as loyal members of the church. It is my impression that the rhetoric of GS struck forcefully on a female population that was ripe for implementing its ideas and carrying them beyond anything anticipated by the Fathers of the Council.[3] My claim here is that the limited vision of social justice articulated by this document paved the way for a more adequate Christian feminist vision of justice among Catholics who might otherwise have felt it necessary to choose between either a traditionally Catholic or a secular feminist philosophy of life and view of justice. What made the difference was the opening of theological education and research to women, which lessened the insularity of male theologians and at the same time gave women the tools to argue our case for justice in the forum that was responsible for legitimating our subordination.

"GAUDIUM ET SPES": PRODUCT OF ANDROCENTRIC CULTURE

There is no reason to suppose that the Council Fathers ever anticipated the sort of contributions Rosemary Radford Ruether, Elisabeth Schüssler Fiorenza, or Margaret A. Farley would make to Catholic theology. It is true that no. 55 recognizes that in general women as well as men are eager to mold the culture of the societies to which they belong:

> In each nation and social group there is a growing number of men and women [*virorum ac mulierum*] who are conscious that they themselves are the craftsmen [*culturae artifices*] and molders of their community's culture. All over the world the sense of autonomy and responsibility increases with effects of the greatest importance for the spiritual and moral maturity of mankind. This will become clearer to us if we place before our eyes the unification of the world and the duty imposed on us to build up a better world in truth and justice.

However, the egalitarian reference to women and men together here is highly unusual; although GS does employ *mulier* alone in various contexts, it generally avoids *vir*, using instead forms of the ambiguous term *homo*, which are nearly always rendered in the generic masculine ("man" or "men") in English.[4] Thus women are not specified in the crucial paragraph that voices the hope that "more of the laity [*plures laici*] will receive adequate theological formation and that some among them will dedicate themselves professionally to these studies and contribute to their advancement," in which the Fathers also declare that "Those involved in theological studies in seminaries and universities should be eager to cooperate with men [*hominibus*] versed in other fields of learning by pooling their resources and their points of view"(no. 62). There is every likelihood that readers of this paragraph would infer a presumption on the part of its authors that intellectual circles were overwhelmingly, if not exclusively, male. For this they could hardly be blamed, given that women were excluded from the early sessions of Vatican II and were admitted only as silent observers during the final two sessions. Indeed, as Albertus Magnus McGrath recalls in her study *Women and the Church*, the noted British economist Barbara Ward was not allowed to address the Council Fathers, her paper instead being delivered at the third session by a man.[5]

During the Council there were, of course, a number of significant statements made concerning justice for women, and Archbishop Paul Hallinan of Atlanta filed a proposal during the final session that women be encouraged to become "teachers and consultants" in theology.[6] But although Hallinan's proposal was widely noted by the press, it never reached the assembly floor, and the text of GS does not specifically promote the involvement of women in theology.

Thus, although the document does represent some progress on the question of justice for women, its tone and contents (especially when rendered in English) betray a decidedly androcentric bias, indeed a blindness to the sexism in its understanding of human rights and dignity. Nonetheless, the language of the document at least leaves open the possibility that women might interpret in their favor statements the text left ambiguous, for there are no passages specifically ruling out the participation of women in theology. Furthermore, by affirming intellectual freedom in theology, the highly significant final sentence of the section on culture states a principle that contributed both to male support of women's involvement in the discipline and also to the development of feminist positions by both male and female theologians:

> But for the proper exercise of this role [of theologian], the faithful, both clerical and lay [*sive clericis sive laicis*], should be accorded a lawful freedom of inquiry, of thought, and of expression, tempered by humility and courage in whatever branch of study they have specialized (no. 62).

Later in this essay, I probe in some detail the document's limitations where justice for women is concerned, but what needs to be stressed first are two factors that offset these limitations and enabled GS to be the ground-breaking document it was. These are essentially theological affirmations, which permeate the document and which make it possible for Catholics who read it to carry its spirit beyond the literal sense of the text.

KEY THEOLOGICAL AFFIRMATIONS

In the first place, it is impossible to exaggerate the import of the document's stress on the essential equality of all persons (*homines*) and of its recognition that " . . . forms of social or cultural discrimination in basic personal rights on the grounds of sex . . . must be curbed and eradicated as incompatible with God's design" (no. 29). Here the Fathers incorporate into their own text a critical principle that continues to be seized upon by their readers as a basis for carrying the spirit of *GS* beyond the implementation envisioned by most of its episcopal authors.

In the second place, along with this important affirmation that God intends a society in which the essential equality of woman is recognized, the Fathers also affirm a more dynamic, historically conscious understanding of God's will for humanity than had previously held sway in post-Reformation Catholicism, with all that this implies in terms of openness to the genuinely *new*. The tone of confidence with which this document speaks of the abiding presence of God's Spirit in history, with the accompanying recognition that even ideals may develop and improve, had the potential to counter a spirituality that feared to transgress static divine orders. Indeed, in contrast to this negative spirituality, *GS* invited believers to look beyond the forms that symbolized past understandings of God's will and concentrate instead on the essential divine values of truth, justice, and love that pulse at the heart of the tradition. Early in *GS*, the words of section no. 11 establish a new sort of piety, one far different from the passive, defensive piety associated with the period following the "modernist crisis," which had sought to protect itself from worldly influences, retreating to the safety of prescribed and seemingly immutable patterns of Christian life:

> The people of God believes that it is led by the Spirit of the Lord who fills the whole world. Moved by that faith it tries to discern in the events, the needs, and the longings which it shares with other men of our time, what may be genuine signs of the presence or of the purpose of God. For faith throws a new light on all things and makes known the full ideals which God has set for man, thus guiding the mind toward solutions that are fully human.

These two theological affirmations—that God wills for society to reflect the essential equality of the sexes and that history is the locus of the activity of God's Spirit—gave expression to a perspective that was already experienced, if not articulated, by many Catholics, especially women and men in societies where God's liberating intent with respect to women had already been felt in "secular" feminist movements for women's educational and political rights. For these women and men, to read GS (especially no. 29) was to discover a powerful rebuttal to the old arguments against women's advancement in society. It was to hear at last a belated disavowal on the part of the international hierarchy of such prejudiced episcopal interventions against social equality as Cardinal Gibbons' 1911 words against women's suffrage in the United States: "When a woman enters the political arena, she goes outside the sphere for which she was intended. She gains nothing by that journey. On the other hand, she loses the exclusiveness, respect and dignity to which she is entitled in her home."[7]

WOMEN AND THEOLOGY

But beyond this, to read GS was to be invited to make connections that even its authors had not made, to move by a logic implicit in the text from affirmation of women's rights in society to affirmation of women's rights in the church, beginning with the right to theological education and to participation in the advancement of theology itself. In the two brief but eventful decades since this document appeared, a profound change in the theological scene has occurred, a change that can be summed up by saying that the nouns "woman" and "theologian" are no longer mutually exclusive terms. This fact that women are now teaching and writing theology as professionals in the Catholic church testifies to tremendous efforts on the part of justice-minded women and men. Risk, sacrifice, suffering, and unflagging labor have been required for women to earn the necessary academic credentials, enter the theological forum, and begin to influence the discussion. These accomplishments, which I briefly review, represent a creative application of the injunctions of GS no. 62 to extend participation in theology beyond the ranks of the clergy and to promote "lawful freedom of inquiry, of thought, and of expression" among theologians.

In 1985, when women can study theology in virtually all the American doctoral programs open to men, it is easy to forget what things were like a generation ago. But relatively equal access to theological education is a very new item indeed for women. All the female members of the Catholic Theological Society of America (CTSA) whose doctorates in theology date from the 1950s are graduates of a single far-sighted program at Saint Mary's College, Notre Dame. These women earned Ph.D.s rather than the traditional canonical degree for Catholic theologians, the S.T.D., and at least one American Catholic woman in the 1950s wanted that traditional ecclesiastical degree enough to go abroad in pursuit of it. Mary Daly recalls her experience in the autobiographical preface to the 1975 edition of *The Church and the Second Sex*:

> There was no place in the United States where a female was allowed to study for the "highest degree" in this field, the "canonical" Doctorate in Sacred Theology. Since I would settle for nothing less than the "highest degrees," I applied to study in Fribourg, where the theological faculty was state-controlled and therefore could not legally exclude women . . . [M]y classmates were nearly all priests and male seminarians . . . in the crowded classrooms there frequently were empty places on each side of me . . . [8]

Another American woman also earned an S.T.D. abroad in the 1960s, namely, Sister Agnes Cunningham, S.S.C.M., who in 1968 completed a dissertation for the theology faculty at Lyons entitled "Toward a Theology of Christian Humanism."[9] Daly, a laywoman, had supported herself in Switzerland by teaching philosophy to American students who were in Fribourg for "junior year abroad" programs. Cunningham's education had been financed by an anonymous lay benefactor who had approached her religious superiors with the idea of backing the preparation of a sister theologian as an experiment. Daly's financial struggle was certainly the more typical experience for women, both religious and lay, who have earned doctoral degrees in Europe, Canada, and the United States in subsequent years.

It is also noteworthy that when women were first admitted to doctoral studies in theology at The Catholic University of America, they were confined to the Ph.D program and were not eligible for the S.T.D., an inequity that was repaired by the early 1970s. Meanwhile, Ph.D. programs had become available to women at Marquette, Boston College, and a number of other Catholic universities by the late 1960s. By this time also a handful of Catholic women had entered doctoral programs in some of the traditionally Protestant schools, including Chicago, Yale, and Union/Columbia, among others. Rosemary Radford Ruether, the most influential Catholic woman theologian today, earned her Ph.D. from Claremont in 1965. In large part this development was an outgrowth of the new ecumenical movement launched by Vatican II, and in many cases it was the result of foresight on the part of leaders of women's religious communities, as well as of initiative on the part of the individual women who undertook to study theology in an ecumenical context. For these women to finance their educations and succeed in situations where most of the students and all the faculty were male was a major accomplishment, whether they studied in Catholic universities or in other institutions of higher learning; the fact that the situation is better for women studying theology today is due in great measure to their pioneering efforts.

Once the degrees were earned, women who wanted to contribute as theologians had to find employment and make their way into the professional organizations. There are now 349 women (approximately 25% of whom are Catholic) listed at doctoral or professional levels in the most recent directory published by the Women's Caucus of the American Academy of Religion.[10] In 1980, this figure stood at 168. Not all these women are employed, but many have found good positions and have contributed to the profession through various publications and through involvement in the College Theology Society, the American Academy of Religion, the CTSA, and in professional groups specializing in such areas as biblical studies, church history, liturgy, and Christian ethics. Jill Raitt, a Catholic theologian who earned the Ph.D. from The University of Chicago in 1970, served as president of the American Academy of Religion during 1981. Anne E. Carr, a 1971 University of Chicago graduate, was the first woman tenured in that university's Divinity School. Monika Hellwig, who obtained the Ph.D. from The Catholic University of America in 1968, became the first woman to receive the John Courtney Murray Award for Distinguished Achievement in Theology in June, 1984. Mary Collins, a 1967 Ph.D graduate from The Catholic University of America, began her term as the first woman president of the North American Academy of Liturgy in January, 1985.

Women's progress in the CTSA has been relatively rapid, given its unpromising beginnings. In *The Church and the Second Sex*, Mary Daly describes in the third person her own disillusioning experience of nineteen years ago:

> In 1966 an American woman who holds a doctorate in theology traveled to Providence, Rhode Island, to attend the annual meeting of the Catholic Theological Society of America, of which she is a member ... When she attempted to enter the ballroom of the hotel in which the meeting was being held in order to attend a buffet for members of the society, she was prevented from doing so by one of the officers, a priest. When she insisted upon her right to enter, the priest threatened to call the police. She replied that in this case it would unfortunately be necessary for her to call the

newspapers. After a long and humiliating scene, she was finally permitted to enter. This was the debut of the female sex in the Catholic Theological Society of America.[11]

Surely this experience contributed to Daly's decision, formalized by the early 1970s, to leave the Catholic church and proclaim herself a post-Christian feminist. Some justice-minded men of the CTSA, however, were resolved to open things up, for by 1969 Agnes Cunningham had been elected to the board of directors of the society, and one or two women have served on the board every year since 1975. Cunningham, in fact, progressed during the 1970s through the offices of secretary, vice-president, and finally president of the society, giving the first presidential address by a woman in 1978. Monika Hellwig, elected vice-president in 1984, will become the second female president of the CTSA in June 1986. About 10% of those attending the meeting where Hellwig was elected were female, and admissions statistics show an increasing percentage of women entering the society. In 1983, for example, more than one-third of the 45 new members accepted were female.

There is no question that the rapid entry of women into the profession has influenced the discussion, for the topics being treated by theologians generally reflect in some measure the agenda that many women have carried into the theological forum. A notable instance is the justice issue of sacramental sex discrimination, often termed the women's ordination issue. The gathering of 1200 women in Detroit at the first Women's Ordination Conference in 1975 was enormously significant, for it was the first time a sizable number of theologically trained female scholars and ministers convened to do theological reflection on the status of women in the Roman Catholic church. Speakers for that occasion included Rosemary Radford Ruether, Margaret A. Farley, Anne E. Carr, and Elisabeth Schüssler Fiorenza, as well as Richard McBrien, Carroll Stuhlmueller, and George Tavard. It is likely that the caliber of the theological papers given at the meeting had something to do with the Vatican's 1977 reiteration of the traditional position against women's ordination.[12] It is also significant that American Catholic theologians responded to the Vatican declaration by publishing a closely reasoned analysis and refutation of its arguments against ordaining women. Forty-four women and men contributed to this project, which was edited by Leonard Swidler and Arlene Swidler and published as *Women Priests: A Catholic Commentary on the Vatican Declaration*.[13] The work bears testimony to the fact that matters were far from settled by the Sacred Congregation for the Doctrine of the Faith, and that American theologians had taken to heart the words of GS no. 62 acknowledging that the "proper exercise" of their role requires "a lawful freedom of inquiry, of thought, and of expression, tempered by humility and courage in whatever branch of study they have specialized."

The influence of women's agenda on the theological discussion is also apparent in the fact that the CTSA commissioned a study of women in church and society, published in 1978, as well as in the fact that many male and female scholars now take care to avoid sexist language in their ordinary discourse and in their references to Divine Reality as well. Other examples of the influence of women's concerns on theology abound. Special issues of journals such as *Liturgy, Theological Studies,* and *New Catholic World* have been devoted to these matters. Raymond E. Brown's Hoover Lecture of January 1975, advertised as an address on New Testament studies and ministry, surprised its ecumenical audience by its content: a discussion of the question of women's ordination.[14] Bernard Cooke's article on "Non-Patriarchical Salvation," which appeared in the tenth anniversary issue of *Horizons* in 1983,[15] and Daniel Maguire's 1982 presidential address to The Society of Christian Ethics, entitled "The Feminization of God and Ethics,"[16] also reflect the influence of feminist theology, as does the fact that when the moral theology seminar of the CTSA took stock of matters it needed to concern itself with during the 1980s, the first item on an agenda proposed by Richard A. McCormick in 1982 was "Feminism in the Church."[17]

It should be clear from the above that the labors of women have had considerable impact on contemporary theological discussion. It should also be apparent that the trend is for this influence to increase, judging from such items as the recent establishment of the Women's Theological Center in Boston, the opening in 1984 of an M.A. program in Feminist Spirituality at Immaculate Heart College in Los Angeles, and the inauguration in 1985 of the *Journal of Feminist Religious Studies.*

Anne E. Carr observes in a 1983 article that the emergence of organized feminist groups of ministers and scholars within the Protestant and Catholic churches over the last two decades has led to a distinctive form of the "theology of liberation":

> Like its Black and Latin American counterparts, feminist theology begins with the concrete experience of women (consciousness-raising), understands itself as a collective struggle for justice (sisterhood), and aims toward a transformation of Church and societal structures consistent with the practical implications of the Gospel.[18]

The literature of Christian feminism, she adds, involves three tasks: critiquing the past, recovering "the lost history of women" in the tradition, and "revisioning Christian categories in ways which take seriously the equality and the experience of women."[19] Carr observes further that the Christian feminist movement is decidedly ecumenical, with Protestant and Catholic theologians alike involved in various aspects of a common project:

> They use the central and liberating Gospel message of equality, mutuality, and service *and* their own experience to criticize those elements in the tradition which capitulate to take-for-granted patriarchal norms. And they use the central biblical tradition of justice and equality to criticize sexist patterns and practices in culture and society.[20]

Another Catholic feminist, Janet Kalven of the Grail movement, describes the project in even more basic terms. What religious feminists are about, according to Kalven, is "simply drawing out the implications of affirming that women are full human beings made in the image of God."[21]

A FEMINIST READING OF "GAUDIUM ET SPES"

To illustrate what feminist theology can involve, I conclude this chapter with a feminist analysis of *GS*, concentrating on Part One and on the chapter from Part Two dealing with "Culture." As I have indicated, there is no question that this document conveyed Good News to the faithful, and particularly to women. Its insistence on the full humanity of woman—fully equal to man and created with him in the divine image— represents a decisive break with a long tradition of misogynist Christian anthropology, which had taught that woman is ontologically inferior to man and less reflective of the divine image. The import of this new understanding of woman's full humanity cannot be overstated, and its articulation by Vatican II in 1965 is to be celebrated.

Nevertheless, the context in which this new teaching is affirmed— the document *GS* and other conciliar and postconciliar documents— makes clear that the *implications* of this new affirmation of woman's full humanity have yet to be recognized and carried out to their logical conclusions in the church. This was not, of course, a task for Vatican II; rather it is an ongoing charge for the faithful who have benefited from the legacy of *GS*, *Lumen Gentium*, *Dignitatis Humanae*, and other momentous conciliar documents. To critique *GS* in light of its crucial insight of woman's full humanity, then, is to affirm as well its other central theological insight, namely, its recognition that it is God's Spirit who moves in the historical quest for fuller solutions to the mystery of ideal human existence on earth (no. 11). In what follows here, then, I draw out some implications of the document's affirmation of woman's equality by describing five limitations of *GS* that a feminist perspective judges in need of rectifying. These concern the areas of language, nature and culture, social analysis, ethical norms, and theological affirmations.

Language. The first thing that strikes a feminist reader of the English translations of *GS* is their use of "generic" masculine nouns in countless instances where a more felicitous rendering of the Latin would have allowed the language of the document to affirm woman's full humanity by including her unambiguously in the *words* about humanity. In view of the fact that as early as 1974 the *Journal of Ecumenical Studies* adopted an editorial policy proscribing the generic use of "man," it can only be regretted that there is not yet available an English translation of *GS* that employs "men and women" or "persons" in contexts where the Latin uses plural forms of *homo*.

To be sure, not everyone recognizes the moral seriousness of the feminist complaint about language. It requires a good deal of empathy and no small amount of moral imagination to appreciate the harm that is done so subtly to the psyches of males and females alike when the very structures of speech imply that one form of human being sufficiently encompasses all that is essential to humanity, that it can stand *in place of* the other form, apparently without significant remainder. Without getting into the question of whether in fact forms of *homo* functioned as generic masculine forms in Latin culture, one can recognize that today nothing would be lost and much would be gained had the opening line of *GS* been translated so as to make it unambiguously evident that the Fathers cared about "The joy and hope, the grief and anguish" of the women as well as the "men of our time."

The issue of language in this document is not merely a matter of translation, however, for the Latin text itself is replete with usages that have the effect of rendering females invisible. Of particular significance is the frequent use of forms of *frater* and *filius* in contexts where the full inclusion of women in the Christian community would require *soror* and *filia* as well. Again, the point is not trivial, though it is not yet universally acknowledged. In a culture where the superiority of males has been assumed, it is taken for granted that "brotherhood" encompasses an ideal for human community and that "God's sons" is an adequate way of speaking of God's children. However, from the perspective of those who appreciate the power that language has over thought and who recognize the injustice perpetuated by sexist language, the words employed in *GS* no. 55 to express the Fathers' interpretation of the duty "to build up a better world in truth and justice" can only be understood as ironic: "We are witnessing, then, the birth of a new humanism, where man [*homo*] is defined before all else by his responsibility to his brothers [*fratres*] and at the court of history."

These words are ironic, albeit unintentionally so, because until people recognize that *the ideal of "brotherhood"*—which excludes half of the world's population from consideration—*is part of the problem of global injustice*, there can only be very limited progress toward the better world for which the authors of *GS* hoped. The wisdom of certain strains of popular Catholicism, which finds it proper to specify both sexes in such classic texts as the Easter hymn *O filii et filiae* and the Litany of the Saints, has something to teach official Catholicism in this regard.

Nature and culture.   A second problematic area concerns the views on nature and culture that undergird *GS*. Here the difficulty is perhaps best described as one involving a "root metaphor" that governs the conciliar understanding of these realities. The metaphor derives from Genesis 1:28 ("And God blessed them, and God said to them, 'Be fruitful and multiply, and fill the earth and subdue it; and have dominion over the fish of the sea and over the birds of the air and over every living thing that moves upon the earth' ") and is essentially a metaphor of domination of nature. Section no. 9 speaks approvingly of "a growing conviction of mankind's ability and duty to strengthen its mastery over nature," and no. 57 refers to a divine design whereby "mankind's" task is "to subdue the earth and perfect the work of creation." The metaphor implies that humanity is superior to "nature" and is divinely authorized to be violent in its regard. What such a concept of culture as "mastery over nature" fails to provide is the sense of humanity's *continuity* with the rest of nature and, indeed, of our interdependence with the earth and the rest of the physical universe. There is an unresolved tension in the document between its several approving references to "conquering," "subduing," and "mastery" in relation to earth and nature (all implying a degree of violence)—see nos. 9, 34, 38, 53, 57, and 63—and the ideal it proclaims at the close of no. 92: " . . . we ought to work together without violence and without deceit to build up the world in a spirit of genuine peace."[22]

Not unrelated to this is the tendency of the document to regard woman's "nature" rather differently from the way it treats the "nature" of "man."[23] When the document speaks of human nature in general, it stresses the element of mystery, the sense that God alone can supply the full answer to the question which each person is to oneself. When *GS* speaks of woman's nature, however, it conveys a sense of fixity that contrasts with an earlier reference to a "dynamic and more evolutionary concept of nature" in general (no. 5). Thus one reads in the chapter on culture (no. 60):

> At present women are involved in nearly all spheres of life: they ought to be permitted to play their part fully according to their own particular nature. It is up to everyone to see to it that woman's specific and necessary participation in cultural life be acknowledged and fostered.

The passage is ambiguous, for were a truly evolutionary view of woman's "nature" intended, it could indeed be a summons to women's liberation. But the term "specific" with respect to woman's participation in cultural life suggests that this is not the case, and subsequent church documents have made it clear that official Catholicism has not applied teachings about the dynamic and mysterious quality of "human nature" so fully to female forms of that nature as to male. Indeed, this became apparent the day following the promulgation of *GS*, when the Fathers of the Council addressed several closing letters to various constituencies. Their message to women indicates that past attitudes were still very much in the ascendency. Even the existence of this message itself is telling, since there is no document addressed simply "to men," although there are messages addressed to "rulers," "men of thought and science," "artists," and "workers." This very arrangement of categories carries the implication that women are thought of primarily in terms of sexual roles, while men are regarded in terms of diversified vocational contributions. Indeed, this is made clear in the opening sentence of the message to women: "And now it is to you that we address ourselves, women of all states—girls, wives, mothers, and widows, to you also, consecrated virgins and women living alone—you constitute half of the immense human family."[24] The message goes on to mention that "the vocation of woman" is in the present era "being achieved in its fulness," a statement whose tone of assurance that the church already knows what this vocation is stands in marked contrast to what is said in the message to workers ("very loved sons"): "The Church is ever seeking to understand you better."[25]

Social analysis. A third area of concern regarding *GS* involves the social analysis it provides, which for all its acuity in so many respects is regrettably limited on two points of importance, especially to women. In the first place, there is a sense in which women are only partly visible to this analysis. While it is good that women's progress toward our rights is generally affirmed by the document, it is cause for regret that the limited nature of this progress, especially in the developed countries, is not acknowledged. Blindness to the real situation of women is particularly evident in the line from no. 9, " . . . women claim parity with men in fact as well as of rights, where they have not already obtained it." Leaving aside for the moment the question of whether "parity," with its weaker connotation of "equivalence" rather than "equality," is an adequate norm for progress toward justice, what amazes a feminist reader of this sentence is the implicit claim that women have achieved a fair situation in some parts of the world. The claim in not documented, and indeed it would be impossible to defend, given the actual status of women worldwide. As the sociologist Constantina Safilios-Rothschild observed *ten years after* the promulgation of *GS*:

> . . . despite some progress in some areas, the status of women is still quite low. . . . If we accept that a society is modern when it "is successful in removing social and structural constraints and in establishing appropriate compensatory mechanisms so that all individuals, regardless of their categorical membership such as age, sex, race, religion, ethnic origin, or social class, can have equal access to a wide range of options in all life sectors," no society can claim to have achieved modernity. . . . [Even in Western, developed] societies . . . sex discrimination has not been eliminated and probably it has not even decreased. It has only changed form: from open, direct discrimination to subtle, sophisticated sex discrimination, which tends to be more effective and difficult to fight.
>   The status of the majority of women who live in the Third World is still low and ongoing social changes either do not affect their status or tend to even further deprive them of options and opportunities.[26]

The factors examined by Safilios-Rothschild in the cross-cultural study that resulted in the conclusion quoted above were educational and vocational training, employment and other economic roles, marriage and the family, power and political participation, and health and nutrition. Today most analysts of women's status worldwide would support her conclusion that it generally remains lower than man's status.[27]

Given that the text of *GS* was approved with such a notable misconception about women's actual status left to stand in no. 9, it is not surprising that other suggestions of the "invisibility" of women occasionally appear, such as the failure of the document to mention rape or domestic violence, both of which are suffered frequently by women worldwide, in its list of crimes against life and human integrity and dignity (no. 27).

A second problematic aspect of the social analysis in the document is its tendency to press the valid distinction between the church and the rest of society so far that the religious institution escapes the criticism that is leveled against the broader society.[28] Whereas no. 26 affirms in general that "the social order requires constant improvement," the more specific sociological reference to the church in no. 44 is considerably weaker:

> The Church has a visible social structure, which is a sign of its unity in Christ: as such it can be enriched, and it is being enriched, by the evolution of social life—not as if something were missing in the constitution which Christ gave the Church, but in order to understand this constitution more deeply, express it better, and adapt it more successfully to our times.

A feminist social analysis, of course, would claim that the church order ought to be a *model* of justice and equality for society in general, rather than simply a gradually enhanced reflection of "the evolution of social life," and would provide detailed practical suggestions toward achieving this goal.

Ethical norms. Paragraph no. 26 also articulates a social ideal that includes ethical norms—particularly justice and love—which are solidly endorsed by feminists. The key passage reads:

> The social order requires constant improvement: it must be founded in truth, built on justice, and enlivened by love: it should grow in freedom towards a more humane equilibrium.

What *GS* fails to acknowledge, however, is the way in which norms of justice and love can themselves paradoxically function to legitimate oppression if they are not subject to criticism from a perspective that appreciates the full humanity of women. In an article supplying just such a critique, Margaret A. Farley demonstrates the need for theology to draw out the implications of the change from " . . . past assumptions regarding fundamentally hierarchical patterns for relationship between men and women and today's growing acceptance of egalitarian patterns of relationship." She points out that "the 'old order' was clearly one in which women were considered inferior to men and in which women's

roles were subordinate, carefully circumscribed, and supplementary."
And this "old order" resulted in *theories of justice* that "systematically
excluded the possibility of criticizing sexism." By contrast, the "new
order," which Farley and other feminists applaud, "is based upon a view
of women as autonomous human persons, as claimants of the rights
which belong to all persons, as capable of filling roles of leadership in
both the public and private spheres, as called to equality and full
mutuality in relation to both men and women."[29]

What Farley then suggests is that theological ethics needs to
develop new interpretations of the traditional principles of love and
justice, interpretations that will give impetus to rather than impede
progress toward a society that recognizes women as full persons.
Whereas GS evinces no sense that Christian ideals of love and justice
have been in any way problematic for women, Farley's feminist
perspective allows her both to critique inadequacies in traditional
understandings of these ideals and to offer constructive alternatives in
their stead. Thus, with respect to "Christian love" she proposes that its
component of "equal regard" is empty if it does not include real equality
of opportunity, that its dimension of "self-sacrifice" is false if tied in with
misconceptions about female "passivity," and that its aspect of "mutuality" is inadequate if based on analogues found " . . . in the mutuality of
relationships between parent and child, ruler and subject, master and
servant" rather than on a full recognition of the equality of women and
men."[30] With respect to justice she argues that adequate understandings
of both individual and common good require a shift from strict
hierarchical models of social organization to more egalitarian ones,
noting that " . . . in fact the good of the family, church, etc. is better
served by a model of leadership which includes collaboration between
[male and female] equals" than one which places a single male leader at
the head of the commmunity.[31] In the end, new understandings of
justice and love are found to be mutually reinforcing norms for this
Christian feminist ethic:

> That is to say, interpersonal communion characterized by equality,
> mutuality, and reciprocity may serve not only as a norm against
> which every pattern of relationship may be measured but as a goal
> to which every pattern of relationship is ordered. Minimal justice,
> then, may have equality as its norm and full mutuality as its goal.
> Justice will be maximal as it approaches the ultimate goal of
> communion of each person with all persons and with God.[32]

Such a perspective would find the ideal of parity expressed in GS no. 9
inadequate insofar as this concept, usually associated with agricultural

economics, implies that less-than-equal shares are just ones. "Parity" is not analyzed in the document, but it is the sort of norm which, when applied to human society, tends to accept unequal distribution of literacy, income, and food on grounds that needs for schooling, remuneration, and nourishment differ according to gender roles, men and boys "naturally" requiring more of all because of their actual or prospective positions of dominance.

A feminist perspective also finds inadequate the ideal of "brother-hood," which is articulated so often in *GS*, precisely because the word reinforces patterns of vision that select out the sisters from our midst (who, across the globe, are less educated, poorer, and hungrier than their brothers in every major society) and thus undermines the very laudable traditional norm articulated in no. 27, the injunction to look upon the neighbor "as another self." So long as one does not *see* the *specifics* of female neighbors, that long will one's neighbor-love remain inadequate in their regard.

Theological affirmations. Finally, a feminist analysis of *GS* must attend to what is said, and perhaps more important, what is implied about Divine Reality in this text. Here again, the problem can best be approached by the avenue of metaphor. It is an accepted theological principle that all language about God involves analogy, which means that no human expressions about Divine Reality are ever adequate to the Mystery to which they refer. In the Western religious traditions the metaphor of human fatherhood, which carries, unfortunately, the weight of longstanding patriarchal associations, has traditionally been emphasized in descriptions of Divine Reality and in the language of worship. Many scholars have pointed out, however, that even ancient biblical texts do not limit their language about God to male images such as father, warrior, and lord (although indeed these predominate), but also employ on occasion female metaphors to describe divine qualities and activities.[33] What is problematic about the language used in *GS* to refer to God is that it relies so heavily on male imagery that it risks reinforcing a naive but widespread tendency to take the metaphor of God as "father" too literally, with the resultant reinforcement of the patriarchal values such language has long legitimated. There are resources within the tradition for countering this tendency, but the Council Fathers, like most Christians two decades ago, were evidently unaware of the connections between societal injustice toward various oppressed groups and patriarchal religious language. Their treatment of atheism can hardly be faulted for not recognizing what was only beginning to be apparent in Western culture, namely, that patriarchal God-language is one of the ways in which "believers" can be said, in the words of *GS* no. 19, "to conceal rather than to reveal the true nature of God." Twenty years later, however, it has become clear that the rejection of Christianity lamented by the Council Fathers is sometimes due to the idolatrous use of religious language that continues to support the "father-rule" so many associate with values and behavior they see as harmful to humanity and threatening to the rest of creation as well.[34]

Thus, were a Council to address the issue of alienation from Christianity today, it would be essential to build on the insights of feminist theologians such as Rosemary Radford Ruether, Elisabeth Schüssler Fiorenza, and Bernard Cooke, who claim that the tradition was originally distinguished by a nonpatriarchal understanding of Divine Reality, which can be expressed in terms of the "Abba" experience of Jesus[35] as well as in terms of the "Sophia-God" experience of Jesus. As Fiorenza concludes from her study of early Christian sources:

> To sum up, the Palestinian Jesus movement understands the ministry and mission of Jesus as that of the prophet and child of Sophia sent to announce that God is the God of the poor and heavy laden, of the outcasts and those who suffer injustice. As child of Sophia he stands in a long line and succession of prophets sent to gather the children of Israel to their gracious Sophia-God. Jesus' execution, like John's, results from his mission and commitment as prophet and emissary of the Sophia-God who holds open a future for the poor and outcast and offers God's gracious goodness to *all* children of Israel without exception. The Sophia-God of Jesus does not need atonement or sacrifices. Jesus' death is not willed by God but is the result of his all-inclusive praxis as Sophia's prophet. This understanding of the suffering and execution of Jesus in terms of prophetic sophialogy is expressed in the difficult saying which integrates the wisdom and *basileia* traditions of the Jesus movement: "The *basileia* of God suffers violence from the days of John the Baptist until now and is hindered by men of violence" (Matt 11:12). The suffering and death of Jesus, like that of John and other prophets sent to Israel before him, are not required in order to atone for the sins of the people in the face of an absolute God, but are the result of violence against the envoys of Sophia who proclaim God's unlimited goodness and the equality and election of *all* her children in Israel.[36]

It is indeed good that Vatican Council II, particularly in *GS*, began a process of restoring to a central place in Catholic piety an appreciation of God's power and presence that stresses the metaphor of the gentle, inviting, and guiding Spirit, who affirms creation and inspires and sustains human hope and community (nos. 11, 93). Surely the fruits of Catholic feminist theology, which the episcopal authors did not anticipate from their work, bear witness today to the truth of the affirmation from Ephesians 3:20-21 with which they conclude the document *GS* (no. 93). In sisterly solidarity with these brothers, then, I also conclude: To this Sophia-God, who by the "power at work within us is able to do far more abundantly than all we ask or think . . . be glory in the Church and in Christ Jesus, to all generations, for ever and ever. Amen."

NOTES

1. My title cites the *Pastoral Constitution on the Church in the Modern World* (*GS*), no. 58. This and subsequent citations of the English translation of this text are from Austin Flannery, O.P., ed., *Vatican Council II: The Conciliar and Post Conciliar Documents* (Northport, N.Y.: Costello Publishing Co., 1975). Citations of the Latin text are from *Sacrosanctum Oecumenicum Concilium Vaticanum II: Constitutiones Decreta Declarationes*, vol. 1 (Vaticanum Typographium, 1967). As to the meaning of "feminist," I employ the term here in a broad sense to indicate a position that involves (a) a solid conviction of the equality of women and men, and (b) a commitment to reform society, including religious society, so that the full equality of women is respected, which requires also reforming the thought systems that legitimate the present unjust social order. Both women and men can thus be "feminist," and within this broad category there is enormous variety in levels of commitment, degrees of explicitness of commitment, and, of course, in opinions regarding specific problems and their solutions. Feminism is a concept that is best understood in dialectical relationship to the concept of sexism. For an insightful analysis of these concepts, see Patricia Beattie Jung, "Give Her Justice," *America* 150 (April 14, 1984): 276-78. In focusing on the Catholic feminist theology that has developed in part as the result of *GS*, I am conscious of the limits of my work. Clearly, many other dimensions of what the document said about "culture" could have been discussed, and clearly, my own perspective is limited by my status as an educated white woman from the United States. There remains a great need for the voices of women of color and of women from less privileged backgrounds to be heard in the theological forum. As long as the voices of nonwhite experience are out of the mainstream of theological inquiry, so long will this discipline risk being skewed and out of line with life. It simply will not do if the justice won by women in theology is shared only by white women from the upper and middle classes of Western society.

2. For examples of positions recently articulated by women that challenge certain Catholic teachings while remaining solidly grounded in the Catholic tradition, see Rosemary Radford Ruether, *Sexism and God-Talk: Toward a Feminist*

Theology (Boston: Beacon, 1983); Joan Timmerman, *The Mardi Gras Syndrome: Rethinking Christian Sexuality* (New York: Crossroad, 1984); as well as essays by women contributors to Robert Nugent, ed., *A Challenge to Love: Gay and Lesbian Catholics in the Church* (New York: Crossroad, 1984); Leonard Swidler and Arlene Swidler, eds., *Women Priests: A Catholic Commentary on the Vatican Declaration* (New York: Paulist, 1977); and the periodical *Conscience.* Catholic women writers, not all of whom are theologians, are by no means unanimous in their analyses, programs, and degrees of dissent from official teachings. In this, of course, they resemble male writers on religious subjects. The above examples are but a sampling from a vast and growing body of feminist literature bearing on Catholic life and thought. I have treated these developments at some length in two articles, from which I occasionally borrow in the present essay, with the permission of Paulist Press. These are: "Women and Religion: A Survey of Significant Literature, 1965-1974," in Walter Burghardt, ed., *Woman: New Dimensions* (New York: Paulist, 1977), 161-89, and "Coming of Age: Women's Contribution to Contemporary Theology," *New Catholic World* 228 (March-April 1985): 61-69. I also want to acknowledge here the assistance given me by two feminist thinkers, Anne E. Carr and Janet Walton, who read an earlier version of this chapter and made valuable suggestions for revisions.

3. Perhaps my own case will help to illustrate the phenomenon of the extraordinary existential impact of *GS* upon some women. I first read the document in the edition edited by Walter M. Abbott, S.J. (New York: America Press, 1966) during a thirty-day Ignatian retreat in the summer of 1967. Schooled in a strict interpretation of the vow of poverty, I had not since 1958 possessed a book like this that spoke so directly to my life and aspirations, and for some reason I felt entitled to take the then remarkable step of underlining and marking this ninety-five-cent paperback so that I could easily find key passages again. Passages that struck home particularly were those dealing with the rights of all, including women, to educational and cultural development. In 1967, I had been teaching high school students for seven years, but despite assiduous application to college extension courses during summers and weekends, I was far from completing my B.A. degree. The words of the document gave expression to my own basic sense of the wrongness of this situation, which I realized even then was tied in with the status of women religious in the church, and they offered a spirituality to counter the prevalent one that legitimated injustice and waste of talents. These words inspired me to take initiatives I would not have considered earlier. I arranged with my religious superiors to be released from classroom duties for three months during the 1968-69 school year, and that spring I completed my B.A. at age twenty-eight, two years earlier than I would otherwise have done and eleven years after I had entered church service. That summer of 1969, I began to study German, the first step in a long program of further study that would finally allow me to become active in the Catholic Theological Society of America in 1978. By 1972, I was heavily involved in organizing Catholic women religious and beginning to publish my developing feminist views. As I reflect on these developments, I feel that had the breakthroughs of *Pacem in Terris* and *GS* not taken place, it is quite likely that my talents and energy would long since have left the world of

institutional Catholicism and been invested instead in "secular" pursuits, a course taken by countless women ahead of me. For another account of the impact of Vatican II and *GS*, see Mary Daly, *The Church and the Second Sex*, both the original and the revised "feminist post-Christian" editions (New York: Harper and Row, 1968 and 1975).

4. Indeed, the term *vir* is not indexed in the Vatican edition of the conciliar documents, although the parallel term *mulier* is included in the index. It is also interesting to note certain other distinctions the index draws or fails to draw: *Fraternitas, Fratres et Sorores Religiosae*, and *Fratres separati* are all listed. The last of these terms, heard often at the Council, inspired Gertrud Heinzelmann to entitle her collection of interventions regarding women made during Vatican II *Die getrennten Schwestern: Frauen nach dem Konzil* (Zurich, 1967).

5. Garden City, N.Y.: Image Books, 1976, 8. This volume appeared earlier under the title *What a Modern Catholic Believes about Women* (Chicago: Thomas More Press, 1972), where the incident is described on p. 5. Mary Daly discusses the place women and women's concerns were given at Vatican II in *The Church and the Second Sex* (1975), 118-31.

6. Daly, *The Church and the Second Sex* (1975), 131. Hallinan's statement appears in George Tavard's *Woman in Christian Tradition* (Notre Dame, Ind.: University of Notre Dame Press, 1973), 127-28.

7. Quoted by Rosemary Radford Ruether in "Home and Work: Women's Roles and the Transformation of Values," in Walter Burghardt, ed., *Woman: New Dimensions* (New York: Paulist Press, 1977), 77.

8. Daly, *The Church and the Second Sex* (1975), 8. As Daly indicates in this post-Christian feminist introduction to her earlier work, she completed doctorates in both philosophy and theology at Fribourg. Had Vatican Council II not taken place, she declares in the same introduction, she might never have written *The Church and the Second Sex*.

9. Mary I. Buckley, now of St. John's University (N.Y.), earned the Th.D. in 1969 from the University of Münster, as did Elisabeth Schüssler Fiorenza in 1970.

10. See Lorine M. Getz and Marjorie L. Roberson, compilers, *A Registry of Women in Religious Studies* (New York: The Edwin Mellen Press, 1984). This directory is available for $10 from Women's Caucus: Religious Studies, c/o Boston Theological Institute, 210 Herrick Road, Newton Centre, MA 02159.

11. Daly, *The Church and the Second Sex* (1975), 141-42.

12. For the proceedings of the Detroit Conference, see Anne Marie Gardiner, ed., *Women and Catholic Priesthood* (New York: Paulist, 1976).

13. New York: Paulist, 1977.

14. This lecture was later published under the title, "The Meaning of Modern New Testament Studies for the Possibility of Ordaining Women to the Priesthood," in Raymond E. Brown, *Biblical Reflections on Crises Facing the Church* (New York: Paulist, 1975), 45-62.

15. *Horizons* 10/1 (Spring 1983): 22-31. This journal is published by the College Theology Society, an organization that developed to meet the needs of growing numbers of Catholic theologians, many of them laypersons, who were not teaching in seminaries. Its membership is not limited to Catholics, and the

organization continues to focus on the concerns of those teaching in colleges and universities.

16. This address is published in the 1982 edition of *The Annual of the Society of Christian Ethics.*

17. "Moral Theological Agenda: An Overview," *New Catholic World* 226 (January-February 1983): 4-7.

18. "Coming of Age in Christianity: Women and the Churches," *The Furrow* 34 (June 1983): 347.

19. Ibid., 348.

20. Ibid., 351.

21. Janet Kalven, "Women's Voices Began to Challenge after Negative Vatican Council Events," *National Catholic Reporter* (April 13, 1984): 20.

22. I suggest that the biblical metaphor should be recognized as suffering from the limitations of the patriarchal culture from which it emerged and the text should be reinterpreted so as to emphasize a different metaphor, one of caring or stewardship. The import of biblical attitudes toward the earth and nature has been amply discussed by Christian theologians since the appearance of Lynn White's famous article, "The Historical Roots of Our Ecologic Crisis," in *Science* 155 (1967): 1203-7. See, for example, Ian G. Barbour, *Technology, Environment, and Human Values* (New York: Praeger, 1980) and Roger Lincoln Shinn, *Forced Options: Social Decisions for the 21st Century* (New York: Harper and Row, 1982), and various works by Ruether.

23. The theme of "nature" is an important and much debated one in feminist writing. For theological contributions to this discussion, see Valerie Saiving's essay of 1960, "The Human Situation: A Feminine View," reprinted in Carol P. Christ and Judith Plaskow, eds., *Womanspirit Rising* (New York: Harper and Row, 1979), 25-42; and Ruether's *Sexism and God-Talk*, especially 72-92. For instances of the secular feminist discussion, see Sherry B. Ortner, "Is Female to Male as Nature Is to Culture?" in M. Z. Zimbalist and L. Lamphere, eds., *Woman, Culture and Society* (Stanford: Stanford University Press, 1974), 67-87; and Penelope Brown and L. J. Jordanova, "Oppressive Dichotomies: The Nature/Culture Debate" in The Cambridge Women's Studies Group, *Women in Society: Interdisciplinary Essays* (London: Virago Press, 1981), 224-41.

24. Walter M. Abbott, S.J., ed., *The Documents of Vatican II* (New York: America Press, 1966), 732-33.

25. Ibid., 735-36.

26. "The Current Status of Women Cross-Culturally: Changes and Persisting Barriers," an article first published in *Theological Studies* 36 (December 1975) and reprinted in Burghardt, *Woman: New Dimensions*, 27. Safilios-Rothschild is quoting her own earlier research in the above passage.

27. For example, Lucille Mathurin-Mair, a Jamaican who is Secretary General of the World Conference of the UN Decade for Women, has recently observed that today, "Women stand in the wings, as political expediency gives lowest priority to those social and economic sectors which serve society's vulnerable groups, of whom Third World women and their families constitute the most numerous and the most vulnerable. Not surprisingly, the current United Nations review of the Decade [1975-85] concludes that ' . . . the

condition of the majority of women in the developing world has changed, at most, marginally . . . ' " See her article, "The Quest for Solidarity," in *New World Outlook* (January 1985): 56. This entire issue of the magazine, a monthly published by the General Board of Global Ministries of the United Methodist church, is devoted to the theme of "Women Challenging the World."

28. The implications of this tendency are evident in such observations as the following passage from the 1977 Vatican Declaration, reaffirming a traditional position against women's ordination: "Thus one must note the extent to which the Church is a society different from other societies, original in her nature and in her structures." Here the distinction between the church and other societies is used to counter arguments that modern social developments indicate the need to alter a longstanding tradition. See "Declaration on the Admission of Women to the Ministerial Priesthood," in Austin Flannery, ed., *Vatican Council II: More Postconciliar Documents* (Grand Rapids, Mich.: Wm. B. Eerdmans, 1982), 342. The tendency also accounts for the discrepancy sometimes noted between official church concern for violations of human rights in various extra-ecclesial political entities and unconcern for violations of human rights within the institutional church. For a recent discussion of this problem, see Leonardo Boff, *Church: Charism and Power* (New York: Crossroad, 1985), 32-46.

29. "New Patterns of Relationship: Beginnings of a Moral Revolution," in Burghardt, *Woman: New Dimensions*, 53-54.

30. Ibid., 56-57.

31. Ibid., 69.

32. Ibid., 69-70.

33. For a rich discussion of this dimension of the Old Testament, see Phyllis Trible, *God and the Rhetoric of Sexuality* (Philadelphia: Fortress, 1978).

34. In *Sexism and God-Talk*, Ruether describes an understanding of patriarchy widely shared by other religious feminists: "By patriarchy we mean not only the subordination of females to males, but the whole structure of Father-ruled society: aristocracy over serfs, masters over slaves, king over subjects, racial overlords over colonized people" (p. 61). Thus, the patriarchal system is understood most fundamentally to be a system in which some dominate others, and besides being associated with sexism, it is also linked with racism, classism, militarism, violence, and ecological irresponsibility.

35. The significance of the NT references to *Abba* and *Pater* remains at issue among scholars. Besides the above-cited works of Cooke and Ruether, see Robert Hamerton-Kelly, *God the Father* (Philadelphia: Fortress, 1979), and Phyllis Trible's critical review of this book in *Theology Today* 37 (1980): 116-19. More recently, Madeleine I. Boucher has provided detailed exegetical evidence to counter the positions of Joachim Jeremias and Hamerton-Kelly regarding the alleged "centrality" of the "father symbol" for God in the religious under-standing of Jesus. In a paper presented to the Catholic Biblical Association of America meeting in New Orleans August 12, 1984, "The Image of God as Father in the Gospels: Toward a Reassessment," Boucher suggests that "the increasing frequency of the father image for God (much more common in Matthew and John than in earlier materials) may have been not so much a theological as a

christological development. It is the understanding of Jesus as 'the Son' that leads to language about God as 'the Father'" (typescript, 19). Boucher is currently preparing a book-length study of the use of *Abba* and *Pāter* in the NT.

36. Elisabeth Schüssler Fiorenza, *In Memory of Her: A Feminist Theological Reconstruction of Christian Origins* (New York: Crossroad, 1983), 135.

RICHARD A. MCCORMICK, S.J.

"Gaudium et Spes" and the Bioethical Signs of the Times

The *Pastoral Constitution on The Church in the Modern World* did not treat bioethics in any explicit or extended way. It did mention abortion and euthanasia (no. 27) briefly and in a very general way as being "opposed to life itself."

The constitution did, however, establish a framework for an approach to bioethical problems, and in two ways. First, it asserted (no. 51) that the "moral aspect of any procedure . . . must be determined by objective standards which are based on the nature of the person and the person's acts." The official commentary on this wording noted two things: (1) In the expression there is formulated a general principle that applies to all human actions, not just to marriage and sexuality. (2) The choice of this expression means that "human activity must be judged insofar as it refers to the human person integrally and adequately considered."[1] "Integrally and adequately" refers to all those dimensions of the person that constitute human well being: bodily health; intellectual and spiritual well-being; social well-being in all its forms (familial, economic, political, international, religious, etc.) Actions (policies, laws, omissions, exceptions) that undermine the human person integrally and adequately considered are morally wrong. Actions that are judged to be promotive and supportive of the human person in all her/his essential dimensions are morally acceptable. It is this personal criterion in all its comprehensiveness that should be the basis of our judgments about the ethical character of various biomedical interventions and policies.

Several things should be noted about the criterion. First, in principle, it calls for an inductive approach based on experience and reflection. Second, there are some things that we have already learned from past experience (e.g., violence begets violence). Furthermore, there are some things that so offend our sense of the proper and the sacred that no experience is necessary to expose their moral character (e.g., the Nazi medical experiments). Yet the principle remains: to judge the moral character of many human actions, experience of its comprehensive impact on persons is essential. Finally, some actions remain ambiguous, because they involve both beneficial and detrimental aspects, or because their impact on persons is unknown, or because they are variously evaluated. Such ambiguity and pluralism call for openness, caution, and a willingness to revise evaluations. This is particularly difficult where a medical technology is involved. As with many phenomena it is extremely difficult to reduce or eliminate once it is in place. Yet the personal criterion used here requires the basic willingness to say no where we have said yes, and yes where we have said no. Finally, in applying the personal criterion, various forms of simplistic shortcuts must be avoided. For instance, the human person is essentially a social being. Hence, what is promotive or detrimental to the person cannot be assessed solely in an individualistic manner but must take account of overall sociological and psychological social impacts.

The second aspect of Vatican II's framework was its emphasis on "the signs of the times," a phrase it adopted from John XXIII's *Pacem in Terris*. After stating (no. 3) that the church seeks only to carry forward the work of Christ himself, *Gaudium et Spes* continued: "To carry out such a task, the church has always had the duty of scrutinizing the signs of the times and of interpreting them in the light of the gospel" (no. 4).

If the "signs of the times" are to be scrutinized in the field of biomedicine, we must begin by identifying significant problem areas, areas that presently engage and will continue to engage the attention of those concerned with the ethical dimensions of our conduct. That will be the purpose of this essay.

When people hear "the signs of the times" used in the medical context, many conjure up the "gee-whiz" problems that are more fancy than fact. They imagine "star-trek ethics" that are so often cast up by the media. I do not. The bioethical problems of the nineties are already with us and provide us plenty to chew on. By saying this, I mean to suggest two things. First, the problems we now have are not going to go away. Second, they are a paradigm. How we go about today's problems will tell us how we will be acting twenty years from now. For the type of moral reasoning employed, its premises, its sensitivity, its precision, its combination of finality of commitment with appropriate tentativeness of formulation will reappear wherever bioethical issues reappear. If we are slipshod now, we will be so twenty years from now. If we relegate ethics to the margin of our consciousness and concern now, we will do so later too. And in doing so, we will hand over the ethos of the ministry that is healing to the dictations of technology. Physicians will transform *themselves* into merchants of the possible. And we will all be lessened by the transformation. To prevent that from happening, I list the following as but samples of possible "signs of the times."

1. THE PERSONAL PROBLEM OF PHYSICIANS

I list this first because the term "ethics" suggests to at least very many people "quandary" or "dilemma" ethics. But far more important than any problem we solve or decision we make is what we ourselves are becoming as persons. The physician who is not a vigorous member of a moral community, a community of nourishment, support, and ideals, is likely to remain a flawed human being, and fall short in his/her greatest ethical challenge.

Let me develop this by contrasting the physician's role and person (or true self). One plays a role in response to environmental influences; but we do not necessarily feel the role in our true selves. We function in roles because it is for the good of society. But functioning in a role cannot be the basis for person-to-person relationships. Let professional actors be an example. We wonder what they are like in real life. We do not expect to get the same image when we see them in real life as when we see them in their roles. Obviously, we need not be actors to function in a role. All of us tend to assume a role in certain environmental circumstances. There is a side to us that others would like to get to know without being filtered through the role.

I am not suggesting that we eliminate roles. Far from it. They are necessary for social structure. They both delimit behavior and give it a stable predictability. We expect a physician or a lawyer to act in a certain way. But the role is not necessarily the true self. There must be times when a person can step out of the role and be the true self.

If an individual is constantly relating to others through a role, that person gradually becomes alienated from his/her true self. If we present ourselves to others in a role, they respond to the role. If the role is alienated from the true self, the role develops, but the self does not mature. Sooner or later that person will discover that he/she is very lonely. That person has presented him/herself to others behind a mask. When he/she wishes to be the true self, it is anemic, immature, infantile. Thus the true self may do some remarkably immature things. One thinks of the established and prominent surgeon who runs off with a cocktail waitress with whom he has absolutely nothing in common.

The physician's role is a kaleidoscope of demands. The physician must be concerned and caring. Yet there must also be a certain detachment from the patient, something less than total emotional involvement. The physician is a father or mother hearing secrets, often of abuse and spiritual malaise. He/she must at times issue gentle orders.

The physician must relate smoothly and coordinatingly with the nursing staff and paramedical personnel—not an easy task when nurses are newly aware of their essential position on the health care team and are shoving physicians around a bit. The physician must be patient. Many patients are not sick or not as sick as they think they are. Yet they must be heard. The physician is a government employee with accountability for medicare, medicaid. He/she is a consoler, a comforter of the dying and their families.

In a word, the physician is under great pressures. There can easily be the tendency to *exhaust* the qualities of other-concern, care, comfort, communication, patience, of father/mother, in the role. When this exhaustion occurs, these qualities do not develop in the person and in personal relationships. When the physician comes home at night, he/she is often met with problems. But he/she has dealt with problems all day in his/her role. Perhaps he/she cannot get out of the role at home, or when he/she does, there is an exhaustion of the reserves needed to deal personally with persons.

We see this phenomenon in many professions. For example, I have known priests who preach forgiveness, yet are vindictive and petty in their own relations. Some preach the poverty of Christ, yet are greedy, money- and luxury-prone personally. I have known priests who in their role are "all things to all persons," yet retain their personal biases and prejudices as persons, who preach beautifully the gift of self, but are hard to reach as persons.

In this light the major moral challenge of the physician is to brings the qualities of his/her role into his/her person. How is this challenge to be met? I have no quick fixes. But I do believe that medicine practiced outside of a moral tradition can quickly become a neutral skill and can easily be "conscripted to serve consumer wants and desires, hired to do the autonomous bidding of the one who pays."[2] The physician's role can quickly be collapsed into the skeletal notions of patient autonomy and privacy. The very same thing can happen to the person. I am suggesting, of course, that for personal growth we need a community of support and solace, of challenge and conviction, of values and valuing.

2. INCREASING DEPERSONALIZATION

There are three factors at work in the way we perceive and respond to health care problems. First, there is the growth of technology. Everything from diagnosis through acute care to billing is done by computer. Check the advertisements in any medical journal and it becomes clear that medicine and the machine are wed. This gives efficiency but inevitably some impersonality.

Second, there is cost and cost-containment. Spiraling costs are due to many factors (e.g., sophistication of services, higher wages, more personnel, cost pass-along systems, inflation). In 1976, for example, expenditures for health constituted 11.4% of the gross national product. Of this sum, 91% went into health care systems, 3% to human biology, 1% to life style, 5% to environmental factors. Obviously, the cost factor will force difficult decisions. Shall we rescind federal coverage of end-stage renal disease? Must we eventually exclude some classes of infants from neonatal intensive care?

The third factor is the multiplication of what I will call "public entities" in health care delivery. I mean attorneys, courts, and legislatures. Thus we have legislated living wills; we have had a series of trial cases: *Quinlan, Saikewicz, Fox, Spring, Severns, Perlmutter, Conroy.* We have the *Wade, Bolton* decisions (1973) of the Supreme Court. These are but the protruding tips of the icebergs.

Together these factors affect the very matrix of the healing profession. This matrix roots in the conviction that patient-management decisions must be tailor-made to the individual, to the individual's condition and values. They are *personal* decisions that must fit the individual like a glove to a hand. Yet the three factors mentioned above are rather *impersonal* factors. When they begin to pre-program our treatment, they tend to depersonalize that treatment. There are those who argue that "fixing" occurs in hospitals but that genuine healing occurs elsewhere. This drift touches every problem area and limits the available responses by framing the questions onesidedly. Adverting to this problem may be half its solution, just as inadvertence will only compound it.

3. THE EMERGENCE OF PUBLIC MORALITY

Nearly everyone has heard the term "public morality" and is vaguely conscious of the need of public morality. But what does the term mean? It suggests that the pursuit of the basic goods that define our well-being has increasingly been shifted from private one-on-one acts and has been put into the public sphere. That means that bioethics will have to have much more to say at the level of policy-making than it has. Until quite recently it has been much more concerned with the level of individual decision. "But," as Daniel Callahan correctly notes, "on a national scale those decisions are going to be over-shadowed by large structural moral and political decisions. It is these decisions that will eventually shape the individual decisions."[3]

I will begin by stating what public morality is not. First, it is not simply public participation in the directions and priorities of medical practice, research, and health care. If public morality is understood in this way, it easily becomes a merely formal affair, a matter of structuring dialogue to include representative participants.

Second, it is not merely law or public policy. One of the prime tests of law is its own "possibility," as John Courtney Murray words it,[4] or its feasibility, ". . . that quality whereby a proposed course of action is not merely possible but practicable, adaptable, depending on the circumstances, cultural ways, attitudes, traditions of a people, etc." Public policy must, therefore, take account of some very pragmatic considerations in a rather utilitarian way. Reducing public morality to public policy would be to undermine public morality.

A clearer grasp of the meaning of public morality becomes possible when we consider the contemporary context of health care delivery. Individual decisions will, of course, remain and will remain important. But increasingly, the services of physician to patient are mediated by institutions. Such institutions have become partners in health care delivery. Thus we have group practice, third party carriers, legislative and administrative controls (e.g., Food and Drug Administration), etc.

Groups (whether universities, insurance companies, or the government) have interests and concerns other than the immediate good of the patient. Thus the government has a legitimate interest in population control, in reducing welfare rolls, in control of illegitimacy, in the advancement of diagnostic, therapeutic, preventive medicine, in balancing the budget, in protecting life. Teaching and research hospitals have a concern for the health of future generations.

This suggests that whenever other values (than the patient's) are the legitimate concern of the mediator of health care, the good of the individual patient becomes one of several values in competition for priority. It further suggests that the individual is in danger of being subordinated to these values.

As I understand the term, "public morality" is the pursuit of these other values without violating the needs and integrity of the individual. It is a harmonizing of public concerns with individual needs. These "other values and concerns" constitute the public dimension of biomedicine because they represent concerns other than and beyond the individual. In Callahan's words: "Ways will have to be found to balance that ethic [patient-centered] off against the legitimate interests of the public. . . ."[6]

Callahan has summarized this matter splendidly. He argues that the allocation of resources, the development of a just health-care delivery system, the adjudication of the rights and claims of different competing groups "are and will be the important moral problems of the future." These problems will "force biomedical ethics to move into the mainstream of political and social theory, beyond the model of the individual decision maker, and into the thicket of important vested and legitimate private and group interests." Establishing the proper balance between individual patient-centered concerns and other legitimate interest is what I mean by the term "public morality."

When biomedicine is mediated by groups with other (than the individual's) concerns, the medical-research establishment is thereby deeply inserted into the value perspectives of society at large, and begins to be shaped by these perspectives and priorities. One need not be a Cassandra to note that in the United States top cultural priorities are technology, efficiency, comfort. This means that these priorities will unavoidably penetrate the "medical-research complex" and shape its decisions. As the late Dr. André Hellegers used to say: "Medicine is increasingly being asked to provide heaven on earth."

Priorities of this type can very easily, if not inevitably, lead to a hierarchizing of values and priorities that is, under analysis, distorted— in the sense that the legitimate needs and claims of individuals are neglected. The ones most likely to get hurt in such policy shifts are the poor, the dependent (elderly, retarded), and the "ordinary patient" who is neglected in favor of exquisite medical virtuosities that consume undue time, energy, and funds.

4. THE EUGENIC MENTALITY

Two recent happenings should not go unnoticed. The first was the *in vitro* fertilization debate in this country. I was privileged to be on the 13-member Ethics Advisory Board, Department of Health, Education and Welfare (HEW), that deliberated on this matter for the federal government. While taking testimony throughout the country, I became aware of an interesting attitude on the part of a considerable number of people. It was the "consumer-item mentality" toward the child. The second incident was the announcement, on May 25, 1982 by Robert K. Graham, of the establishment of the Repository for Germinal Choice. Graham was seeking out the sperm of superior individuals (e.g., Nobel Prize winners like Dr. William S. Shockely) to produce—I use the word deliberately—genetically superior persons. "We only go with the most superlative males," boasted Graham.

These two events occurred in a twofold cultural context. First, there is the increasing sophistication of prenatal diagnosis. We have amnio-centesis, ultrasonography, fetoscopy, maternal serum alpha feto-protein testing for neural tube defects. Second, there is the cultural acceptance of abortion as an acceptable form of health care.

The consumer-item mentality toward children combined with increasingly sophisticated prenatal diagnosis will lead to an increasing emphasis on eugenics. There are already in place telling symptoms of this mentality. We hear people refer to "the right to a healthy child." Implied in such loose talk is the right to discard the imperfect. What is meant, of course, is that couples have a claim to those reasonably available means to see that their children are as healthy as possible. Furthermore, recently we have seen two cases of "wrongful life" (California, 1982, *Turpin v. Sortini*; Washington, 1983, *Harbeson v. Parke-Davis, Inc.*) where *the child herself* is the plaintiff. Recent neonatal intensive care cases have revealed an alarming attitude on the part of some people, including physicians. The options narrow to a healthy child or a dead child. We have donor insemination. Fairly soon, we will likely have genetic correction for some diseases (e.g., Lesch-Nyhan Syndrome) and undoubtedly researchers will contemplate a more thorough cure, that of correcting the defective gene in the germline cells (ova or sperm). As *The New York Times* noted: "Repairing a defect is one thing, but once that is routine, it will become much harder to argue against adding genes that confer desired qualities, like better health, looks or brains. There is no discernible line to be drawn between making inheritable repairs of genetic defects, and improving the species."[7]

"Improving the species" belongs to what we call "positive eugenics." It raises a host of unanswerable questions: what qualities are to be maximized? Who decides? Which defects are too burdensome? Who decides? Every thoughtful commentator runs from questions like these as if they were the plague. Bentley Glass speaks for nearly all when he calls them "frightful dilemmas."[8] These are just some of the dilemmas of positive eugenics—the preferential breeding of superior individuals to improve the genetic stock of the race. Far too few people advert to the fact that when we program for high IQ, we can begin to value the person in terms of the quality. In other words, we reduce the whole to a part. People who do that are on their way to doing other things civilized societies should abhor.

This eugenic mentality is powerfully supported by the developing notions of disease and health. The term "disease" has had an interesting evolutionary history and therefore so has the term "health."[9]

"Disease" first meant an identifiable degenerative or inflammatory process which, if unchecked, would lead to serious organic illness and sometimes eventually to death. The next stage of development was statistical—at least some diseases being identified by deviation from a supposed statistical norm. Thus we referred to *hyper*thyroidism or *hypo*cholesterolemia, *hypo*glycemia, etc. One was said to be unhealthy, to have a disease, if he or she were *hypo* or *hyper* anything; not in the sense of an existing, tangible degenerative process, but in the sense that the individual was more than others likely to suffer some untoward event, what my colleague Dr. André Hellegers was fond of calling "hyperuntowardeventitis."

The third notion of disease is inability to function in society. For instance, there is a good deal of surgery being performed to enlarge breasts, to shrink buttocks, to remove wrinkles—in brief, to conform to someone's notion of the attractive and eventually of the tolerable. We live in a society that cannot tolerate aging. At some point, then, this question arises: Who is the patient here, who is sick—the individual, or society? I mean, of course, that this broad understanding of "health" can too easily reflect a sickness of society, in its judgments about the meaning of the person. In our time and in some societies, people are hospitalized because of nonconformity. That suggests that the notion of "health" is becoming increasingly nonsomatized and getting out of control.

The final stage of development is the definition of health popularized by the World Health Organization. Health is a "state of complete physical, mental, and social well-being, not simply the absence of illness and disease." This description of health was adopted in the *Doe v. Bolton* abortion decision of the U.S. Supreme Court. The Court stated that the "medical judgment may be exercised in the light of all factors—physical, emotional, psychological, familial, and the woman's age—relevant to the well-being of the patient."[10] Following this notion of health, the quite preposterous situation could arise where a person's sense of well-being is threatened by the size of his or her car. The appropriate medical judgment would be a prescription of a Chrysler Imperial to replace one's Dodge Dart.

Through the expansion of the notions of health and disease, contemporary medicine is increasingly treating the desires of people in a move toward a discomfortless society. Desires, of course, are notoriously the product of many suspect sources. Whatever the case, it is clear that parents *desire* the "perfect baby."

5. CARE OF THE DYING

There are several problems that will continue to vex us in the years ahead. But before outlining them, it is important to remember that it is all too easy to get lost in the casuistry of decision-making. This can blunt our sensitivities to what is surely our first moral mandate when dealing with the dying: to reduce the human diminishments that accompany the dying process. Or more positively, what we ought above all to be trying to do is to maximize the values the patient treasured during life.

That being said, there are three areas that present serious problems. First, how should we conceptualize our duties toward the dying? Traditionally, we have become accustomed to speaking of ordinary and extraordinary measures. If a medical intervention had to be qualified as ordinary, it was seen as morally mandatory. If extraordinary, it was not morally mandatory. It was said to be ordinary if it offered a reasonable hope of benefit to the patient *and* could be used without excessive inconvenience (risk, pain, expense, etc.). If it offered no reasonable hope of success *or* was excessively burdensome, it was extraordinary.

Many (e.g., Robert Veatch, Paul Ramsey, James Childress) believe the terminology has outlived its usefulness. There are several reasons for this. First, the terminology too easily hides the nature of the judgment being made. The major reference point in factoring out what is "reasonable" and "excessive" is the patient—his/her condition, biography, prognosis, and values. The terminology, however, suggests that attention should fall on the means in an all too mechanical way. Second, many people erroneously interpret the terms to refer to "what physicians ordinarily do, what is customary." This is not what the terms mean. In their ethical sense, they simply must encompass many more dimensions of the patient than "what physicians ordinarily do" allows. Thus the terms have been badly abused in our recent history, especially as the vehicle for involuntary homicide, and at the other end, as mandates for the fruitless and aimless prolongation of dying.

Many suggestions for replacements have been made. For instance, Paul Ramsey continues to suggest a "medical indications policy" (medically indicated, not medically indicated). This obscures the fact that we are dealing with a *moral* judgment, not a scientific one. Rome's Sacred Congregation for the Doctrine of the Faith suggests "proportionate," "disproportionate" means. Still others opt for "reasonable or fitting," "unreasonable or unfitting," all things considered. I myself believe that we avoid many misunderstandings by using the terms "obligatory" and "optional." The matter is more than semantic. Loose language can be abused, which in this case means that people can be hurt.

The second area of remaining unclarity is the treatment of the incompetent. As a background, it should be noted that the competent patient is acknowledged to have the right, except for a few marginal instances, to accept or reject medical treatment. But what about the incompetent? Who decides for them and on what basis?

Let the case of Brother Charles Fox illustrate the problem. Fox, at the age of 83, underwent hernia surgery during which he suffered cardiac arrest followed by diffuse cerebral brain stem anoxia. He was maintained on a respirator. Reverend Philip Eichner, his superior, after consulting Fox's surviving relatives (nieces and nephews) appealed for relief, a relief opposed by the district attorney. It was granted on

December 6, 1979 by Judge Robert Meade. Fox died January 24, 1980, and, as far as I know, was still on the respirator as Meade's decision was appealed.

Eichner had appealed to the right of privacy as found in the *Quinlan* and *Saikewicz* cases. Meade refused to pass on this, arguing that there must be state action to constitute an intrusive violation of privacy. Furthermore, privacy is insufficiently defined and invites abusive interpretation.

Rather, Meade appealed to the common law notion of self-determination. However, Fox clearly could not exercise this. In *Quinlan* and *Saikewicz*, a substituted judgment was allowed for such cases. Meade rejected this, for self-determination is precisely the right to make up *one's own mind*. However, he granted the relief on the grounds that Fox had expressed himself on the Quinlan case ("none of that extraordinary stuff"). Therefore the decision was truly that of Brother Fox.

The implication of such reasoning is that the vast majority of incompetents will be unable to get off of respirators. They have not expressed themselves on *Quinlan*, or at least not in a public, witnessed way. This is *a fortiori* true of those who have never been competent.

I believe that one could argue, therefore, that Meade is correct as far as he goes. He just does not go far enough. We need more than self-determination to deal with those incompetents who were never competent, or never expressed themselves. I will not develop the analysis here (since I have done so elsewhere).[11] But the two further principles we need are patient benefit and family self-determination.

The third area that will remain vexing is the treatment of seriously defective newborns. May we ever conclude that it is morally acceptable to forego life-saving interventions in these cases? The matter was brought to national attention by the "Infant Doe" case (Bloomington, Indiana). On April 15, 1982 "Infant Doe," a week-old Down's syndrome baby, died. The parents had obtained a court order barring doctors from treating or feeding him. The infant suffered from tracheosophageal fistula, which, unless surgically corrected, prevents ingestion of food.

On May 18, 1982, then Secretary of Health and Human Services Richard Schweiker stated that "the President has instructed me to make absolutely clear to health care providers in this nation that federal law does not allow medical discrimination against handicapped infants."[12] This was then followed by a letter from Betty Lou Dotson (Director, Office for Civil Rights, HHS) to the nation's 6400 hospitals, reminding them of the applicability of section 504 of the Rehabilitation Act (1973) to these cases. That section stipulates: "No otherwise qualified handicapped individual ... shall, solely by reason of his handicap, be excluded from the participation in, be denied the benefits of, or be subjected to discrimination under any program or activity receiving federal or financial assistance."

On April 14, 1983, Federal District Judge Gerhard A. Gesell struck down the new rule as "arbitrary and capricious" and in violation of the Administrative Procedure Act.[13]

On April 15, 1985, after months of jostling, cajoling, lobbying and arm-twisting, there finally appeared the Final Rule (Child Abuse and Neglect Prevention and Treatment Program). Exception to the requirement to provide treatment may be made only in three instances: (1) the infant is chronically and irreversibly comatose; (2) provision of treatment would merely prolong dying, or not be effective in correcting all of the infant's life-threatening conditions, or would be futile in terms of infant survival; (3) provision of treatment would be virtually futile in terms of survival and would itself be inhumane.[14] These regulations look tight and tough. But there are qualifiers ("virtually futile," "inhumane," "appropriate nutrition") that provide some room for flexibility.

The problem, then, that we face and will continue to face is to find a middle ground that will protect newborns but not overprotect them, that will stem abuse without creating new forms of it. We are not there yet. The solution lies in guidelines that will provide outlines in which prudence should operate (thus providing protection) without trying to replace prudence (thus providing a range of flexibility that is appropriate).

6. DISTRIBUTIVE JUSTICE

I can be brief here because the matter is so utterly intractable. In 1969 the American Medical Association stated: "It is the basic right of every citizen to have available to him adequate health care." John XXIII made a similar statement in the encyclical *Pacem in Terris*. In 1981 the American Catholic bishops issued a pastoral letter, "Health and Health Care." It stated: "Health care is so important for full human dignity and so necessary for the proper development of life that it is a fundamental right of every human being."[15] Such statements probably resonate harmoniously with our own sense of fairness and justice.

But that is where the problem begins. How do we equitably distribute a limited resource? It must be recalled that under the term "health care" fall all kinds of things: artificial hearts, psychiatric care, transplantation, hemodialysis, cardiac surgery, reproductive technologies, cryogenic techniques, cosmetic surgery, dental care, prenatal diagnosis, etc. Does everyone get everything, and as a right? What principles do we use to provide fair access to our available health care? Do we attempt to stipulate a "decent minimum" for all, as Harvard's Charles Fried suggests? Or do we adopt an egalitarian principle whereby the sickest get what they need, even the most sophisticated interventions, if they can benefit by it? As I noted in citing Daniel Callahan, these are and will be the important moral problems of the future.

James Childress has summarized our macro-allocation problems succinctly with the following three questions.[16]

(1) What resources (time, energy, money) should be put into health care and into other social goods (education, defense, poverty elimination, environment)?

(2) Within health care, how much time, energy, resources go to prevention vs. crisis or rescue medicine?

(3) Within either category (prevention, rescue) who should receive resources when we cannot meet all needs?

7. THE PROBLEM OF PATERNALISM

Some patients are not likely to reach reasoned decisions about their own treatment. One thinks of those who are depressed and of some addicts. Even the fully competent do not always act in their own best interest. Whether to intervene in such decisions is the problem of paternalism.[17] The problem exists because some think the duties of beneficence should take precedence over patient autonomy in certain cases. That is, the person's preferences or wishes should or may be overridden in order to visit a benefit or prevent harm to that person.

I will not enter here into the niceties of this discussion. James Childress has done that most adequately. But two things should be noted. First, as Childress words it, "the conflict between professional paternalism and patient autonomy pervades health care."[18] Nor does it require much imagination to suggest that it will assume institutional forms when/if the government assumes a greater partnership role in health care delivery. Second, individual physicians should be well acquainted with this discussion and develop precise and well thought out principles upon which to structure their responses. Failure to do this will constitute a further invitation to the legal profession to deepen its prosecutorial role in medicine.

8. THE PROBLEM OF EUTHANASIA

The problem I want to raise here is the distinction between killing and allowing to die, between a potassium chloride injection and removing a respirator. This distinction is becoming increasingly muddy in the public forum. I was recently consulted on the case of a woman devastated with metastatic carcinoma. She was given two weeks to live at most, but was maintained on a respirator. She wanted nothing to do with it and begged to be freed of it. The physicians refused on the grounds that it would be murder. In the Karen Quinlan case, Judge Robert Muir asserted that removal of Karen from the respirator would be subject to the homicide laws of New Jersey.

Another example is the case of Melanie Bacchiochi, a 23-year-old Connecticut woman. She suffered cardio-respiratory arrest while having her wisdom teeth extracted. Resuscitated and rushed to a local hospital, she was placed on a respirator, and after several days of testing, she was declared brain dead. Her physician then announced that he would never remove the machine without a court order. Some 43 days later, in response to the trial judge's admonition that the doctor should proceed on the basis of the appropriate medical response to the patient's physical condition, the physician removed the respirator. Commenting on the Bacchiochi case, Dr. Allen Douma, assistant director for health education for the American Medical Association, stated that because there is no law establishing a definition of death in Connecticut, doctors who would disconnect Miss Bacchiochi "would be open for a suit."

Instances like this can be multiplied. For instance, Carol A. Smith, Assistant Attorney General of the State of Washington, gave (1977) this opinion regarding the law with respect to withdrawing or withholding life support from a dying patient: "Under the present law, an attempt to bring about death [sic] by the removal of a life sustaining mechanism would constitute homicide, first degree."[19] Such an interpretation of things struck home dramatically in the murder trial of Clarence Herbert's physicians (Neil Leonard Barber, M.D. and Robert Joseph Nejdl, M.D.), who had removed their patient from a respirator and IV support after he had suffered a massive anoxic insult to his brain and was left in what appeared to be a vegetative state.

What does all this mean? Most people, and assuredly virtually all bioethicians and moral theologians, would agree that it is morally appropriate to withdraw or withhold life-sustaining interventions if they are of no benefit to the patient—e.g., if they merely prolong the dying process. Yet when others call this murder, then this has eventually the effect of making murder itself more thinkable, and of confusing killing with not prolonging dying. This simply adds to the public confusion and increases the difficulty of removing people from useless technology and allowing them to die in peace.

The ethical problem at the bottom of the euthanasia discussion is the moral difference between killing and allowing to die. Robert Veatch lists five different arguments for holding the two morally distinct: (a) actions and omissions are psychologically different; (b) active killing conflicts with the role of the physician; (c) there is a difference in intent; (d) the long-range consequences are different; (e) the cause of death is different.[20] Veatch admits that some of these arguments are more persuasive than others. He concludes that even though the differences between commission and omission are much more subtle than some traditions would indicate, still "the wisdom of the common judgment is sound. There are significant moral distinctions between actively killing and simply omitting an action. . . . "

I agree with this judgment. But it will be extremely difficult to make this judgment persuasive in the public forum. Americans are an extremely pragmatic people with an interventionist bias. At some point and in some cases (of dying) a corpse is a corpse, and it matters little how it became such.

These, then, are *some* of the problems in bioethics for the eighties. Many others could be listed: genetic therapy, reproductive technologies, transplant innovations (e.g., artificial heart). My own response to them is—depending on the problem—a mixture of conviction, puzzlement, alarm, confusion, more questions, regret, intrigue, hope. Of one thing I am sure: if the questions surrounding these issues are not asked—not asked in dead earnest, not asked publicly, not asked continually, not asked humbly—we gamble with our own future by identifying the humanly and morally good with the technologically possible.

But here I am above all interested in such problems insofar as they may constitute "signs of the times" to be interpreted in the light of the gospel. What does that mean? It does not simply mean a pious construction put on contemporary events or problems. M.D. Chenu has stated:

> When, then, Christians, as a body, a Church, want to interpret events according to God or the Gospel, they cannot subconsciously sever them from their actual, "worldly" reality; they cannot merely "spiritualize" them. These events are signs in their own full and inner meaning. It is in these events, as they are in *reality*, that the Church sees something that cries out for the Gospel. These facts must therefore be respected and are not to be used for apologetic purposes. They must be listened to according to their own nature; they must not be glibly given a supernatural varnish, which leads too easily to "mystification."[21]

M.C. Vanhengel, O.P. and J. Peters, O.C.D., have pointed out that if the expression "signs of the times" is to be truly significant and not theologically trivialized, two elements must be presupposed: (1) an accumulation of facts that all point in the same direction; (2) the fact that people are aware of this direction.[22]

In what direction, then, do the bioethical problems outlined point? They have two key characteristics: ever-changing and complex. No one individual can master them and draw firm ethical conclusions valid for all times and cultures. They demand a convergence of competences to discover what is truly humanly promotive or destructive.

The very nature of these problems suggests the manner of the church's reflection on and contribution to them. I want to suggest here that such problems call for a modification of the church's magisterial function. The church must be deeply present to and thoroughly immersed in the messy and confusing details of these problems. This the church can do only through her members competent in these areas. Competence combined with deep faith should have a shaping or transforming effect on biomedical events. Only if this shaping or transforming effect is present will the church be able to interpret such events in the light of the gospel.

In the very recent past, the church has been accustomed to teach by declaration—and declaration usually emanating from a centralized Roman authority (e.g., the Congregation for the Doctrine of the Faith). It is, I believe, a "sign of the times" that teaching-by-declaration is not the first step in giving shape to modern biomedicine, but rather the last. Declaration must be the result of a painstaking process that is inductive, ecumenical, collegial, tentative. Without such a process, declaration will cease to be true teaching. It will open no eyes and will fail at what teaching ought to be: corrective vision.

NOTES

1. *Schema constitutionis pastoralis de ecclesia in mundo huius temporis: Expensio modorum partis secundae* (Vatican Press, 1965), 37-38.

2. Allen Verhey, "The Death of Infant Doe," *Reformed Journal* 32 (June, 1982): 10-15.

3. Daniel Callahan, "Shattuck Lecture: Contemporary Biomedical Ethics," *New England Journal of Medicine* 302 (1980): 1232.

4. John Courtney Murray, *We Hold These Truths* (New York: Sheed and Ward, 1960), 166.

5. Paul Micallef, "Abortion and the Principles of Legislation," *Laval Théologique et philosophique* 28 (1972): 267-303.

6. Cf. note 3.

7. "Whether to Make Perfect Humans," *The New York Times*, July 22, 1982.

8. Bentley Glass, "The Human Multitude: How Many Is Enough?" in Darrell S. English, ed., *Genetic and Reproductive Engineering* (New York: MSS Information Corpo., 1974), 119.

9. These reflections I owe to the late Dr. André Hellegers (Charles Sumner Bacon Lecture).

10. *Doe v. Bolton*, 410 U.S. 179, 192 (1973).

11. Robert Veatch and Richard A. McCormick, S.J., "The Preservation of Life and Self-Determination," in Richard A. McCormick, S.J., *How Brave a New World?* (Washington, D.C.: Georgetown University Press, 1985), 381-89.

12. *Washington Post*, May 19, 1982, A21.

13. *The New York Times*, April 15, 1983.

14. *Federal Register*, April 15, 1985.

15. *Health and Health Care* (Washington, D.C.: United States Catholic Conference, 1981), 5.

16. James F. Childress, *Priorities in Biomedical Ethics* (Philadelphia: Westminster Press, 1981), 76.

17. Cf. James Childress and Tom Beauchamp, *Principles of Biomedical Ethics* (New York: Oxford University Press, 1979) and James Childress, *Who Should Decide? Paternalism in Health Care* (New York: Oxford University Press, 1982).

18. Childress, *Who Should Decide*, vii.

19. Cf. John Paris, S.J. and Richard A. McCormick, S.J., "Living-Will Legislation, Reconsidered," in McCormick, *How Brave a New World?*, 423-30.

20. Robert Veatch, *Death, Dying and the Biological Revolution* (New Haven: Yale University Press, 1976), 82-93.

21. M.-D. Chenu, "Les signes des temps," *Nouvelle revue théologique* 87 (1965): 29-39, at 34.

22. M.C. Vanhengel and J. Peters, "Signs of the Times," *Concilium*, no. 25 (Ramsey, N.J.: Paulist Press, 1967): 143-52.

PART III

Politics

*Political Hopes and Political Tasks: A Reading
of "Gaudium et Spes" after Twenty Years*

*From Conciliar Aula to Senate Floor:
Reflections on "Gaudium et Spes"*

John Langan, S.J.

Political Hopes and Political Tasks: A Reading of "Gaudium et Spes" after Twenty Years

> The joys and the hopes, the griefs and anxieties of the men of this age, especially those who are poor or in any way afflicted, these too are the joys and hopes, the griefs and anxieties of the followers of Christ.[1]

It may seem strange to begin a reflection on the political aspects of *Gaudium et Spes* by concentrating on this first sentence of the document with its direct sympathy, its sweeping universalism, its stress on the temporal and the emotional. But it is here that, like the Fathers of the Council, we must begin. For what is most remarkable about this document and its subsequent influence on Catholic social teaching and political action is the way it expresses a moment of hope and desire, a moment that nearly all those bishops, theologians, religious leaders, and activists who shaped the conciliar age in Roman Catholicism lived through as a time of supreme fulfillment and aspiration. But it was equally a moment that spoke to millions of Catholics and non-Catholics around the world as they witnessed the extraordinary revitalization of an institution long perceived as obdurate in its rejection of the central features of modern culture and in its continuing embrace of antiquated notions in theology, in philosophy, in the social sciences, and in political action. The majority of those who were most exhilarated by the drastic changes in this central but conservative pillar of Western civilization had probably failed to discern the many subtle (though often frustrated) tokens of profound change that had come to the surface in Catholicism during the eighty years from the death of Pius IX (1878) to the death of Pius XII (1958). The long, checkered development of a more open, less defensive, less authoritarian, more cosmopolitan style of Catholicism had been going on since the time of Lammenais in France in the 1830s. Important scholarly advances and an increasing appropriation of both biblical and patristic sources, as well as of contemporary forms of historical and critical consciousness, had been proceeding quietly since the 1920s.

But Roman Catholics of all ages generally perceived a sharp division between the church before and after "the Council," even when they were bitterly divided in their evaluations of these two periods. All were agreed that a profound change had occurred during the time between the opening of the Council by John XXIII in October 1962 and its conclusion under Paul VI in December, 1965. For a vast number of Catholics, however, this transition was more wrenching and more liberating than the mere recognition of a significant event in external history such as the independence and partition of India (1947) or the ascent of Sputnik (1957). It was a process in which personal and social identities were adopted, transformed, repudiated. It was a time of profound gain and loss, a time in which choices were both open and forced. Especially for the young, it was a time like the great revolution of 1789 as Wordsworth describes it in a famous passage of *The Prelude*:

> Bliss was it in that dawn to be alive,
> But to be young was very Heaven! O times,
> In which the meagre, stale, forbidding ways
> Of custom, law, and statute, took at once.
> The attraction of a country in romance!
> When Reason seemed the most to assert her rights
> When most intent on making of herself
> A prime enchantress—to assist the work,
> Which was then going forward in her name!
>   . . .
> What temper at the prospect did not wake
> To happiness unthought of? The inert
> Were roused, and lively natures rapt away!
>   . . .
> Now it was that *both* found, the meek and lofty
> Did both find, helpers to their heart's desire.
> And stuff at hand, plastic as they could wish.
> Were called upon to exercise their skill,
> Not in Utopia,—subterranean fields,—
> Or some, secreted island, Heaven knows where.
> But in the very world, which is the world
> Of all of us,—the place where, in the end,
> We find our happiness, or not at all.[2]

Wordsworth's lines express a rationalist and secularist program, but one actually pursued in a spirit of visionary excitement. The special interest of *Gaudium et Spes* is that more than any other of the Council documents, it expressed and produced a similiar excitement in many active members of the church, both lay and clerical. Unlike the declaration on religious freedom, *Dignitatis Humanae*, it looked primarily to the future rather than to the rectification of past errors and historical embarrassments. Unlike the dogmatic constitutions on the church and revelation, *Lumen Gentium* and *Dei Verbum*, which signalled the breaking of the hold of neo-Scholastic formulae and the official acceptance of a more historical and biblical way of doing theology that had already achieved a certain intellectual maturity, *Gaudium et Spes* was a mandate to build a new and better future. This mandate was drawn up in terms that did not repudiate the natural law tradition of Catholic teaching in social ethics but that stressed the importance of collaboration across ideological, confessional, and national lines for the sake of a universal common good.

Gaudium et Spes was a theological document that resembled the charters given by European states to the explorers and merchants seeking to found new settlements in the Indies and the Americas; for it required the exploration of a new world and the establishment of new ways for dealing with problems. At the same time, it expressed a liberation of generous hope and feeling in a church that had seemed to be both victim and proponent of nostalgia and *ressentiment* and that had alternated between regarding itself as the despised prisoner of the modern world and as the stern admonitor of that same world. It was a document that, like the Council itself, surprised both members and critics of Roman Catholicism with its freshness, its friendliness, its vulnerability. It was evidence that Rome would not be like Oxford, where, as one Cambridge wit put it, the Oxford Movement was so called because it was unique. The old church, supposedly nailed to its gilded throne, showed life in a way that amazed and enticed even "the cultured despisers" of religion.

At this point I should make an autobiographical confession. When the Council closed in 1965, I was a twenty-five-year-old Jesuit teaching philosophy, and I had had enough exposure to both traditional piety and neo-Scholastic philosophy and theology to be profoundly grateful for the very different future which the Council opened up, without feeling that I had spent years in study and work that rested on essentially mistaken premises. During the twenty years since, I have studied and taught philosophy and theology and have been an observer of the American political and religious worlds. Most of my thinking and writing during that time has moved along lines that extend the Council's desire to acknowledge "the rightful independence of earthly affairs" and to reflect on these affairs in the light of that "innermost truth" about human beings which is to be found in the Catholic faith.[3] The reason for mentioning my own situation is that I take it to be not untypical for many American Catholics of my generation. *Gaudium et Spes* is neither the earliest nor the deepest nor the ultimate expression of those forces of modernity and faith that shape our life projects. But it does have a special place both because of the moment in our lives and in the life of the church in which it was issued, and because of its status as an expression of the mind of the universal church. The time of the Council, the early 1960s, was also a time of achievement in a special way for Catholicism in the United States. The Catholic share in the enormous post-World War II prosperity and power of the United States had reached a pinnacle in the election of John Fitzgerald Kennedy as the thirty-fifth president. American Catholics, for long an excluded and self-enclosed group in American society, were ready to make their distinctive contribution in a special way to American institutions and movements ranging from General Motors and the AFL-CIO to antiwar protests.

The way in which an American Catholic of my generation now reads *Gaudium et Spes* has to be influenced both by how he or she understands and evaluates continuity and change in the social teaching of the church, and by how he or she reads the political struggles and debates of the last twenty years in the United States. It is neither appropriate nor likely that a reflective American Catholic between the ages of thirty and seventy will be able to treat this document with pure scholarly detachment, for it was too successful in speaking to the joys and the hopes, the griefs and the anxieties of several generations. On the other hand, precisely because of its influence and its intimate connections with other important documents of the conciliar and postconciliar period (including both liberation theology and the recent pastoral letters of the United States hierarchy), *Gaudium et Spes* requires and deserves critical scrutiny at a time when the course of events both inside and outside the church has brought forward questions which call for more complex answers than simple affirmation or rejection.

ALASDAIR MACINTYRE'S CRITICISM OF MODERN CULTURE

The special character and spirit of *Gaudium et Spes* are emphasized when it is compared with the somber picture of our society's moral landscape given in one of the most influential recent presentations of the fundamental issues of ethics, Alasdair MacIntyre's *After Virtue* (1981). MacIntyre is a Scot who has resided for several years in the United States; he has written as a Barthian Christian, a Marxist, and a maverick analytic philosopher who takes both sociology and the history of ethics seriously. He offers the following summary of his indictment of the contemporary condition of morality:

> The language—and therefore also to some large degree the practice—of morality today is in a state of grave disorder. That disorder arises from the prevailing cultural power of an idiom in which ill-assorted conceptual fragments from various parts of our past are deployed together in public and private debates which are notable chiefly for the unsettlable character of the controversies thus carried on and the apparent arbitrariness of each of the contending parties.[4]

This view of our moral universe as fragmented and incoherent corresponds with MacIntyre's view of our political life as not "a matter of genuine moral consensus" but as "civil war carried on by other means."[5] He gives a complex and controversial account of how we came to this pass, an account which puts great stress on the general philosophical abandonment of Aristotelian teleology and on the inevitable failure of the Enlightenment attempt to justify morality independently of beliefs about human nature.

There is a great deal in MacIntyre's critique of modernity with which Cardinal Ottaviani and other curialist conservatives would have agreed, even though they would have regarded many of his arguments with abhorrence. Although MacIntyre is writing fifteen years after the Council Fathers, he and they are responding to what is generically the same world, the world of liberal capitalist democracies with an originally Christian but now largely secularized culture. MacIntyre and many conservatives would look on the pluralism, the permissiveness, and the inability to bring moral debates to a satisfactory resolution as evidence of a fundamental crisis in the moral life of Western civilization. Over the last twenty years, we have grown accustomed not merely to religious leaders denouncing departures from traditional ethical norms and threatening us with the possibility of spiritual ruin and eternal damnation, but also to a whole series of secular moralists who are appalled by the prospects of nuclear war, environmental catastrophe, worldwide famine, the collapse of the international financial system, the disruptive effects of transnational corporations, the increasing burden of world population, the exhaustion of scarce natural resources, the vulnerability of urban centers and essential systems to technological breakdown and terrorist attack, and who in response denounce the bankruptcy of the Western cultural tradition which has brought us to our present state of opulent apathy and self-destructive power, and announce the prospect of irreversible material ruin. Like Macbeth, too many of us "have supped full of horrors"—not so much in real life as in the prophecies and imaginings of war which emanate from secular sources even more frequently than from religious authorities.

What renders these negative possibilities so burdensome to the Western conscience is not that they have happened or even that they are unavoidable. It is rather, I would argue, that they put in question the worth and sustainability of the technological, interdependent, energy-intensive kind of society that Western civilization has aimed to become, especially over the last century. They point to limits and costs that are inherent in reliance on technological systems, but also to the weaknesses even of our strengths. Taken together, they constitute a radical challenge to confident, quasi-religious affirmations of the inevitability of progress and even to a more modest pragmatic confidence that we, the engineers and managers of the Western world, can keep the engine of history on the tracks and out of the surrounding quagmire.

The issue is not merely the future factual one of whether our political and technological elites can keep us from extinction, but a retrospective moral one of whether some fundamental flaw in our system of values and in our understanding of ourselves has brought us close to the edge of disaster. There is no lack of suggestions as to where we have gone wrong—in accepting the biblical view of man as called by God to exercise dominion over the earth, in rejecting the biblical understanding of man as called to obedient service to the Lord, in accepting some primal form of patriarchal domination, in rejecting the authority of the church, in aspiring to subject the order of the universe to human reason, in lapsing into a nihilistic denial of meaning and value in the world, in espousing various forms of individualism and subjectivism which disrupted social order and made common good unattainable, in developing large institutions and corporations which left individuals helpless and alienated, or in our continuing refusal to subordinate the rights and interests of individuals to the pressing needs of an imperiled community. As one can readily see, there is some plausibility in almost all these diagnoses; but they are not easy to reconcile with each other and they often come from an ideological *parti pris.*

The long string of potential catastrophes that have been rehearsed for us by a generation of secular apocalypticists and the equally long string of diagnoses of the malaise of our culture by secular moralists leave most people unsurprised by MacIntyre's criticisms of modern culture. MacIntyre's work had more of an impact within the world of academic philosophy, where the dominant analytic tradition has been interested either in reductive or piecemeal analyses of the uses of moral language, or in the rational reconstruction of a new system of morality.

This academic world carefully insulated itself from trends and aspirations in what it perceived as "the soft underbelly" of culture. What is perhaps most remarkable and unstable about MacIntyre's position is its religious character. In the controversial final chapter of his book, he compares the present situation with the decline of the Roman Empire in the West. He writes:

> A crucial turning point in that history occurred when men and women of good will turned aside from the task of shoring up the Roman *imperium* and ceased to identify the continuation of civility and moral community with the maintenance of that *imperium*. What they set themselves to achieve instead—often not recognizing fully what they were doing—was the construction of new forms of community within which the moral life could be sustained so that both morality and civility might survive the coming ages of barbarism and darkness. If my account of our moral condition is correct, we ought also to conclude that for some time now we too have reached that turning point. What matters at this time is the construction of local forms of community within which civility and the intellectual and moral life can be sustained through the new dark ages which are already upon us ... This time however the barbarians are not waiting beyond the frontiers; they have already been governing us for quite some time. And it is our lack of consciousness of this that constitutes part of our predicament. We are not waiting for a Godot, but for another— doubtless very different—St. Benedict.[6]

This passage is a counterthrust to Gibbon's famous characterization of the fall of the Roman Empire as the triumph of "religion and barbarism." What makes it remarkable and unstable is that MacIntyre arrives at this point not from the confidence of faith, but from the exhaustion of skepticism and unbelief. Unlike those religious moralists who feel the vulnerability and cultural isolation of conservative religious groups in an age of science and secularization, and who have been inclined to stress the necessity of adapting the church's message to the world's ability to respond, MacIntyre insists on the incoherence and moral rootlessness of the dominant secular and pluralistic society.

It is a shrewd and significant move on MacIntyre's part that he evokes the figure of St. Benedict, the founding father of a monastic tradition that developed a rich tradition of spirituality and also provided much of the intellectual and material basis for the subsequent flowering of medieval culture in the universities and urban centers of the West. The Benedictine tradition lacks the aspiration to a comprehensive political order that is found in Ambrose, Augustine, and Gregory the Great, as well as the architectonic intellectual drive that is so prominent in both Augustine and Aquinas. MacIntyre's intention is not to provoke a religious takeover of the dominant society with all its unsolvable problems, much less to endorse a religious legitimation of this society with its emotivist interpretation of morality and with its dominant characters of the aesthete and the manager; rather, what MacIntyre seems to counsel is the establishment of small but coherent moral communities, and a long period of waiting during which the collapse of the larger society would open the way for the formation of a new moral universe, the special character and direction of which is left to the reader's imagination. But we would not be amiss in thinking that these communities would inculcate values of frugality, modesty, cooperation, fidelity, respect for both manual and intellectual work, and sexual restraint. They would restrain greed, promiscuity, and violence. They would avoid a centralized concentration of power but would encourage patterns of imitation and mutual criticism which would contribute to their coherence and stability. Such a picture has a profound religious attraction; but, as MacIntyre himself seems to admit, it needs a profound religious experience to sustain communities against the pressures and the temptations of the larger society, however troubled and erratic that society may be, and to preserve them from the conflicts that customarily rend both monastic and utopian groups.[7]

MacIntyre's vision of the survival of religious communities or cells in a future of darkness and barbarism may be attractive to theological conservatives who wish to preserve the faith from secular contamination and to religious radicals who want "to convict the world of sin" (John 16:9). It is less attractive to institutional conservatives and pragmatic reformers who exert themselves to sustain and improve the existing institutions of society, which they would justify in terms of the human needs they meet (even if incompletely) and the way in which they express the values of an imperfect but still living culture. His vision is also unacceptable (both because of its religious indeterminacy and its political radicalism) to those who would build a new Christendom or who, in a spirit of greater modesty, would attempt to put an explicitly religious mark on what they regard as key social institutions. The vagueness of this vision—which makes sense, given his views about the dependence of moral views on long-term social change—also frees him from the burdens and failures of concrete historical communities, whether these be religious or secular.

The intention of this essay, however, is neither to expound nor to criticize MacIntyre's views but to use them as a point of reference for assessing the moral teaching of Vatican II on the central worldly activity of politics and, more broadly, for appraising the attitude of the bishops of the Council to the modern world. For MacIntyre gives a reading of the current situation of the modern world that takes history seriously and that exerts a powerful appeal precisely to those within the Christian tradition who are making a transition similar to MacIntyre's from confidence in the course of the larger society to despair about its future, and who choose to direct their imaginative energies and moral passions in a sectarian direction. This is not a surprising reaction in those Americans who came of age in the early 1960s in the euphoria of Camelot and the Council, in the era of confidence and good will crystallized in the lives and gestures of John XXIII and John Kennedy. For the course of events since 1965 both in the church and in American society has been so full of changes, illusions, and disappointments that a contemporary reader of *Gaudium et Spes* must wonder whether the Fathers of the Council rightly understood either the church for and to which they were speaking or the world with which they aspired to collaborate. In order to answer this question, we must turn our attention to the text, but we must also interpret that text in the light of the Council's own aspiration to carry out "the duty of scrutinizing the signs of the times and of interpreting them in the light of the gospel" (no. 4).

"GAUDIUM ET SPES" AND THE LIFE OF THE POLITICAL COMMUNITY

The teaching of *Gaudium et Spes* on political subjects actually falls into two parts. The connection between them is expounded in general terms:

> The Council has set forth the dignity of the human person and the work which men have been destined to undertake throughout the world both as individuals and as members of society. There are a number of particularly urgent needs characterizing the present age, needs which go to the roots of the human race ... Of the many subjects arousing universal concern today, it may be helpful to concentrate on these: marriage and the family, human culture, life in its economic, social and political dimensions, the bonds between the family of nations, and peace. On each of these may there shine the radiant ideals proclaimed by Christ. By these ideals may Christians be led, and all mankind enlightened, as they search for answers to questions of such complexity (no. 46).

This text makes clear the fundamental structure of the document in a way that the introductory section does not attempt. What the Council is offering can be divided into four levels: (a) a theological anthropology (the dignity of the human person), (b) Christian ideals, (c) moral norms, (d) policy directions and recommendations ("answers to questions of such complexity"). Admittedly, the moral norms are not explicitly mentioned here, but they are clearly operative at key places in the argument (for instance, in statements on the rights and duties connected with various institutions, or in the presentation of just war theory and the condemnation of total war and countercity warfare); and they are, moreover, an integral part of any presentation of Catholic social ethics. This division of levels represents an incipient deductive framework for conducting a Christian moral argument about general matters of public policy and social life; and some of what I shall say will take it in that way.

But the Council was also eager to communicate a vision of humanity and of the place of the church within human history and society. That vision is holistic and hope-filled; it is neither captured nor refuted by syllogistic arguments. It attempts to persuade, to broaden understanding, to deepen a sense of shared experience and shared values, rather than merely to instruct in a deductive fashion. The Council was also very much impressed by the interconnection of the various parts of its vast theme; and so it did not shrink from covering a large number of topics and from stressing the fundamental importance of culture and history for the positions taken on particular issues.

For this reason, theological anthropology enjoys pride of place in *Gaudium et Spes* and provides a basis for the treatment of specific issues. Part One of the document, "The Church and Man's Calling," which is preceded by an introductory section, "The Situation of Men in the Modern World," as well as by the preface affirming the bonds between the church and mankind, is marked by a fundamental dialectic of identification and distinction in the treatment of the relationship between the church and humanity. It is in this section, where the Council reflects on what the church can say to a world predominantly non-Christian, to a European society that is in many respects post-Christian, and to powerful social movements that are often explicitly anti-Christian, that real differences are more clearly expressed. The effort to achieve a clear unity with regard to ethical content is set forth in Part Two, "Some Problems of Special Urgency," which treats the specific issues listed in no. 46. This concern for unity of ethical content has a double source: it is inherent in the tradition of Catholic moral theology and social teaching; and it is a requirement that arises from the demands of action and social collaboration. Thus the Council addresses the oppressors of the Church: "Therefore if we have been summoned to the same destiny, which is both human and divine, we can and we should work together without violence and deceit in order to build up the world in genuine peace" (no. 92).

The presentation of theological anthropology and Christian ideals in Part One of *Gaudium et Spes* is intended to provide a basis for all the special problems treated in Part Two. So I proceed by beginning with Chapter Four of Part Two, which deals with the life of the political community; and then I point to some of the politically significant passages in Part Two before taking up those themes in Part One which constitute the foundation for the Council's understanding of political life.

The chapter on politics is quite short and consists of four long paragraphs. The Council begins by adopting an optimistic and progressivist interpretation of recent political changes. It points to an increasing desire to protect human rights, to achieve active participation in political life, and to develop integrated national communities in which the rights of minorities are respected. It does, however, acknowledge that there are governments in the world "which block civil and religious liberty, multiply the victims of ambition and political crimes, and wrench the exercise of authority from pursuing the common good to serving the advantage of a certain faction or of the rulers themselves" (no. 73). We should recall that the Council was writing at a time when the breakup of the Western colonial empires was entering into its final stage (particularly in Africa), when the European Economic Community was providing a framework for a vigorous expansion of the European economy, and when the United States was promoting democratization and economic development in Latin America through the Alliance for Progress. Expressing high hopes at such a time was not a matter of religious naiveté; rather, it was one way in which the Council accomplished its task of speaking for a developing world church.

The Council reminds its readers of the necessity of both virtue and political wisdom for the attainment of "a truly human political life," and then sets forth certain "basic beliefs about the true nature of the political community, and about the proper exercise and limits of public authority"(no. 73). It holds that the political community is a natural necessity—given the insufficiency of individuals, families, and groups to establish "a fully human condition of life"—and that the authority of this political community is not unlimited but exists to serve the common good, which is defined as "the sum of those conditions of social life by which individuals, families, and groups can achieve their own fulfillment in a relatively thorough and ready way"(no. 74). Authority is to be exercised within the bounds of morality and creates a moral obligation in citizens to obey, though they remain free to defend their rights against abuses of authority. The precise form of government is "left to the free will of citizens," and the way in which the political community functions varies "according to the particular character of a people and its historic development."

The particular value in the political order which the Council wishes to promote is "the chance to participate freely and actively in establishing the political bases of a political community" (no. 75). Participation is maintained by the rule of law; by a limited government which does not hinder "family, social, or cultural groups, as well as intermediate bodies and institutions"; and by an active government which intervenes to bring about "conditions more likely to help citizens and groups freely attain to complete human fulfillment with greater effect" (no. 75).

The Council goes on to urge Christians to fullfill "their special and personal vocation in the political community," to accept a legitimate pluralism of political views, and to enter "the difficult but most honorable art of politics"(no. 75). But a distinction between the political community and the church must be maintained. Both serve "the personal and social vocation of the same human beings," but they are to be "mutually independent and self-governing"(no. 76). The special function of the church is to be "a sign and a safeguard of the transcendence of the human person." It is not to be bound to any political system, and does not seek privileges from any. In fact, there is even an explicit declaration that the church is willing "to renounce the exercise of certain legitimately acquired rights if it becomes clear that their use raises doubt about the sincerity of her witness or that new conditions of life demand some other arrangement"(no. 76). But the church demands the right to preach the faith and "to pass moral judgments, even on matters touching the political order, whenever basic personal rights or the salvation of souls make such judgments necessary"(no. 76).

Chapter Four of Part Two of *Gaudium et Spes*, then, contains little that is particularly controversial or illuminating. It is basically a combination of the church's insistence on the natural and "divinely foreordained" character of the state, an affirmation of human rights and the common good (thus opposing both collectivism in its authoritarian and totalitarian forms, and excessive individualism), and an acceptance of participation as a value in the political community. Participation can be seen as the democratic and individual complement to the classical doctrine of the natural character of the state; it is essential to the attainment of what Aristotle spoke of as "the excellence of a worthy citizen" which includes "knowing both how to rule and how to obey."[8] Politics, as understood here, however, is not merely about politics in the narrow sense, the processes and structure of the political community. It is also about the other "problems of special urgency": the family, the development of culture, economic life, and the attainment of world peace. The Council affirms with regard to each of these areas a general duty and responsibility of public authority to do those things which promote the common good and which protect relevant rights and values.[9]

But it is the problems involved in the avoidance of war and fostering of peace that call in a special way for political judgment, action, and resolution. The Council, however, treats the task of avoiding war primarily in terms of "universal natural law and its all-embracing principles" (no. 79), and on this basis condemns total war and countercity warfare. This treatment of the task of creating a right international order which would not collapse in outbursts of violence is put in more vague and less vigorous terms than those used by John XXIII two years earlier in his encyclical *Pacem in Terris*, where he had called for "a public authority, having world-wide power and endowed with proper means for the efficacious pursuit of its objective, which is the universal common good in concrete form."[10] The Council is significantly less firm and pointed when it says:

> The universal common good needs to be intelligently pursued and more effectively achieved. Hence it is now necessary for the family of nations to create for themselves an order which corresponds to modern obligations, particularly with reference to those numerous regions still laboring under intolerable need (no. 84).

There is actually in no. 82 an affirmation of "our clear duty" to work for the outlawing of war "by international consent," and it is granted that "this goal undoubtedly requires the establishment of some universal public authority acknowledged as such by all, and endowed with effective power to safeguard, on the behalf of all, security, regard for justice, and respect for rights." But this is deferred until after the resolution of the problem of international security.

The Council does acknowledge that there is a continuing need to eradicate causes of dissension among peoples; these it identifies as injustice stemming from "excessive economic inequalities" and a quest for power which involves "human jealousy, distrust, pride, and other egoistic passions"(no. 83). It calls for more and better international cooperation, especially in economic matters, and commends existing international agencies. The church's own presence in the international arena is to contribute to "strengthening peace and to placing brotherly relations between individuals and peoples on solid ground" (no. 89), and is to be achieved both through its public institutions and through the collaboration of Christians.

The Council's treatment of international relations manifests a profound and understandable reluctance to think of international conflicts in political terms. Both the recommended solutions and the conception of the church's contribution to these solutions show a strong desire to speak from a suprapolitical point of view. This desire is not inappropriate, given the understandable unwillingness of the Fathers of a Council representing the universal church to say anything that would show partisanship in international conflicts or rekindle the fires of ideological dispute and denunciation. But this produces a split between what I would call the voice of the celestial spectator, deploring the arms race and the continuing disagreements among nations and offering incontestable reflections about the necessity of finding a better way to regulate the affairs of the world, and the voice of moral counsel instructing leaders and citizens in the norms of natural law and just war theory and urging cautious restraint in a perilous time. This split, I would argue, lies behind such remarkable juxtapositions in the Council's argument as can be found in the insistence that "peace must be born of mutual trust between nations rather than imposed on them through fear of one another's weapons" and the recommendation that the arms race is to be concluded not through unilateral disarmament, but through disarmament "proceeding at an equal pace according to agreement, and backed up by authentic and workable safeguards"(no. 82). This leaves political leaders and also citizens with two distinct imperatives, which have contradictory presuppositions. The two statements both point in the same general direction of less reliance on weapons, but they cannot be combined into one coherent program. Far from applying a general value or norm to the making of a policy recommendation, *Gaudium et Spes* here offers a policy recommendation that presupposes the unreliability or inadequacy of the general norm of trust.

THE COUNCIL'S VISION OF THE HUMAN COMMUNITY

However, *Gaudium et Spes* does not draw its power to persuade and inspire from its treatment of international relations or from its straightforward presentation of political life as a natural and valuable exercise in achieving the common good. It draws this power rather from reliance on a vision of human community and destiny that does not divide Catholics from those in other traditions who are working for the common good. Such a vision not merely legitimates but mandates an active, autonomous involvement in working out the problems of contemporary society. Much of the document's impact on contemporary Catholic involvement in political life stems from its promise of overcoming the internal divisions within individual Christians who are often torn between an attitude of passive acceptance of established evils, apparently ordained by God's will, and a passionate desire to remedy injustice, and who are also drawn to both contemplative union with God and an active effort to contribute to the betterment of society. In the most fundamental way, however, the task of combining religious commitment (which always stands in need of renewal and purification) with political activism is something that cannot be accomplished by any document. Rather, it must be undertaken by individuals and groups who are willing to bear the trials and share the graces of such an enterprise.

But *Gaudium et Spes* contributes to this task in several important ways. First, it insists on the obligatory character of the task:

> This Council exhorts Christians, as citizens of two cities, to strive to discharge their earthly duties conscientiously and in response to the gospel spirit. They are mistaken who, knowing that we have here no abiding city but seek one which is to come, think that they may therefore shirk their earthly responsibilities. For they are forgetting that by the faith itself they are more than ever obliged to measure up to these duties, each according to his proper vocation (no. 43).

As the rest of the section makes clear, this injunction applies both to "professional and social activities" and to the necessarily political efforts of Christians to see "that the divine law is inscribed in the life of the earthly city." Second, it does not merely command or admonish, but offers an attractive picture of the harmony of earthly and spiritual values toward which Christians are to work. The Council says of Christians: "In the exercise of all their earthly activities they can thereby gather their humane, domestic, professional, social and technical enterprises into one vital synthesis with religious values, under whose supreme direction all things are harmonized into God's glory" (no. 43). Third, the document itself sets an example of engagement and dialogue with the contemporary world. The Fathers of the Council give up the defensive, admonitory, regretful, alienated tone that has so often shown up in church pronouncements about the state of the modern world. They show more readiness to learn and less to condemn, more inclination to respect the complexity and worth of the world on its own terms, and less inclination to treat it as simply the object of religious imperialism. They also manifest a recognition (now common but then so rare as to be newsworthy) that the finger pointed in accusation is less persuasive than the hand striking the breast in contrition or extended in friendly collaboration.

Fourth, *Gaudium et Spes* brings into question the adequacy and necessity of efforts to fashion a purely Catholic culture in which secular activities are given religious value by being conducted in a separate counterpart society. The organizations and institutions that carried on these efforts were not in most cases abandoned; but they did lose their claim to an effective monopoly on Catholic involvement in key areas of society. In the United States, of course, there was no tradition of explicitly Catholic political activity, nor was there any tradition of explicitly antireligious political activity of either a liberal or Marxist character. So in this regard there was no separate Catholic counterpart organization that had to be abandoned or modified; rather, there was an ongoing pattern of participation in political coalitions spanning religious and ideological differences. This actually constitutes a fifth way in which *Gaudium et Spes* contributed to overcoming the problems of dualism and separatism in Catholic life, namely, by formulating and ratifying in general terms many of the aspirations and projects that had existed in different countries and cultures for some time. These efforts had been most articulate and most venturesome especially in France, but they were also important in northern Europe and the English-speaking world. The Council was seen as a decisive breakthrough for the development of a more liberal form of Catholicism better adapted to a pluralistic environment but not departing from the fundamental Catholic tradition. The efforts of such a Catholicism to find a satisfactory formulation of its hopes and to achieve legitimacy within the church had been subject to many checks and reverses during the century from Pius IX to Pius XII. One of the most important results of *Gaudium et Spes* and of Vatican II in general was to provide a magisterial charter for the many well-educated Catholics in advanced industrial societies to explore a very wide range of possibilities. This did not mean that the laity, the theologians, or the political activists were given a completely free hand to reshape the political agenda of Catholicism, especially when such reshaping involved doctrinally sensitive subjects such as birth control and abortion. Similar restrictions applied to situations involving conflicts with the local hierarchy, overly close collaboration with Marxist political movements, or projects that seemed to jeopardize the unity or freedom of the church as a whole. But these restrictions, while often quite real and important, have had to be imposed with a view to a significant degree of lay autonomy in many areas. The admission in *Gaudium et Spes* that pastors did not have readymade solutions to complex problems, combined with encouragement for the laity to take on their own distinctive role and warnings against identifying partisan solutions with the gospel message (no. 43), effectively cut the ground from under any direct clericalism in politics. In fact, these considerations have been used by those who have attempted to deny the legitimacy of politically relevant church teaching on issues currently under debate, as for instance, in the pastoral letters of the United States bishops on war and peace and on the economy.[11] The possibilities for conflict between church teachers (mainly bishops and priests, but also theologians and church organizations) and Catholic political leaders, as well as for collaboration between Catholic and non-Catholic political groups, have been greatly increased by the Council's positions on the autonomy of the laity and on the proper independence of the political community. This is, in fact, just what one should expect in a situation of political pluralism in a democratic polity.

THE THEOLOGICAL ANTHROPOLOGY OF "GAUDIUM ET SPES"

But more basic than the Council's reflections on these ecclesiastical topics is what enables it both to accept the prospects and uncertainties of democratic politics and to believe confidently that the church would be able to proclaim its message and carry on its ministry with integrity. This, I would argue, is its theological anthropology, that is, its understanding of the dignity and vocation of the human person before God. Some of the terms that I use in discussing this anthropology are taken over from political philosophy; but I think it would be a fundamental mistake to interpret the anthropology as a whole on reductively political lines. (This would be somewhat like dismissing all the paintings in San Marco and the Doges' Palace as simply propaganda for Venetian imperialism.) Rather, this type of theological anthropology attempts to draw together some major aspects of our current reading of the human situation and some major themes from the theological tradition which deal with the human situation as grasped by the community of believers. It does not offer a value-free account of the human situation as some social scientists and philosophers have proposed to do. Instead, the move from the theses of theological anthropology to normative conclusions is simple and direct, since these theses themselves usually have considerable normative content.

The primary affirmations of the theological anthropology set forth in Part One of *Gaudium et Spes* that are relevant for an understanding of political life are the following. First, humanity shows great power and creativity but is also troubled by a series of anxious questions about ultimate reality and meaning (no. 3). This points humanity to a destiny revealed in Christ.

Second, the form and language in which these questions are expressed are subject to historical change. The most important of these questions today arise from an increase in human knowledge and power combined with growing uncertainty about how this is to be directed to human welfare (no. 4). We are living through a crisis of growth and development marked by profound imbalances within individuals and groups, and by distrust and conflict between groups (no. 8). Third, humanity is both the cause and the victim of social evils (no. 8). Fourth, humanity is called on to establish control over creation and to set up "a political, social, and economic order which will . . . help individuals and groups to affirm and develop the dignity proper to them"(no. 9).

Fifth, the human being is "the center and crown" of "all things on earth" (no. 12) and is created "to the image of God." This image is especially manifest in the exercise of human freedom (no. 17). Sixth, all human life is "a dramatic struggle between good and evil, between light and darkness," in which human beings need divine assistance (no. 13). Seventh, conscience is "the most secret core and sanctuary" of the human person and presents a law which is not merely self-imposed but requires our obedience.

Eighth, death presents the riddle of human existence in its most acute form. Across it, God calls us to the resolution of this riddle in "an endless sharing of a divine life beyond all corruption"(no. 18). This ultimate vocation to be with Christ does not, as we have already seen, justify an abandonment of earthly responsibilities. The church's teaching on eternal life provides human beings with hope and with "fresh incentives" to accomplish their duties (no. 21). Ninth, the human task of bettering this world is one to which Christian faith makes a positive contribution, especially by activating people to justice and love; but at the same time it is one in which believers and unbelievers can join, informed by "sincere and prudent dialogue" (no. 21). Tenth, the mystery of human existence is illuminated by the mystery of Christ, who struggles against evil, dies for all, and makes possible the one ultimate vocation of all (no. 22). Eleventh, the spiritual dignity of persons is realized not on the level of technical progress, but on the deeper level of interpersonal relationships (no. 23). Twelfth, all human beings have God as their one ultimate goal and constitute "one family" (no. 24). This implies a rejection of racism and any exclusionary ideology.

Thirteenth, there is a systemic interdependence of person and society in such a way that the person "stands completely in need of social life" even while the person is at the same time "the subject and goal of all social institutions," whose rights are to be safeguarded (no. 25). Human beings have not been created "for life in isolation, but for the formation of social unity"(no. 32).

Fourteenth, evil done by human beings is a result of social circumstances and of the influence of prior sins, but at a deeper level it is a result of "man's pride and selfishness" (no. 25). Fifteenth, achieving the common good, "the sum of those conditions of social life which allow social groups and their individual members relatively thorough and ready access to their own fulfillment" (no. 26), is a task that is increasingly complex and requires "constant improvement."

Sixteenth, the human person has "rights and duties that are universal and inviolable" (no. 26). This implies that human beings must have access to "everything necessary for leading a life truly human " and that violations of human life and human dignity are to be condemned. Seventeenth, Christian love and forgiveness are to be combined with respect for truth and goodness so that in conflicts error is condemned but not the person in error (no. 28). Judgment of the person rests with God. Eighteenth, human beings have "basic equality" in virtue of their possession of a rational soul and their creation in God's image. This point must "receive increasingly greater recognition" (no. 29); it requires a humane minimum for all in society but does not imply the abolition of "rightful differences."

Nineteenth, human beings find fulfillment by freely playing an active role in common endeavors (no. 31).

Twentieth, human activity aimed at bettering the lives of human beings "accords with God's will" and continues the Creator's work (no. 34).

What this brief statement of major points in the theological anthropology of *Gaudium et Spes* makes plain is that complex balancing of opposing tendencies underlies the Council's approach to political and social life: personalism, but not individualism; a communitarian ethos but not collectivism; an equality of rights but not the comprehensive elimination of inequality; universalism without uniformity; pluralism without harm to the common good; affirmation of the spiritual and involvement in the world; acceptance of historical change and conceptual development along with preservation of doctrinal and normative continuity; an insistence on the primacy of moral values in the shaping of human affairs while avoiding both cynicism and fanaticism. This complex, multidimensional balancing is like the positioning of a dome above the arches of the crossing of a great baroque church: the stability of the dome depends on the balancing and distribution of forces in opposing directions. The balancing so characteristic of Catholic social teaching, however, lacks the precision of the architectural model.

Once it is granted that there is no unique solution to the problem of achieving justice in society and that key terms in the problem are subject to regional variation and temporal change, a certain element of slack and indeterminacy is introduced into the system. But this is what we should expect, given the vagueness of many of the key terms in the points listed earlier and in the oppositions just mentioned. The element of indeterminacy is, of course, crucial in enabling people with quite different political programs and interests to make legitimating appeals to Catholic social teaching as presented by the Council and by national bishops' conferences as well as in papal social encyclicals. Most policy conclusions, other than extreme cases such as total nationalization of the private sector of the economy or the denial of equal status to a racial group, require a step beyond the purely normative. This step involves a reading of the complex of facts relevant to a given problem in a particular social situation; it also calls for a decision that estimates the urgency or importance of the problem being addressed and chooses means that are judged appropriate and sufficient to achieve the end without incurring unacceptable costs or risks. It is generally impossible to present this decision as logically entailed by the preceding complex of considerations, let alone by the moral principles or value judgments taken in isolation. One way of understanding the "option for the poor" so widely spoken of since the Puebla meeting of the Latin American bishops (1979) is as an effort to overcome this indeterminacy by at least a general instruction to weigh certain of the considerations in a different fashion than heretofore, but even this is not normally enough to eliminate the element of indeterminacy.

The persistent presence of indeterminacy in Catholic social teaching on politics, along with the steady rejection of extremism in *Gaudium et Spes* and more generally in the teachings of the modern popes, allows for a fairly wide range of positions and combinations within the central band of the ideological spectrum. An important and controversial aspect of the two recent pastoral letters on social questions by the U.S. bishops is that they make more specific judgments, e.g. on weapons and welfare systems. These judgments do not flow deductively from the moral principles and fundamental judgments of value which dominate most Catholic social teaching. Rather, they constitute one line of development on the basis of those principles. Two of the most interesting questions about the future status and effectiveness of these pastorals are (1) whether they will succeed in establishing a definite Catholic position on such central issues of political life as national security policy and economic policy, and (2) whether such a development would bring about fundamental changes in the internal life of the church or the political life of the United States.

The American bishops correctly affirm that their pastoral letters are not conceived as partisan political documents. They clearly aim at a more fundamental and more consistent kind of discourse than is commonly found in American political debate or in the statements of the great composite coalitions that are our major political parties. But they do argue for specific policies on the part of the federal government in a way that eliminates the element of indeterminacy even while they pledge not to impose such positions as part of their teaching authority. At the same time, these positions are part of the subject matter of ordinary political debates and can only be made effective policy through political processes. Whether the bishops or the public believe that they have crossed a critical line is unclear, just as it is also unclear how far they propose to use political means to achieve their political objectives. It is at least possible that these two pastoral letters will remain an isolated phenomenon and will not lead to a comprehensive politicization of the Catholic church in the United States.

Another way of dealing with the problem of indeterminacy is to think of it as partially soluble in particular cases by political leadership (which can in some exceptional cases come from the church). The precise form which the maintenance of the balance of values should take in view of the pressures of human needs and social changes is not a matter that yields to a purely deductive approach from principles; rather, it requires a concrete act of political imagination which recognizes the shaping power of historical tradition and context and is prepared to work with the often intractable material of conflicting interests and personalities. This act of imagination can be the work of a single leader or can be shared by a group. In this approach there is room for both prudence and art, for the application of principles to the uncharted complexities of cases, and also for the use of persuasive and enlightening symbols. The function of the church in this view is to serve as a critic of political leaders, groups, and programs when they move to violate the fundamental values which are to be protected in and by political life; it is not to attempt to realize a particular social Gestalt or program. This leaves the resolution of indeterminacy outside the church, even while it leaves the church free to fulfill a critical and "prophetic" function in political life.

Both this critical approach and the more positive approach of the American bishops indicate ways to prevent the political message of *Gaudium et Spes* and Catholic social teaching from becoming a utopianism of the center.

The broad array of social ideals proposed in the pastoral constitution is an expression of human Christian hope for the modern
world, but it does not give guidance on how the objects of this hope are
to be realized. *Gaudium et Spes* enkindles enthusiasm for what is an
idealized version of the program of constitutional democracy and the
welfare state. It preaches a universalist egalitarianism compatible with
liberty and Christian humanism. It presents a synthesis of freedom and
order, of equality and pluralism. After the ideological debacle of the first
half of this century, it restates core values of the Western religious and
political traditions.

But can it provide an alternative to the division and incoherence
which MacIntyre finds to be characteristic of our culture in the second
half of the century? There is no easy, straightforward answer to this
question. But comparative reflection on the social directions proposed
in MacIntyre's *After Virtue* and in *Gaudium et Spes* suggests that in both
there is a sense of the tensions that mark modern culture and an
insistence on the need to bring harmony out of these tensions. The key
difference between them lies in their different assessments of the
capacity of modern culture to achieve this harmony. For MacIntyre, this
is impossible, and so modern culture must undergo destruction with a
hope of resurrection and transformation, whereas the Fathers of Vatican
II believed that modern culture, once purified of extremist tendencies
and of its antireligious elements, could provide a basis for the future not
merely of the West but also of the entire human community. That
historical project has proven more difficult and more painful than the
Council and the church movements inspired by it expected. It has been
undercut in various ways by East-West rivalry, by regional antagonisms
and conflicts, by the continuing power of nationalism, by the profound
intractability of the problem of poverty, by a renewed sense of financial
constraints, by dramatic exhibitions of human cruelty and depravity, by
the debilitating burdens of materialism and greed. Disappointment,
pessimism, retreats into vindictive fantasy are all understandable, but
such a reaction would be unfaithful both to the American character and
to the hope of Vatican II. For we as a people have been able to draw
strength from statements of ideals that seemed to many to be utopian.
The aspirations of Washington and Jefferson, of Lincoln and Wilson
were not realized simply by being conceived or by finding expression in
public rhetoric. They coexisted for long periods in our history with
harsh and bitter social realities, which provoked difficult political
struggles. But at the same time they gave birth to new forms of political
action and cooperation, to movements of social protest and transformation, to new strategies for dealing with ills undreamt of by earlier
generations, and to a creative internal development of the American
political tradition. The words of *Gaudium et Spes* should fulfill a similiar

function for the Catholic community around the world, for the document is a statement not about concrete political programs nor about what is within our reach if only we will be converted, but a statement of the outlines of a truly just society whose full realization in perfect harmony is not attainable by us now, but which we cannot forget as a goal for our present societies and as a good for our consciences.

Vatican II may indeed offer a utopianism of the center, and it may give rise to utopian temptations and delusions. It sometimes speaks as if the achievement of peace with justice, freedom, and economic abundance required only an act of political will, a few direct and well-intentioned programs and agreements. Our experiences of the last twenty years as American Catholics and as persons involved in both political and religious life should convince us that the goal is much farther away than that. But this should be all the more reason for us to look with longing on the goal and to acknowledge our need for imperfect, intermediate measures, measures which will keep alive our hope for a society that is a foretaste of the kingdom.

NOTES

1. Vatican II, *Gaudium et Spes (Pastoral Constitution on the Church in the Modern World)*, in *The Documents of Vatican II*, ed. Walter Abbott (New York: America Press, 1966), no. 1. Hereafter, section numbers in parentheses are used to refer to the document.

2. William Wordsworth, *The Prelude*, Book XI, lines 108-116, 122-124, 136-144.

3. *Gaudium et Spes*, nos. 36 and 41.

4. Alasdair MacIntyre, *After Virtue* (Notre Dame, Ind.: Notre Dame University Press, 1981), 238.

5. Ibid., 236.

6. Ibid., 245.

7. For presentation and appraisal from a number of viewpoints of the values, aspirations, and limitations of a number of such communities in the contemporary United States, see James Hug, S.J., ed., *Tracing the Spirit: Communities, Social Action, and Theological Reflection* (New York: Paulist Press, 1983).

8. Aristotle, *Politics*, III, 2.1277-27-28.

9. See *Gaudium et Spes*, nos. 52, 59, 66, 71, 79.

10. John XXIII, *Pacem in Terris*, no. 138 in Donald Campion, S.J., ed. (New York: America Press, 1963).

11. National Conference of Catholic Bishops, *The Challenge of Peace: God's Promise and Our Response* (Washington, D.C.: United States Catholic Conference, 1983); *Pastoral Letter on Catholic Social Teaching and the U.S. Economy*, second draft, October 7, 1985 (Washington, D.C.: United States Catholic Conference, 1985).

Patrick J. Leahy

From Conciliar Aula to Senate Floor: Reflections on "Gaudium et Spes"

In accordance with the plan of this book to provide a variety of responses to the *Pastoral Constitution on the Church in the Modern World* on its twentieth anniversary, the editor invited Patrick J. Leahy, a Catholic and Vermont's junior Senator, to offer his reflections on what the Council had to say about political life in light of his own experience in politics over the last twenty years, eleven of them in the U.S. Senate. John B. Breslin, S.J., of Georgetown University, conducted the interview with Senator Leahy.

Breslin: Senator Leahy, as you know, "Questions of Special Urgency" is the title of the second section of the *Pastoral Constitution on the Church in the Modern World (Gaudium et Spes)*. In that section, the Council Fathers take up a number of specific issues that seemed particularly important and particularly troublesome at the time of the Council. One of them is political life, and what I'd like to do this morning is to get your own reflections on certain of the questions that are raised in this section. The Council Fathers begin by applauding what they see as a number of positive signs in modern political life: protection of personal rights, concern for the rights of minorities, respect for differing religious and cultural views, strong disapproval of violations of these civil rights. In general they see these developments as a positive sign. My question to you is, from where you sit, do you see an equally positive picture today, twenty years later? Are things getting better or worse in terms of civil rights, protection of divergent political and religious views, concern for minorities, and universal disapproval of regimes that violate these rights?

Leahy: Well, I think this ebbs and flows somewhat. The bad news is that it does ebb and flow, the good news is that at each cycle the concern for personal rights and individual freedoms tends to be stronger than in, say, the decade before, or the generation before. Right now, in the United States, individuals seem largely concerned only for themselves as individuals. We lack a sense of history, of how we got here, of how the civil and political rights we cherish were arrived at; we've forgotten the struggles, whether they were civil rights struggles or religious struggles—during the 1920s, the 1930s, even into the 1960s—that this country faced. Now that many of those rights are more and more assured, we forget how long a road it was to get where we are.

What we're hearing a lot today may not be isolationism, but it's at least an attitude that says we'll worry about our situation here in the United States and let other countries worry about themselves. One effect of this is a curious syndrome we get ourselves into. If certain countries say they're for us and against the Communists—whether Chile or South Africa or countries closer to home, like Guatemala— we're less curious about what they're really doing with their political prisoners and less upset about it when we do find out.

Breslin: That ties in with another way the Council Fathers describe political development: they use the criterion of political life becoming more or less human. Is there a perceptible trend toward the political life of people in this country, but also of people around the world, becoming more human?

Leahy: I think we sometimes have a hard time looking at the human aspect of it. We tend to see things too much in the abstract, too much in terms of numbers, and less in human terms. Maybe it's because of the busy world we live in—I'm not sure of the reason—but we have seen less concern in the last few years with basic human rights, whether it's civil or religious rights or problems of hunger. There have, of course, been notable exceptions to this, for example, when people's consciences get pricked by something like the photographs of Ethiopia—all those crises we talk about, and read about and hear about through the media. Suddenly the issues become real, and people say, "We'd better do something about this."

Similarly, if a house burns down in a neighborhood, people respond to that, so it's clear that the basic feelings are there. I firmly believe there is an essential goodness present in people today, however you define it. What I think we lack, once again, is a sense of history to give us a better idea of what we need to do to make sure that human rights, civil rights, and the right to religious liberty will best be preserved in the long run. One problem we have in the case of religious liberty today has to do with the real meaning of the separation between church and state. It's an area where I think we face one of our greatest dangers today, and I think that the Catholic Church has probably stumbled as badly as anybody in the past few years in that area.

Breslin: You wrote about that in an op-ed piece that appeared in the *Washington Post* in March of 1984. In that article, entitled "The Church We Love Is Being Used," you argued that a de facto political alliance had been formed between the Catholic Church in the United States and extremely conservative Christian evangelical groups like the Moral Majority. The link was opposition to abortion, a genuine point of agreement for the two groups, but the danger you saw was that the Catholic Church's position on other right-to-life issues like human rights, arms control, economic assistance for the poor here and abroad, would be compromised by the alliance, since many on the "Christian Right" were vigorously attacking supporters of those issues. As an example of the danger this poses in electoral politics, you quoted Father Theodore Hesburgh: "We have witnessed the fact that political candidates who agree 95% with Catholic principles of social justice in most issues of public policy have been defeated by their opposition on this one issue and have been replaced by candidates who, agreeing superficially on the issue of abortion, disagree with us on almost every other issue bearing on justice and equality." Do you still feel pretty much the same way a year later?

Leahy: I do. I think in the presidential election last year, the Catholic church made a very bad mistake. Some of the church leaders got themselves very much involved in the election, and they made it even worse when, like Archbishop John O'Connor in New York, they stood up and claimed that they were not really involved at all, though they made a point of saying all the nice things they could imagine about Ronald Reagan and a number of damaging things about the Democratic candidates, in particular, Geraldine Ferraro. This is not just a partisan issue from my perspective. I suppose I felt it more strongly because the Democratic party was suffering from this kind of church involvement, but I'd feel exactly the same way if the positions were reversed. I just think that church leaders should stay completely out of this kind of politics.

Breslin: This brings us directly to one of the questions that comes up in the last section of the Council's treatment of politics. They're talking about the relationship between church and state, and they make the point that there is an inevitable tension between affirming the autonomous character of each in its own sphere, while insisting on the church's responsibility to speak out on moral issues, even when these moral issues have political implications. How do you see this tension being worked out, for instance, in the pastoral letter the United States bishops wrote on the nuclear arms race, or in the letter they're currently writing on the American economy? Both areas clearly involve serious moral issues, but they also touch directly on political issues, and very sensitive political issues at that.

Leahy: I have no problem with the bishops speaking out on those topics or on abortion, or on any other moral issue. There are, however, certain questions within these general areas that I don't think it appropriate for them to speak on, because they fall totally within the political realm. For example, I wouldn't want them to speak out on specific tax cuts unless they were arguing that some specific tax proposal was going to so egregiously shift the economic balance in this country as to create the likelihood of class struggle, or something along that line. But I have no problem at all, whether I agree or disagree with the bishops, when they speak out on an issue that is clearly morally significant. Indeed, they should speak out; they have a duty to do so. What bothers me is when they step over the political line and urge almost as a duty that people should vote in a certain way. I think some of them did that in the last election, and very clearly, too.

Breslin: They would deny that, of course.

Leahy: Yes, but they can't deny it with a straight face. Every time the White House wanted to have a photo opportunity, they'd round up a highly placed cleric in colorful and flowing robes to say wonderful things about the President. They even got a prominent Catholic cleric to stand on the platform and praise Mr. Reagan's humanitarian character as he was dedicating a housing project that he had tried to cancel. The problem with all of this is that church leaders lose their credibility with a lot of people whose support they need if they get too deeply involved or appear to be too deeply involved in partisan politics.

Breslin: In the draft of their letter on the economy, the bishops make the statement that the disparity of income in the United States is now so great that it is morally unacceptable. Where does that fall on the spectrum of what is justifiable moral comment, and what constitutes getting overly involved in the political process?

Leahy: I think that's a good example of what I was talking about before. I have no problem with their making a statement like that, provided they don't go on to say that to rectify the situation Congress must pass a redistribution of wealth law. When they do that, when they get that specific, I think they've stepped over the line by telling the citizens' representatives how they should vote. But the issue itself, the disparity of wealth in this country, is certainly something that they should be talking about because it's an important moral question. Separation of church and state in America does not mean that our religious leaders should become moral neutrals, or that pastoral letters from Catholic bishops should only be about eating meat on Fridays, or revising the list of holydays of obligation. Such a retreat into the sacristy would cost the church dearly in its influence on American life. I think bishops should be moral leaders, and there will be times when the bishops will be out ahead of the people in the pews, and other times when they'll be somewhere behind them. That's no problem so long as they are not with the people in the voting booth.

Breslin: To move now to a more general theme, the Council Fathers talk frequently in the early part of this section about what they call "the common good." They don't spend much time defining it in the document itself, partly because the phrase has a long history in Catholic social and political teaching, and indeed in our own political life. They use it as a touchstone for judging individual policies, but also for deciding about the legitimacy of a government itself—is it in fact promoting the common good? Do you think that this global concept of the common good motivates actual decisions that get made in government? I guess I'm thinking in particular about the common good versus special interests: how does the balance work out?

Leahy: Every so often, the common good actually does seem to take precedence, for example, in the decision about public lands in Alaska, and other large questions like that; but too often, it seems to me, Congress rises above principle and votes for special interests. There are a number of reasons for that. Special interests have the capacity to do targeted mailings and fundraising, and at times they seem to have an unholy grasp on the legislative process. This is an area where I think the church could play a positive role, precisely because it can speak for the common good without wading into politics and church leaders could speak out with a powerful voice that could drown out some of the special interests. Unfortunately, what seems to have happened is that there is at present a kind of war going on within the church about its own special interests. And the result is that church leaders appear to have decided not to speak about the broader issues of the common good within such and such a district, whether arms control or hunger, because it may embarrass a candidate who supports the church on something like tuition tax credits. I've seen a lot of members of Congress who get themselves off the hook on the broader issues of the common good that the church has always supported by saying, for instance, "Well, I'll support you on tuition tax credits." In that situation, I think the church—and indeed, the community at large—end up being the ultimate losers. I'm not at all suggesting that the church lives in some kind of ivory tower and that it can afford to make light of political realities, but if the church gives the impression of being just another lobbyist with its own special interests, then it loses credibility on the larger issues, and perhaps surrenders too much in the interest of short-term gains.

Breslin: Let me follow up on that for a moment. I was just talking with someone last night, and she was discussing the Catholic church's lobbying efforts on the Hill. How would you rate the lobbying efforts of the U.S. Catholic Conference, both in terms of content, the issues they're pursuing, but also in terms of how they go about lobbying?

Leahy: Maybe the Catholic members are treated differently from non-Catholic members, but in my experience the church's lobbying efforts on specific bills are poorly done. The attitude seems to be "Here are your marching orders." And the result is that they've pushed a lot of Catholic members of the House and Senate into a position of having to prove their independence or toward wondering whether they can be in government or in Congress at all and still be Catholics. When this approach is taken, there's no respect for the separation of church and state, and it renders much of the work done ineffective, something that shouldn't have and needn't have happened.

Breslin: Again, more specifically, what about the lobbying done by the Catholic bishops on policy in Central America?

Leahy: That's been somewhat better. But even there, it owes a lot to certain individuals who have worked very hard with the Congress on it. That's a good example of what can be done without in any way interfering with the separation of church and state. For example, if church people were to say to members of Congress of a particular state, "We're having this conference on human rights, or abortion, or whatever, and we'd like you to come and express your views and hear some of our views," that could be a very effective means of lobbying.

A lot of this comes back to a constant concern of mine about one of our biggest failings as a nation; we lack a sense of history, and it leads to a great shallowness. Now, the churches have been through an amazing history over the past 200 years. The Catholic church was dominant in some areas, like Maryland for a while, and suffered repression in lots of other areas. The principle of the separation of church and state represented for the church a guarantee of independence, and it had to be fought for. If our church leaders now begin to blur that distinction, they stand to lose far more than they'll gain. What they should be doing is stressing what has been learned from the struggle over separation, but they should also be stressing those basic human rights that concern us as church, and that the Catholic church in this country has always espoused: concern for the poor, for housing, for refugees, in short, for the needs of all those people left out by our society. Identifying with these people is really identifying with our own past, and I think the church could provide the nation with a useful service, reminding people where we come from and how far we still have to go in order to create a just society.

Breslin: You're speaking here, I think, about a teaching role that church leaders can fill in American society. In speaking about the common good, the Council Fathers speak also about a teaching role for public officials. Do you find that there's much interest among the general public in having their attention directed to the common good, or are they more concerned about the specific things that interest them?

Leahy: I probably am in a unique situation, coming from a state like Vermont. We're small enough that people tend to know each other and respect the individual as an individual. When I came to the Senate eleven years ago, I began to see my role as that of a teacher and a leader. That meant going back home and discussing difficult issues. The political experts told me, "You really don't want to stir those up." But I found that, as a result of regularly talking with my constituents about serious matters, I ended up with a very issue-oriented constituency in Vermont. We'd have public town meetings all over the state, and we'd wind up with half the audience in agreement and the other half in disagreement, but the discussion would be great, and at the end everyone would agree on one point, that it was great fun thrashing out ideas like that.

That's one way in which elected officials can be teachers and leaders—by stimulating public debate, and taking a definite position on the issues. Now it's true that we have members of both parties in Congress who simply can't be called leaders. They ask for the latest opinion poll results at 10:00 in the morning so that at 11:00 they can announce its findings as their long-held beliefs. Similarly, we have people in the Senate who think they own a seat here. Well, that simply isn't true. All of us in the Congress, but especially in the Senate, have a responsibility to be the consciences of the nation, and I'm afraid we've moved away from that. We've got great privileges here: there's no other parliamentary body in the world where you have more freedom to discuss and debate, but we don't use it enough anymore.

Breslin: Do you think that the New England tradition of town meetings has helped you in Vermont to get the issues discussed? Are people more ready in Vermont for that kind of thing than they might be in other parts of the nation?

Leahy: Very much so. People come and actually debate things. I was reminded of it one night watching the Bob Newhart show. They had one episode about a town meeting in which the moderator was reading the minutes of the last one. It went something like this:

> "Well, we voted to pave the road past the Widow Smith's house."
> "Ayup."
> "And we voted to put a new roof on the schoolhouse."
> "Ayup."
> "And we voted to fix the bridge down by Farmer Jones's house."
> "Ayup."
> "We voted to have the Israelis get out of Sinai."
> "Loud debate on that one."

When I saw that, I roared out loud. He really had caught a Vermont town meeting.

That's one way of expressing concern about issues beyond the merely parochial. And that's one of the things I bring with me out of my own background to the Senate. Similarly, Catholic members bring other things with them as well, their own cultural background and their moral upbringing, and what they do in Congress should reflect that. They have to be true to their own moral sense of what's right and wrong, just as any member does. So on a very fundamental level, what the church should expect is that Catholic members should bring with them the moral sense that has been instilled in them over the years and is still being instilled by the teachings of the church. Counting on that is far more important than attempting to direct members how to vote on this bill or that bill.

Breslin: Could you expand on that a bit? I'd be interested in knowing how your own sense of moral values is connected with your understanding of what it means to be a Christian. Put another way, is there a clear connection in your mind between your Christian vocation and your public vocation as a senator?

Leahy: Elected officials are not here just to represent themselves, and to represent an entire state requires a sense of vocation. Growing up as a Catholic during the time I did meant you inevitably thought about vocation, and boys would think about the priesthood at some point. But I think I always knew since I was a little boy that I wanted to be in government. In fact, I remember telling my grandfather when I was five years old that's what I was going to do. Having that kind of sense of vocation doesn't mean that everything falls neatly into place, or that you always live up to it, but it reminds you that you have a responsibility to a lot of people, especially a lot of people who don't have the same voice in government that you do. There are 225 million Americans, and I'm afraid there are some senators that know and care a lot more about their own future than they do about the futures of those 225 million constituents. To be honest, we all do that at some point or another; it's simply basic human nature, but the best public officials are those who get the ratio right, who in general worry more about the 225 million than about the one. That's the real tie between my vocation as a Christian and my vocation as a senator.

Breslin: In a later section of their political discussion, the Council Fathers discuss the powers of government, and in particular the relationship between the smaller units of government and the larger ones. They're carrying on a kind of balancing act here, with totalitarian governments clearly on their mind when they argue that government should not have complete control of society. What I was wondering, in terms of the American political scene, is what your own feelings are about the current relationship between the federal government and the state and local governments. Reducing the size and influence of the federal government has been a rallying cry with the present administration for the last four-and-a-half years. What do you think about the idea behind it and the way it's been done?

Leahy: Frankly, I find the administration's policies in this area somewhat contradictory. On the one hand, they say they want to get the federal government out of the local scene, but they also want to ensure that.we'll have state-sponsored school prayer which, to my mind, is intruding government into an area where it has no place being; prayer should be the responsibility of parents and of whatever church a person belongs to. In addition, they want to intrude government regulation into a number of medical areas of the most intimate kind. On the other hand, the administration seems to want to keep government out of those areas where it has historically been most effective, civil rights, for example; and their argument is that, if left alone in this kind of social area, people will display their basic goodness. Unfortunately, this hasn't been the case in an area like civil rights. History has taught us that these improvements have to be encouraged and directed by government, or else minorities will continue to suffer discrimination. Furthermore, there are a number of other issues, especially ones concerning social welfare, where you need to have the federal government involved simply because we have fifty states with widely varying populations, and widely varying levels of affluence. It's somewhat disingenuous of the President of the United States to say, as President Reagan did during his campaign, that people can vote with their feet: if they don't like a state they can leave. That's a good piece of rhetoric, but it's also rather cruel in the burden it imposes on individuals who have needs; moreover, it tends to pit one state against another and undermines the very federal system that Mr. Reagan claims to support.

I believe in state and local governments as the building blocks of our democracy. I think in general that the federal government should allow states to determine their own programs and make choices for the people, and the more the federal government does this, the better. But there are certain overriding concerns where the federal influence is needed and can be applied in harmony with smaller units of government.

Breslin: What, in the economic area, do you think constitutes a good balance between civil and local control?

Leahy: Taxation is probably the most important contribution the federal government can make to economic justice. What we need is a fair and rational tax program, but what we have is one so riddled with individual special interests, even good special interests, that it's not a fair program. This is one place where the federal government can help, indeed where only the federal government can help. Moreover, if we at the federal level can come up with a just and equitable tax plan, then we can have influence as well on the taxation policies of state and local governments in a way that could lead to a generally more equitable system across the country.

Breslin: I have one other question about the common good, and this moves it beyond the domestic scene to the international scene. The Council Fathers claim that the doctrine of the common good also empowers people to resist governments that violate the common good, even to replace them. What I'm interested in is your reflection on U.S. involvement in situations where people are attempting to gain their rights by resisting oligarchies of various kinds. Here, it's not so much a question of special interests versus the common good, but of our perceived national security or national interests versus what people in other countries see as their common good. How do you find that those two values get balanced out in practice?

Leahy: Well, that's a difficult one, because our federal government has a definite responsibility to protect our security, that is, once again, the security of 225 million people. Does that mean we are allowed to do *anything*? I think not. For example, after World War II, we were the only nuclear power in the world, and so in planning our long-range security we could have said,"Let's destroy nation X which poses a potential threat to us." In a purely strategic sense, that kind of plan might have been considered. But it would have been entirely immoral, going beyond the bounds of what was acceptable to protect our national security.

That's why nuclear weapons and nuclear war have become such a tangled moral issue. On the one hand, there is a responsibility to protect the nation. I for one do not think we are required or justified as a government in embarking on a course of unilateral disarmament, for example. But, at the same time, we have a great moral responsibility to push very hard for real arms control, arms control aimed at one thing: to reduce the possibility of a nuclear war, because in such a war not only would we be destroyed as a nation, but so would the Soviets, and hundreds of millions of other people as well. It's a grave moral question, the gravest of all the moral questions that face us, and the moral imperative that follows from it is that, if we're going to have nuclear weapons as a primary part of our national defense, then we must also find ways to eliminate the possibility of their ever being used.

Breslin: I guess I was thinking more particularly about Third World situations in that question. How do you see the tension between a people's right to pursue their common good and our own national security interests working itself out in the underdeveloped world?

Leahy: In talking about our relation to Third World nations, I think it's important for us to look at what our real situation is in this country. We have slightly over 5 percent of the world's population, but we consume between 30 and 40 percent of the world's resources. That imposes on us, I think, a moral imperative to help the Third World nations to share in the world's bounty. On that level, I don't think there can be much debate about the moral issue. We simply can't sit here on this planet as human beings and say we have a right to all these resources, as if our good fortune didn't impose on us a moral obligation to help others. The notion that we've been specially blessed as God's favored children always struck me as specious at best, if it means that we can be selfish with what we have. I for one have never been able to understand how we can sit here with enormous surpluses of food, spending millions and millions of dollars storing it in warehouses, while the world is filled with starving people. I've also always opposed food embargoes to the Soviet Union, despite the fact that I get terribly angry at many of the things the Soviet Union does—Afghanistan, for example. But I am completely opposed to using food as a weapon. This is a moral issue for me, and I don't think the wealthiest, most powerful and best-fed nation in the world can morally justify using food as a weapon, with the possible exception of a country we're actually at war with.

Similarly, if through the use of our power and influence we can improve the human rights situation in a country, then I think we have to look at the moral implications of that. Can we morally say that we have no right or no interest in doing that? That doesn't mean there won't be some rocky sliding for a while, nor does it mean we'll always be right; sometimes our involvement ends up with disastrous results, for example in Iran. On the other hand, we've also had some very good results, as in the case of Argentina.

In addition, I think our power and influence also impose on us an absolute duty to set an example for the rest of the world. When we violate human rights, it gives a lot of other countries around the world an excuse to justify their own violations. We have to show the world that we protect minorities, we protect human rights and freedom of speech, indeed we protect all the rights that are guaranteed in our Constitution, so that we can then say to others with a clear conscience that we expect the same level of moral behavior by them.

Breslin: The final part of the discussion of politics in *Gaudium et Spes* deals with political participation. The Council Fathers talk about both the right and the duty of people to participate, to vote. One of the perennial political questions in this country is about voter apathy. Do you see that changing, getting better or worse, and what kind of practical effects does this apathy have? For example, have you seen any really negative things that have happened because of voter apathy?

Leahy: Actually, I'm rather proud of our voter turnout in Vermont; it's about 70 percent, which is very good indeed, one of the best in the country. Of course, I'd like to see it 100 percent. Nationally, however, voter turnout is about 50 percent, and that's disgraceful. The reason for it, I think, goes back once again to our lack of a sense of history, our failure to teach the people that they are the government; it's not just the people who are in office, but all of us together who form the government. Somehow we have to get across to people that their vote really does make a difference, that all of us have a voice in the way things are done and not just the special interests.

Finally, we've got to attract better people to office in general. As I said before, it has to be seen as a real vocation, a real calling, in order to attract better people. And if we can do that, then we should be able to get more people interested in voting. I don't see any easy solution to this, but it has to begin with education and with lessening the influence of special interests in the election process. To do that we have to get away from these terribly expensive elections with their emphasis on media and image, and get back to real debates. Ironically, television is the thing that's making elections so expensive, but it's also a possible medium for having real debates, especially with all of the channels now available. We've got to start at the local level and get people interested in local elections, like the local school board, and then we can begin to make people realize that they do have a stake in all elections and that their vote really does make a difference. Another benefit, of course, in reducing the expense of elections would be to get people who do not have great personal financial resources to get involved in the elective process without committing themselves to special interests.

Breslin: What about making voting mandatory, which is the case in a number of countries? Would that work?

Leahy: I don't know. I worry about the need in a democracy to protect not only the freedom to vote but the freedom not to vote if you don't want to. There's that cynical remark, "I've never voted; it just encourages 'em," but I'd hate to think that we've reached that point in this country.

Breslin: You touched on the question of education, and that brings up another issue of the Council Fathers, namely, the responsibility of government to educate the people so that they can assume their rightful place as citizens. Do we do that kind of education well in this country, do you think?

Leahy: I just had a civics teacher down here with a group of kids, and they said they had one question they wanted to ask. They'd been able to find out that Vermont has two senators, but they wanted to know how many senators does a state like New York have. Well, that kind of basic ignorance about our government worries me a great deal. We just don't spend enough time teaching history and civics in our school.

Breslin: I wonder myself sometimes what the feeling behind such apathy is, and it sometimes seems to me that it can arise from contradictory impulses. One is that nothing I do is really going to make any difference, and no one's really going to help me, so why should I get involved. On the other hand, a lot of it comes, I think, from a sense people have of feeling basically content; things are going okay, and therefore why bother?

Leahy: Yes, I've heard that argument myself. We've all got worries of our own, mortgage payments to make, kids whose teeth need fixing. How can I find time to worry about the International Monetary Fund or Trident submarines when I'm trying to scrape together enough money to pay for immediate things like that? But that's again where education and a sense of history come in. If a democracy like ours is going to work, citizens have to become involved in the process and concerned about the issues. And I do think that if people are treated maturely and presented with the issues in an understandable way, they will become concerned.

Breslin: Along the same lines, I wonder, too, if we're not the victims of our own success in another sense. When you have a country like Italy or a number of Latin American countries where there's a great variety of political parties, each of which has its own passionate supporters, there is more excitement about political life. Our two-party system has provided us with a great deal of stability, but it also makes politics somewhat less interesting.

Leahy: It does make it less interesting, but it's also true that in our system the individual counts for more than party affiliation. Now, I can argue this one both ways, whether our system is better or not. But I think in the end—and this may be my American bias—I prefer the emphasis on the individual, and on the individual candidate. Then your decision as a voter is not simply an ideological one, but it has to do with the quality of the person, the quality of his or her mind and character. This, of course, puts a very large burden on the person who wants to get into public life, because the whole person becomes involved in political decisions, not just following the party line, but considering the moral implications of a particular policy, the way it affects the lives not only of Americans, but of people around the world. In our system, you're electing not just a rubber stamp for party policies, but an individual whose intellectual capacities and moral character will count for more than any ideology in the decisions that are made. I think that at its most profound level, that's the kind of political animal the Council Fathers were talking about and hoping for in their deliberations—an integrated human person with a heart as well as a mind and a finely developed set of moral instincts as well as a party platform.

PART IV

Socioeconomic Life

The Church and the Economy in
the Modern World

"Gaudium et Spes" and the Development of
Catholic Social-Economic Teaching

DANIEL RUSH FINN

The Church and the Economy in the Modern World

Very few church documents are widely read and broadly influential. Even fewer are celebrated on an anniversary of their publication. The *Pastoral Constitution on the Church in the Modern World, Gaudium et Spes,* is one of a handful of that rank in this century. Its significance lies in its creativity within continuity, in its forging of new approaches to problems while remaining largely faithful to the prior tradition.

It has its limitations, of course, as must this reconsideration of its treatment of socioeconomic life. Its language is unabashedly sexist, particularly in the authorized English translation. Quoting even otherwise inspiring texts is today like hearing good music on a piano that needs tuning; listening requires greater than normal effort. And our consideration of this document in this volume focuses attention more narrowly on our own faith tradition than can ever be sufficient for a full consideration of the significance of Christian faith for the economic realm. Still, the effort is well worth it.

This essay begins with an overview of the document's vision of socioeconomic life in the context of Catholic social teaching prior to Vatican II. It includes a brief review of some of the developments in the world and the church since that time which are relevant to a moral assessment of economic activity. It considers the influence of economic science on public moral discourse, and concludes with four critical questions that remain on the agenda for Catholic social thought twenty years after the document was released in its final form.

"GAUDIUM ET SPES" ON SOCIOECONOMIC LIFE

Gaudium et Spes begins its treatment of socioeconomic life with the two fundamental principles elaborated in its earlier, introductory section: the dignity of the human person and, flowing from this, the welfare of society (no. 63). In basing its arguments in this way, the

Council continued the line of ethical development that has led to the situation today where these two are the most frequently cited elements in the orthodox Catholic formulation of social teaching on economic matters.

The document's chapter on socioeconomic life is divided into two sections. The first section addresses an issue of worldwide importance in the decade of the 1960s: economic development. The second section outlines certain principles, including several "principles of justice and equity" (no. 63), which ought to govern socioeconomic life as a whole.

In the first section, economic development, technical progress, and a better standard of living for the world's people are affirmed as positive goals—provided that these occur in the service of humanity (no. 64). The obligation of all to reduce the "immense economic inequalities" (no. 66) in the world is stressed. This, of course, was the standard Catholic position at the time of the Council.

Within the discussion of development, the document raises a broader, self-reflective question about the role of the church in economic policy by affirming the relative autonomy of economic activity: it is to be carried out "according to its own methods and laws" (no. 64). But even the more thorough treatment of "the autonomy of earthly affairs" in the earlier portion of the constitution leaves several crucial questions unanswered, no doubt indicating the Council's own lack of consensus.

The earlier treatment begins by posing the problem in a general and very helpful way: "Now, many of our contemporaries seem to fear that a closer bond between human activity and religion will work against the independence of men, of societies, or of the sciences" (no. 36). The document's answer, however, is not nearly as valuable as its formulation of the question. As we will see later in this essay, this is one of the key problems stressed by contemporary Catholic critics of church teaching on the economy.

Gaudium et Spes identifies one meaning of "the autonomy of earthly affairs" as totally appropriate: "that created things and societies themselves enjoy their own laws and values which must be gradually deciphered, put to use, and regulated by men" (no. 36). It also identifies an erroneous meaning: "that created things do not depend on God, and that man can use them without any reference to their Creator" (no. 36). However, the distinction between these two meanings begs the basic question: to what extent should ecclesiastical authorities refrain from comment on the practicalities of "earthly affairs" (or in particular, economic affairs) *because of* the rightful independence of this realm of human activity? In turn, this question is most often interpreted to mean:

at what level of generality are Christian principles authoritative (at least for Christians) and at what level are applications from general principles (even applications made by popes and bishops) simply one interpretation among many, where nonreligious criteria (such as efficiency) are the only appropriate means for the adjudication of disputes?[1]

The difficulties exhibited in sorting out the issues concerning the autonomy of "earthly affairs" have roots in the question of the church's mission and, of course, also in its theological vision more generally. *Gaudium et Spes* represents a clear development in the church's understanding of its mission in socioeconomic affairs:

> Christ, to be sure, gave His Church no proper mission in the political, economic, or social order. The purpose which He set before her is a religious one. But out of this religious mission itself come a function, a light, and an energy which can serve to structure and consolidate the human community according to divine law (no. 42).

The meaning of "religious" implicit in this statement is considerably narrower than theological discourse today would find appropriate. However, the statement is an important development. The inclusion of the words of Pius XII, in a footnote, may indicate that the Council bishops were themselves aware of this. As Pius had put it, "Its divine Founder, Jesus Christ, has not given [the Church] any mandate or fixed any end of the cultural order. The goal which Christ assigns to it is strictly religious ... The Church can never lose sight of the strictly religious, supernatural goal."[2] Unlike Pius' formulation, the conciliar phrasing leaves room for "a mandate" in the cultural order, just as there would later be room for a real "mission" of the church in the political, economic, and social order.[3]

Whatever other ambiguities exist in the relation of religion and the economy, the document is clear that economic development "must be kept under the control of mankind" (no. 65). Procedurally, this means that "at every level the largest possible number of people [should] have an active share in directing that development" (no. 65). In addition, the document proposes two fundamental cautions. Economic growth "must not be allowed merely to follow a kind of automatic course resulting from the economic activity of individuals." Similarly, however, " ... it [must not] be entrusted solely to the authority of government" (no. 65).

This implicit comparison of the classic solutions of capitalism and communism is as close as this document comes to engaging directly the arguments about these two rival economic systems. It indicates the Council Fathers' awareness of these debates within and among nations concerning economic development but it likewise demonstrates their unwillingness to enter the ideological fray directly. As we will see later, this ambiguity in church documents about engaging and clarifying ongoing theoretical arguments between capitalism and socialism remains a significant element in ecclesiastical deliberations on economics today.

Section Two, on the principles relevant to economic life, begins with the notion of human dignity. In this, *Gaudium et Spes* represents a key step in the development of Catholic social teaching. The predominance of the logic of natural law ethics in *Rerum Novarum* (1891) and *Quadragesimo Anno* (1931), with only passing reference to the dignity of individuals, was already giving way in the letters of John XXIII.

In *Mater et Magistra* (1961), John observes that the principles of social teaching derived from the social nature of human beings do, in fact, affirm and defend the dignity of the human person.[4] Two years later, in *Pacem in Terris* (1963), he relies more substantially on the concept of the dignity of the person. This dignity still arises, in accord with the natural law tradition, from the fact that the human person is "endowed with intelligence and free will."[5] But once established, the principle operates with greater independence, for example: "From the dignity of the human person there also arises the right to carry on economic activities according to the degree of responsibility of which one is capable."[6]

Gaudium et Spes carries this development even further, as is indicated by the title of the first chapter in Part One: "The Dignity of the Human Person." Employing in the section on socioeconomic life a construal of the issue that John Paul II would later elaborate in detail in *Laborem Exercens* (1981), the document moves from the dignity of the person to the status of human labor in the economy. Thus, it identifies human labor as "superior to the other elements of economic life. For the latter have only the nature of tools" (no. 67). Through work, the person becomes "a partner in the work of bringing God's creation to perfection" and by offering that work to God, the laborer "becomes associated with the redemptive work itself of Jesus Christ" (no. 67). Because the stakes are so high, the document sets a high standard: "The entire process of productive work, therefore, must be adapted to the needs of the person and to the requirements of his life, above all his domestic life" (no. 67).

The document reaffirms existing teaching on the rights of property ownership within the natural law tradition. Private property is a critical expression of human freedom, and it has "a social quality" due to the communal purpose of the possession as a created thing (no. 71). Public ownership of property, however, is also defended. No distinction between *types* of property is made. Presumably, the Council authors intend to continue the twentieth-century papal approbation of appropriate forms of both private and public ownership of productive assets such as tools, machines, and factories.[7]

Of all the presumptions of Catholic social teaching that irk its North American critics, probably the most fundamental is the conviction that even impersonal institutional relationships should occur in accord with moral principles. Phrases like "the distribution of goods should be directed toward . . . " (no. 70) are fundamentally inimical to a view that the distribution of goods (or income or wealth) takes place through an impersonal market where no individual or group *decides* how it is to happen. Church teaching has always presumed that all human activity should occur in accord with moral norms. In the extension of moral theology to include a vigorous social ethic for institutional life in the modern world, the application of this persevering conviction to economic policy has led more "conservative" economic critics to assert that stressing moral standards too strictly in the economic realm will endanger the economic productivity that the moralists take for granted.

We will return to this theme later, but should also note the document's continuation of the trend to greater stress on human rights and more robust use of the Scriptures in ethical argumentation.[8] While generally referring to the New Testament rather than quoting it, *Gaudium et Spes* is clear that "by virtue of the gospel committed to her, the Church proclaims the rights of man" (no. 41). With a very important exception, the list of human rights is fairly standard within prior social teaching, including the right to adequate food, clothing, and shelter and to employment (no. 26), to safe working conditions and to labor unions (no. 68), and to far broader "participation" of workers in the running of the enterprise (nos. 68 and 65). As always, the Catholic tradition of substantive rights extends far beyond the boundaries of what are often called "political" or "formal" rights of the British liberal tradition, where "rights" were generally limited to rights to noninterference only and did not include rights to positive assistance.

Conspicuously absent from the list of human rights in *Gaudium et Spes* is any reference to a "just wage." Leo XIII had argued that a just wage should be sufficient "to support the wage-earner in reasonable and frugal comfort." He went on to argue that "If through necessity or fear of a worse evil, the workman accepts harder conditions because an employer or contractor will give him no better, he is the victim of force and injustice."[9] These are strong words. Pius XI insisted that the wage be sufficient "to meet adequately ordinary domestic needs" and to allow the [male] worker's spouse to remain at home.[10] Fewer than five years before *Gaudium et Spes*, John XXIII had insisted that justice requires a wage "sufficient to lead a life worthy of man and to fulfill family responsibilities properly."[11] But this central document of Vatican II does not insist on or even discuss a just wage.

In order to understand the reasons behind this shift, one that has been upheld in subsequent church documents, we need to understand the degree of dissonance between the idea of a just wage and the market system that characterizes the economies of most of the nations of the globe. This must be postponed until we later deal with the contributions of contemporary economic science. We might for now observe the political infeasibility of any specific assessment of a minimum wage as a proxy for an appropriate just wage. In the United States, for example, the federal government's measure of the poverty level might be taken as a rough dollar measure of the sort of standard the above definitions of the just wage indicate. In 1985, an urban family of four needed an income slightly above $10,000 to be above the poverty line. Since some families would have only one wage-earner, the minimum wage necessary to guarantee this standard would be in excess of five dollars an hour. In an era when the minimum wage of $3.60 an hour is under attack, it is no wonder that the second draft of the United States bishops' pastoral letter on the economy advocates means other than the minimum wage to meet the requisites of justice.[12]

SOME IMPORTANT DEVELOPMENTS SINCE VATICAN II

Any view of *Gaudium et Spes* from a perspective twenty years later must take into consideration the changes in the world and the church over that time. Such an effort would be daunting even within the scope of a whole volume dedicated only to that purpose; it is impossible to accomplish in a single essay. Still, there are a number of developments that, because of their importance for the world and/or for the church, must be at least touched upon in our retrospect of the Pastoral Constitution's view of socioeconomic life.

Within the realm of economic activity, there has been continued economic expansion, severe gyrations in long-held attitudes of economic optimism, a growth in the number of people in poverty in the world and, at the same time, a sharp rise in the assertiveness of nations in what has come to be known as the Third World.

Technological change has not only continued but accelerated from the already rapid pace prior to Vatican II. Immense technical improvements have occurred in transportation, communication, automation, and the management of information. The productive capacity, the wealth-creating ability, of the nations has continued to rise: in manufacturing, in agriculture, in the service industries. The global economic interdependence addressed by *Gaudium et Spes* has deepened and become more intense.

In this same twenty-five years, however, there have also arisen confidence-shaking events that have vividly reminded humanity, particularly in the industrialized nations, of our finitude. In 1973, a little-known organization founded a decade earlier shocked the world by imposing an oil embargo on certain nations friendly to Israel and by raising the price of petroleum dramatically. Taking the United States as an example, the Organization of Petroleum Exporting Countries (OPEC) caused economic insecurities about the nation's control of its own economic destiny that had not been felt since the great depression.

About the same time, the first crude empirical studies on the "limits to growth" were published by the Club of Rome.[13] The debates which followed[14] illustrated some of the same fundamental differences to appear later in the explicit debate over economic structures within Christian social ethics. One group objected to the predictable depletion of resources and creation of pollution that would be caused by the unfettered market, while another pointed out past problems that the market had resolved (without *too* much suffering) and expressed confidence that the price mechanism would allocate costs and benefits in an orderly and relatively equitable manner. Further development of the theme of limits has led to analysis of the *social* limits to growth, recognizing that part of what many people want is based on their position relative to other people.[15]

Meanwhile, those countries known at the time of Vatican II as "the developing nations" came to be called "the Third World," distinct from the industrialized Western nations of the First World and the mostly Eastern European, communist nations of the Second World. This very terminology signified a significant shift in consciousness. Modern medicine and basic sanitary conditions greatly lengthened the expected life-span of people in the Third World, and along with historically high birth rates, this caused high rates of population growth. New nations had been forming from earlier colonial possessions since World War II and the United Nations underwent an historic shift in its "center of gravity" in the General Assembly: from the developed nations of the North to the less developed nations of the South. This new majority in the world began demanding a new world economic order, and the nations of the First World found themselves "stuck" between feeling insulted by the Third World's lack of gratitude for loans and largesse and feeling threatened at the potential damage to worldwide credit systems should Third World nations begin defaulting on their immense debts.

Additionally, by the 1980s, the United States in particular has been feeling increased pressure from nations once clearly weaker economically. Unemployment rates have grown higher in each decade since World War II. Even U.S.-based multinationals have been closing facilities at home and moving operations elsewhere in pursuit of cheaper labor and lower taxes. The popular response to these strains has taken a turn toward conservatism, individualism, and chauvinism, a real challenge to the social teaching of the church. Arguments about the business climate have threatened or weakened much of the "social legislation" designed to soften the blows of the market for the less powerful in our society. United States foreign policy in the eighties has eschewed or defied the intervention of United Nations agencies and has all too often been defended by claims that our (superior) values allow us exceptions to widely held rules of international conduct (like nonintervention) which we refuse to allow to our rivals. The similarity to the logic of terrorism is unmistakable and disheartening.

But for all the significant changes in the world and the nation that have occurred since Vatican II, there have been equally basic shifts within the Roman Catholic church. Perhaps most significant has been the influence of the experience of the Third World within the church as a whole. Subsequent papal statements, particularly *Populorum Progressio*, have carried on and amplified the concerns of John XXIII and the Council bishops. The number of Third World bishops and cardinals has risen significantly. The emphasis that Vatican II put on national and regional conferences of bishops created the conditions where the deliberations of Third World bishops, for example at Medellín, Colombia (1968) and Puebla, Mexico (1979), have had an unprecedented impact on the church in the rest of the world.

Clearly, theological developments have been critical in the postconciliar church, and nowhere is this more true than in the Third World. Liberation theology has transformed the theological landscape of Latin America (and to a lesser extent, Africa and Asia) and has had strong influence on theological development in Europe and North America. The most important single work of the vast literature known as liberation theology, Gustavo Gutierrez's *A Theology of Liberation*, is founded theologically on two critical themes of Vatican II which I have already noted. On the one hand, there is the commitment to justice, to the poor, and to actively striving to transform the world, which the 1971 Synod of Bishops termed "constitutive" of, and not simply important for,[16] the preaching of the gospel. On the other hand, there was the shift to a more inductive method for theological reflection, beginning with the signs of the times and the experience of Christian faith rather than with ageless truths. Thus, Gutierrez argues that Christian theology, at least in the Third World if not everywhere, must begin in and arise from prayer, Scripture study, and conversation *with the poor and oppressed themselves.* Much more would have to be said than is possible here, but liberation theology's vision of economic and political liberation as one of the dimensions of salvation in Christian belief has become an undeniable influence in the theological discussion of socioeconomic life since Vatican II.[17]

Within the Catholic church in the United States, the rise in the number of Hispanic Catholics, the action by the institutional church in favor of the poor (for example, the Campaign for Human Development), and the drafting of statements and pastoral letters on a multitude of social, political, and economic issues, have altered the context from within which we look at *Gaudium et Spes.* The growing public discussion of the ethical dimensions of economic policy and structures has also been important. The discussion is as widespread as during the great depression and the discussants have generally more economic sophistication than in previous eras. The debate among Catholic theologians and social ethicists over socioeconomic issues has proceeded in fairly close dialogue with peers within Protestantism.

The most helpful introduction to the major alternatives for economic systems (including centralized and democratic socialisms and laissez-faire and "social market" capitalisms) is J. Philip Wogaman's *The Great Economic Debate: An Ethical Analysis.* Wogaman uses the term "ideology" to mean "a pattern of beliefs and concepts (both factual and normative) which purport to explain complex social phenomena."[18] This is especially helpful in the light of the use of that term in Catholic social teaching, where it is never applied to any truly Christian view of life and is usually used in the pejorative sense to refer to the failures of both liberalism and Marxism.[19]

Among the theologically based literature supportive of capitalism, the best (though not the best-known) single work is Robert Benne's *The Ethic of Democratic Capitalism: A Moral Reassessment.* Using John Rawls and Reinhold Niebuhr to supplement his reading of the Christian tradition, Benne argues for the realism of a largely free market. While he defends democratic capitalism, his commitment to justice leads him to support various government programs that many conservatives today would find objectionable. Such programs—for example, vouchers for schooling—tend to rely on market forces but are aimed at overcoming the effects of chance in life, which are arbitrary from a moral perspective. In Benne's words, "In summary, then, we would argue that undeserved inequalities at both extremes need earnest social attention. But, for the great middle of American society, we should let the market deal out its rewards for contribution."[20]

As the title indicates, *The Spirit of Democratic Capitalism* by Michael Novak is less systematic from an ethical point of view. Novak appeals to Christian principles, but leaves the reader unsatisfied when, in a chapter entitled "A Theology of Democratic Capitalism," his list of six theological doctrines includes "competition" but omits "justice."[21] In the midst of much that is quite helpful, he begs several basic questions, such as what are the demands of justice within Christian belief and what role do markets, governments, and voluntary associations *each* play in their implementation?

Among those works helpful in understanding the theological issues inherent in seeking an alternative economic system, there are volumes of diverse scope. Arthur F. McGovern's *Marxism: An American Christian Perspective* traces the relationship of Marxism and Christianity and argues that several of the classic Christian objections to Marxism (e.g. property, violence, class struggle, democracy) are not, when both sides are properly understood, grounds for a necessary split between the two.[22] *The American Journey*, by Joe Holland, is a retelling of American history self-consciously employing Marxian analysis; it outlines the struggles of American working people and implicitly points to less competitive social and economic structures.[23] John W. Houck and Oliver F. Williams are editors of a volume incorporating several helpful essays, *Catholic Social Teaching and the United States Economy.*[24] *Toward a Christian Economic Ethic*, by Pemberton and Finn, attempts an overview of economic ethics in the history of Christianity and an analysis of some of the major issues in contemporary economic science and policy.[25]

The debates on what *should be* the teaching of the church on socioeconomic life continue. In addition to theological and moral reflection, the insights and analyses of contemporary economics have had and will increasingly have a significant impact, and to this I now turn.

THE INFLUENCE OF ECONOMIC SCIENCE ON PUBLIC DISCOURSE

There has never been much direct and sustained contact between professional economists and members of the hierarchy. Still, there has been some and it is clearly increasing. And since the development of the discipline of economics has had a tremendous effect on how economic life is viewed by both policy makers and the public, a brief review of some of the facets of economics is critical for understanding certain changes in church teaching and for informing further developments in Catholic social ethics.

1. The Economist's View of Economic Activity.   One of the key issues in ethical reflection on socioeconomic life is the role of self-interest in economic activity and its relation to the process of wealth-creation. Adam Smith, the Scottish moral philosopher of the eighteenth century, set out to address this issue in his famous book: *An Inquiry into the Nature and Causes of the Wealth of Nations.* The two main causes for an increase in the wealth of any nation were the "division of labor"[26] and what we today call technological progress.

The division of labor is the specialization of function in the production process. Early in human history this meant that not every person or family would produce all they needed to survive, but instead some would specialize in, say, growing crops while others hunted. In the modern world, even within the production of a single item, different workers specialize in different phases of production. People tend to choose the work they're best at and, as Smith argued, they usually get better at that job than they would if they did it only infrequently. In addition, he pointed out that individual workers are more likely to be able to think of new ways to improve the production process (technological change) if their attention is concentrated on only a part of it. Smith's example of the production of pins in his day remains vivid. Few of us would *have* pins if we had to produce them ourselves.

But what is the real meaning of all this? Is this "wealth" and is it worth having?

There are two interrelated ways to view this wealth-making. From the point of view of individual workers, the more they produce in a day, the more things they can buy, either by exchanging goods (in a barter economy) or by spending the money they earn (in a wage-labor economy like ours). Economists point out that the single most important reason that workers today have a higher standard of living than their grandparents is that they produce more in a day's work—because the workers are more skilled and/or because they work with more productive tools and machines.

Just as importantly, the same process of wealth-creation must be seen from the outside, from the point of view of the others in society who will buy the product that these workers now make more productively. The nearly inevitable result of such greater productivity in a market economy is that the product is sold for a lower price.[27] Thus, every other person who buys that product enjoys a small increase in wealth, since the lower price will leave some "extra" money to be used as that consumer wishes.[28] When a myriad of such changes occurs over long periods of time in an economy, the overall effect is that the wealth of the nation and of nearly all of its citizens increases.

When Smith asked himself just what made all of this happen, he concluded that it was the self-directed action of individuals which was the motive force behind the creation of wealth, or what we now call economic development. Individuals choose to specialize and make the effort to invent new methods and tools largely because it will have good effects in their own lives. Buyers and sellers alike, Smith reminds us, act out of their own interests.

This "self-interest," for which Smith is so famous, can be a very detrimental force if it is not reined in. The debate over capitalism can be interpreted without much distortion as a debate over whether self-interest can, in fact, be allowed to flourish without significant harm to the less powerful and to the common good more broadly. In Smith's scheme, self-interest is controlled by the competing interests of other selves involved in producing or selling the same goods. Since any one merchant or manufacturer knows that consumers can go elsewhere to buy, each must work at gaining and keeping customers by means of modest prices and/or good service. When competition works as it should, according to Smith and the later defenders of the market system, the economy grows more productive and the people more wealthy.

Religiously sensitive critics of capitalism have often argued, as the National Catholic Welfare Conference did in the depths of the great depression, that generalized competition is folly: "It assumes that this 'enlightened selfishness' will automatically bring about the maximum of justice for all. It assumes that evil trees will bring forth good fruit."[29] Today's critics of capitalism argue that regardless of whatever competition existed among the bakers or brewers of Smith's time, the gigantic corporations of the late twentieth century have a degree of market power that obviates many of the benign effects of competition on which Smith depended.

This question of the degree of competition existing in contemporary capitalism is an important one, but since it is perennial in public discourse and since it is treated in far more detail elsewhere, I now turn my attention to other issues within economic science which have slowly influenced economic thinking more broadly. One of the critical changes in mind-set that occurred fairly early in modern economic thought was the disappearance of support for the idea of "just price," a development that foreshadowed the later resistance to the idea of a "just wage" which we have already noted in *Gaudium et Spes* and later Catholic social teaching.

2. The Just Price and the Just Wage. The basic view of the economist on the relation of self-interest and the creation of wealth led to a universal rejection of the idea of a "just price" for commodities which had characterized earlier thinking about economic matters. The shift is significant even though the economist's view here is not typical of all people, even in modern society. The issue for the average citizen is quite straightforward. There certainly are times when a seller can charge an unusually high price for a product because of a temporary shortage. Adam Smith noted the rise in the price of black cloth immediately after the death of a monarch.[30] Nearly everyone's sense of justice is violated when unscrupulous vendors sell food at exorbitant prices during a famine. Many will judge such prices to be "unfair" or "unjust." Economists assert that while one might make this judgment on moral grounds, there is no way to do so within economics itself.

Prior to the modern era, nearly all economic thought came from philosopher-moralists. A typical medieval position on the just price can be found in Thomas Aquinas. Buying and selling are established "for the common good of both parties," and since "whatever is established for the common advantage should not be more of a burden to one party than to another . . . ; to sell a thing for more than its worth, or to buy it for less than its worth, is in itself unjust and unlawful."[31] Thomas recognizes that the just price for a thing is not a precise amount and that "a slight addition or subtraction would not seem to destroy the equality of justice." Additionally, Thomas recognizes that a thing may "be worth less in itself" (i.e. it may cost less to produce) than it is worth to its owner (for the owner's own use) due to current circumstances. In this case, the owner may charge more than what the thing is worth "in itself." However, if a prospective buyer can derive a great advantage by acquiring the thing while the seller would be at no particular loss through being without that thing, the seller should not raise the price above "the worth of the thing in itself."[32]

Much has been written about the "just price," and as most economists have pointed out, whatever the moral interpretation of the arguments, the "just price" of a good generally meant what economists call the long-run average cost of producing it. This is the cost of producing the good after producers have had ample time to adjust their production facilities and workforce to the most efficient level, given the level of consumer demand.[33]

From the orthodox economist's point of view, the fundamental problem with the idea of a just price is the underlying difference presumed between the value of a good and its price. Economists argue that there no consistent criterion suitable to distinguish between price and value. On the one hand, if the "value" of a thing were to be associated with its cost of production, there is no single cost of production for any type of product.[34] On the other hand, the economist asks, if one kind of product becomes temporarily more highly sought after by buyers (like Smith's black cloth after the king dies), isn't it *worth* more then? And why shouldn't the merchant get a higher price? There are definite costs in carrying an excessive inventory, and shouldn't the merchant receive some payment for the risk borne by keeping a large quantity on hand in case of a royal death—since the monarch might have lived another twenty years and the cloth might turn out to be a bad investment? In sum, the "value" of a thing may be quite different to different people (and to any one person at two different times, depending on that person's resources). In place of an equivocal meaning of "value," economists have come to use "price" as the only interpersonally verifiable measure of what a thing is "worth."

This has become true not just for economists, but for most people in the industrialized countries. If you ask someone "What is that worth?", most people will answer "in dollars and cents." Few will give any equivalence in other goods (as would be true in a barter economy) and few would articulate its worth solely in terms of their own use of the thing. This same general consciousness has, predictably, had an effect on economic thinking within the Roman Catholic church. Already by the time of Leo (more than a century after Smith), the just price had passed from its earlier importance.

Although Leo XIII held several views that would later be abandoned by his successors,[35] he was part of a shift in Catholic social teaching when he treated the problem of poverty not on the basis that prices were too high, but that incomes were too low. Unjust prices were not the problem. In fact, goods produced by the new industries and technologies were cheaper than they used to be. The issue was more fundamentally employment—its availability and conditions. That is, the underlying moral value of justice for the poor was retained even though some of the analysis through which it had been traditionally preserved had shifted.

The shift in *Gaudium et Spes* away from any discussion of a "just wage" can be traced to two distinguishable factors. On the one hand, there occurred in the writing of *Gaudium et Spes* a critical shift of emphasis in theological ethics. As others have made clear,[36] this document of Vatican II marks a clear move away from sole dependence on the creation-based natural law tradition and depends heavily on themes of redemption and the demands of Scripture. As a result, the just wage, depending as it had historically on the logic of natural law, was less attractive than it had been. On the other hand, the idea of the just wage had lost the support that economic analysis had once provided.

As economists point out, of course, the wage is simply the price of an hour's labor. The idea of a just wage is a particular case of the idea of a just price more generally. Underlying any discussion of a just wage, economists argue, must be some distinction between the price of labor (the wage-rate per hour or day) and the "worth" of an hour's or a day's work. Here, too, such distinctions are hard to maintain.

As we saw earlier, papal teaching has tended to associate the just wage with what it takes to maintain a worker's family in modest comfort. This sort of thinking was far more appealing in an era such as Adam Smith's when the "labor theory of value" prevailed. According to this theory, the value of labor is equivalent to what it takes to maintain the laborer's family.[37] It is not a large step from this descriptive notion to the normative idea of Leo XIII or John XXIII that a *just* wage for labor is one that is adequate to maintain the worker's family in frugal comfort.[38]

The idea of a just wage runs counter to orthodox economic analysis today and contemporary economists show little support for and much opposition to the idea. This, I judge, is one of the central reasons for the eclipse of the notion of the just wage in recent ecclesiastical documents on socioeconomic life. Although it would be a mistake to put too much emphasis on developments in economic science as causes for shifts in Catholic social teaching, careful attention to this connection could prove quite helpful in understanding issues where further development in social teaching could and ought to occur. While there are many possible candidates for consideration, I would identify two presumptions of the economic view of things that Catholic social teaching probably will (and certainly should) come to appreciate more: the relation between scarcity and tradeoffs, and the place of consequentialist analysis in policy making.

3. Scarcity and Tradeoffs. Mainstream economists today universally understand their discipline to be the study of scarcity, or more explicitly, the study of the allocation of scarce resources to attain competing ends. The very meaning of "scarcity" for economists is rooted in the excess of our goals beyond our means. A resource is "scarce" if we would like to have more of it but have to pay (that is, give up) something to get it. Obviously very few things are *not* scarce. Clean air in the Canadian Rockies and fallen leaves in the autumn in New England may be "free," but most things are not. Thus, the economists remind us that tradeoffs characterize human choice. If we want to accomplish one thing, we'll be giving up the chance to accomplish something else, even if only because in doing so we'll be using up our own time (one of the most scarce resources for modern people).

One of the fundamental conflicts between the moral analysis of the church and the economic analysis of orthodox economists has been the church's defense of moral values without apparent assessment of the costs or tradeoffs that this entails. Whether it is Leo's defense of the just wage[39] or the defense in *Gaudium et Spes* of the right to employment (no. 26), the effects of the laws necessary to secure these goals are, we Catholics must admit, rarely outlined.

Often, this oversight is described by critics of church social teaching as "impracticality." Just how would the nation ensure that every worker in a market economy received a wage adequate to the requirements of frugal comfort for the number of people in that worker's family? If workers with large families had to be paid more than those with small, clearly the latter would be more sought out by employers, to the detriment of those very workers the "just wage" approach was intended to assist. Just how would the nation guarantee a job for each person who wanted one? While the role of the national government in job security is crucial, never alluding to the obvious costs (to taxpayers and employers) damages the credibility of church documents among those who are already doubtful that popes and bishops are aware of the complexities of the situation.

Nearly every introductory economics textbook warns its readers that the secondary effects of any economic policy are often as important as its primary intended effects. This is one of the most significant blind spots of well-meaning people who try to shape public policy to humanize the economy. It is a basic requirement of good policy that the negative effects be anticipated. There are times when a reader must wonder whether the authors of various church statements were aware of such effects.[40] In other cases, the authors may have been quite aware of the negative side effects, may have been willing to encounter them, but were unwilling to address them publicly out of concern that this may diminish the persuasive power of their arguments.

To be fair, it is not just Catholic bishops who avoid addressing the costs or tradeoffs implicit in their proposals. The realities of mass media campaigns ensure that candidates for political office will distance themselves from the "bad news" which their positions will entail. Still, church statements would do well to state the tradeoffs explicitly for two reasons: to set an example for more honest public debate and to enhance their own credibility among others who doubt the authors' competence in the field.

4. Ethics and Policy Assessment.   A second element of orthodox economics that will and should come to have greater influence in church documents in the future is the economist's view of public policy. This is not to say that this approach should displace others completely, since the economist's view has its own shortcomings. Still, traditional church teaching on socioeconomic issues has much to gain. From the point of view of the discipline of ethics, the economist's perspective is rooted in utilitarianism, the school of thought within ethics which, by and large, holds that the morally proper choice between any two alternatives is the one which will lead to the greatest amount of good for humankind.[41] The single greatest difference between utilitarian ethics and the ethics of the natural law tradition which has characterized the Roman Catholic approach concerns the possibility of doing evil to achieve a good result. When the evil is small and the subsequent effects very good (e.g. using nonlethal force to disarm a would-be murderer), the two approaches agree. When the evil is great (e.g. taking an innocent life), the Catholic tradition has forbidden this course regardless of how much good would subsequently flow from it (e.g. preventing scores of other deaths).[42] The utilitarian approach would approve, providing that the good effects outweighed all the bad ones.

Economists rarely deal with such life and death issues directly, but they do presume that the best policy is the one which has the best effects overall—even if it does have bad effects. Church documents at times speak as if even relatively minor evils prevent the moral approbation of economic policies or whole economic systems. *Gaudium et Spes*, for example, asserts that "any way of organizing and directing [economic] activity which would be *detrimental to any worker* would be wrong and inhuman" (no. 67, emphasis mine). Being subject to the human condition, any conceivable economic system will be injurious to some workers (at least in comparison to what the position of those workers might be under some other system for organizing economic activity). On the face of it, this norm from *Gaudium et Spes* would seem to brand every possible economic system as "wrong and inhuman."

The danger, more generally, is that ethically sensitive people often press for the complete implementation of all moral standards and reject compromises. The economist responds that the optimal policy in a world of scarcity (and hence, of tradeoffs) is not the policy that aims at perfection.[43] Striving to attain perfection in any one area will almost always entail serious losses in another. Air pollution in major cities is very bad, but passing a law banning all auto pollution would wreak havoc, since it would end virtually all auto travel and certainly the poor would suffer the most from the much higher cost of pollution-free cars. Banning industrial pollution or all toxic chemicals, reducing the national highway speed limits to 45 or 30 miles per hour, and legislating healthier diets would all reduce the number of deaths each year in the nation. But these measures would also have other seriously harmful effects (shutting down factories and farms, decreasing the efficiency of our transportation system, and violating our civil liberties) which prevent us from choosing to implement them. Perfection in any one area is not optimal under the conditions of scarcity which characterize economic life.

This confronts church leaders (and anyone else interested in public policy) with the need to ask just what values are so basic that they must be respected even at heavy costs. Obviously, we as a nation have already identified many such values in our Constitution, Bill of Rights, and the many laws of the land. No matter how much "inefficiency" they cause, civil liberties and laws prohibiting murder must be respected, and policy makers are not free to suspend these, regardless of the "benefits" that might be attained. Other basic standards proposed by religious leaders (and others) that were once opposed by many as "inefficient" restraints on the market are now taken for granted as permanent parts of the economic landscape: child labor laws, social security, unemployment insurance, workman's compensation, the forty-hour work week, the right to unionize.[44] In their concern for "efficiency" in cost-benefit analysis, economists and other policy advisers often forget that many such absolutes are already incorporated into our socioeconomic system.

But if economists often forget how long the list of such absolutes is, church leaders have historically tried to lengthen it. As we have seen, some principles, such as the just price (matching the price to the cost of production) and the just wage (matching the wage to the need of the worker) have fallen from the list even within church social teaching. Today the debate concerns such matters as the right to a job and the continued existence of a meaningful minimum wage.

If church leaders were to ignore the costs of such efforts, they might simply insist that the national government guarantee a job for every citizen who wants one and that the minimum wage be raised to the point where one worker could support a household of four without falling below the poverty level. But, as economists would caution, a straightforward government jobs program for all who lack employment would cost on the order of a hundred billion dollars a year, and more importantly, a program of that magnitude would have serious negative effects on the job market in the private sector. Similarly, raising the minimum wage to the approximately five dollars an hour needed to keep a family of four out of poverty would, quite predictably, eliminate at least hundreds of thousands of current jobs which employers would not be willing to offer at the new wage.

When church leaders allow such negative effects to dissuade them from supporting policies which would directly implement such basic goals as "the right to employment," they indicate that these goals are not absolutes to be achieved regardless of their effects but are relative values, among others, which should be striven for amid a consequentialist ethical analysis. Of course, the natural law tradition has always had a stronger consequentialist flavor to it than the deontological (or "ethics of duty") tradition so closely associated with Immanuel Kant.

It is in this vein that the U.S. Catholic bishops call for a broad ranging strategy for job creation within which direct public service employment should play a significant though not an overriding role.[45] Such a set of policy proposals would certainly bring down the unemployment rate significantly. However, it would not guarantee a job for everyone who wants one (which, presumably, is the literal meaning of "the right to employment" (*Gaudium et Spes*, no. 26)). There are other examples of shifts in social teaching toward the economist's cost-benefit approach, but before turning to several major questions remaining for the further development of Catholic social teaching, I would note one further characteristic of the policy-making situation which presents its own difficulties to church leaders.

Policy makers usually have very little influence over the motivations of the citizenry. Presidents can successfully appeal to the higher instincts of the people in times of crisis, but most policy decisions simply alter the set of conditions within which individuals go on making their own choices in accord with the values and standards they already hold. This puts church leaders in an awkward position. Their efforts to preach the gospel directly to people must entail the demand for a change of heart. Their efforts to help structure an ethically responsible public policy must presume that many people for whom the policy is intended will be acting only out of baser motives which ought not be endorsed. Entering into the "logic" of public policy appears as a compromise of fundamental values, which is why many Christian sects historically refused to do so.

Thus, for example, while a moral appeal for frugality is appropriate at the time of an energy crisis such as the United States experienced in 1973, the public policy response ought not be based on the presumption that people will be virtuously frugal. After immediate steps to cushion the blow of abrupt change on those least able to adjust, a responsible public policy must combine reliance on the incentive of higher prices (e.g. people will drive less with higher gas prices) with adjustments in government support programs for the poor in the face of higher prices of this essential commodity.

5. Dangers in the Influence of Economic Ideas.   As we have seen, economic science is having, will have, and should have an increasing influence on church teaching about socioeconomic life. This is not to say that the economist's view of things should prevail. Rather it says that the ethics of economic life has much to learn from the economist's perspective. It is and will remain critical, however, that the Christian vision of justice be articulated in the midst of the greater "realism" engendered by this change.

Some within the Catholic church have adopted all too much of the "economic perspective," at times without being conscious of it. The best evidence for this is the discussion surrounding the U.S. bishops' pastoral on the economy.[46] All too many people have responded to the drafts more or less along these lines: "I agree with the bishops on their general principles but disagree on the concrete policy proposals." Such a position is, of course, an intellectually and morally respectable one. The problem is that most who think they hold it actually don't. Many, in fact, do not hold the church's position on social justice and economic rights at all; most often, social justice is redefined and diluted while economic rights are restricted or denied altogether.

The "Lay Letter" published simultaneously with the first draft of the U.S. bishops' pastoral on the economy is a good example. The Lay Letter defines social justice as " ... the distinctive virtue by which individuals freely associate themselves with one another to pursue goods held in common, especially public goods, which cannot be achieved by individuals on their own."[47] This has a strangely individualistic "ring" to it. The letter goes on to say that "social justice has two aspects: it is both a virtue practiced by individuals, and a thrust toward improving the social order."[48] In neither of these formulations nor in subsequent discussion is it at all clear that social justice entails an *obligation* toward the poor on the part of, for example, those of us who are economically well off (except *perhaps* an obligation not to spend our profits profligately but to reinvest them in the economy to produce more wealth and jobs). The letter does not explicitly assert that concern for the poor is optional, but as a later section puts it, "a Jewish and Christian society will wish to help the poor," and "the generosity of the American people in wishing to help the poor ... has been immense."[49]

The cutting edge of justice, evident from the Old Testament prophets to the twentieth century popes, is nowhere to be found in the Lay Letter. Even *Gaudium et Spes*, by no means the most forceful Catholic statement on socioeconomic life, is far and away clearer on our obligations:

> At the same time, however, there is a growing awareness of the exalted dignity proper to the human person, since he stands above all things, and his rights and duties are universal and inviolable. Therefore, there must be made available to all men everything

necessary for leading a life truly human, such as food, clothing, and shelter; the right to choose a state of life freely and to found a family, the right to education, to employment, to a good reputation . . . (no. 26).

The list goes on. While more recent formulations depend less on the language of universality deriving from natural law and more on gospel demands, the content of these obligations has not changed.

Neither economists nor "the economic way of thinking" should be seen as the sole or ultimate source of the tendency to pull back from a robust understanding of social justice and economic rights. Philosophically, this tendency in American and British political theory can be traced to the liberal tradition extending from Thomas Hobbes and John Locke. Still, economists are particularly inclined toward this orientation for three reasons. The first is that mainstream economists focus on marginal changes within stable institutional structures. Thus they tend to overlook the more or less "absolute" moral norms incorporated in some of those structures and now taken for granted. The second is that economists are broadly convinced that minimizing outside government interference (whether based on moral ideals or entrepreneurial self-interest) assists economic growth. And the third is that orthodox economists aim at doing "value-free" social science. This latter element embodies an admirable hope of preventing a researcher's own convictions from biasing the results of scientific study. However, it supports the dangerous illusion held by many economists that their concepts and analyses are "value-neutral." In fact, as was observed earlier, orthodox economic analysis incorporates an a priori proclivity toward consequentialist ethics.

The key to an appropriate inclusion of economic science in the church's moral reflection is to retain the tension between the demands of a moral vision and the "realism" of economic efficiency. Economists do rightly stress the importance of the latter. But anyone, economist or other, who has only a weak sense of the demands of social justice does not notice the truly significant tradeoffs between justice and "economic efficiency"; and the value of increased production, not counterbalanced by other social values, is the only voice heard or heeded.

REMAINING QUESTIONS FOR THE CHURCH
ON SOCIOECONOMIC LIFE

In dealing with problems of the socioeconomic realm, one is always struck by how large is the canvas and how small the paintbrush. Out of the many questions facing Catholic social thought today as we look back at *Gaudium et Spes*, I will outline four issues that are particularly critical. The scope of an essay such as this does not allow for a thorough treatment of the variety of current positions held today on each of them. However, I will make particular reference to the work of perhaps the best-known participant in the discussion in the United States, Michael Novak. His own talents and his substantial efforts to relate the American and Catholic traditions makes him an appropriate choice.

    1. The Relative Autonomy of Economic Life. As we saw earlier, *Gaudium et Spes* acknowledged "the rightful independence of earthly affairs," at least in the sense that social, political, and economic realms "enjoy their own laws and values which must be gradually deciphered, put to use, and regulated by men" (no. 36). This means that church leaders should not just make up their own minds about how the economy or society should operate and then try to impose such a vision in public policy. At one level, the empirical reality of how things really work is a set of constraints within which moral reflection occurs. Thus, for example, the creation and operation of jumbo jets, oil refineries, and large universities will entail shortcomings inevitable in large organizations; and morally sensitive people who see the value of these three elements of modern life will have to be realistic about what is possible and not advocate, say, the personalized relations among employees that might be feasible in small-scale institutions.

    But, of course, this ought not be understood simplistically. Many of the things that occur in the economy do not merit moral approbation. Sin taints human activity and institutions, and a part of "how things work" in any economy or society must be rejected or reformed. Here lies one of the basic issues in the current debate over Catholic social teaching on the economy. Just how much of what is at odds with Christian values in the economy is due to the laws and values of economic life and must, therefore, be (reluctantly) lived with? And how much should be opposed vigorously in the interest of human values?

    Michael Novak has argued for a greater respect by the church for the inherent dynamics of the economic system. In *The Spirit of Democratic Capitalism*, he outlines a view of pluralistic societies as consisting of three separate "systems": a political system, an economic system, and a moral-cultural system.[50] Each has its own ethos and interacts with the other two, with necessary and desirable tensions among them. Each would, of its own impetus, make the other two subservient. But, Novak argues, the essence of the pluralistic society is that no one of the three is allowed to dominate. In effect, Novak sets out to structure the discussion about the "autonomy" of the economic order. If one accepts his construal of these human institutions, the simple existence of three systems of roughly equal importance supports the idea of relative autonomy addressed in Catholic social teaching. However, even here one is led to ask under what conditions and in support of what values should the church, an institution of the moral-cultural system, formulate potential economic policies and marshal political support to effect them? Novak never really sets out to answer this question. While this may be because his work aims at reducing the tendency of ecclesiastics to intervene in economic affairs through the political system, the oversight is unfortunate.

Whatever conception of pluralistic society one begins with, most of the participants in the discussion of Christian ethics and economics understand the Christian tradition to demand that certain fundamental values be respected by any economic system. That is, church documents are almost universally expected to formulate general principles for economic life.

Obviously, the more general the principle, the greater the autonomy implicitly allowed to the economic system in implementing it. For example, if the general principle is "concern for the poor" or "the freedom of the individual," capitalist systems might be defended on the grounds that in the long run the poor will do better, or socialist systems might be defended on the grounds that public ownership of factories means that the freedom of individual citizens is defended. If the principle is more focused and concrete, less autonomy is implicitly allowed. Thus, if the principle is that "the poor have the right to shelter" or "individuals have the right to own productive assets like tools and factories," then capitalist and socialist governments would be more clearly challenged to set up structures to counteract elements of the basic logic of capitalism or socialism, respectively.

This issue is more easily stated than resolved: How concrete should be the policy proposals put forth in church teaching? The answer given recently by the U.S. bishops in their economics pastoral is, I believe, the correct one. National bishops' conferences should articulate their view of general principles and also of the policy conclusions flowing from them, with the clear statement that the authority of the latter is significantly less than that of the former.[51]

2. Analyzing Competing Economic Ideologies. In spite of the reluctance of church documents to apply the term "ideology" to the conceptual and moral framework they themselves bring to socio-economic deliberations, most of the documents of the social teaching of the church have engaged in sorting out and evaluating the conceptual and moral frameworks underlying capitalism and socialism. *Gaudium et*

Spes was different in this regard, and the recent pastoral by the U.S. bishops represents another exception to this trend, apparently designed this way to focus attention on the economy as it operates and not on competing theories. While this may be a prudent move in light of the American situation at the time, I believe it would be a mistake if it became the norm. Intellectuals on both sides probably overestimate the power of ideas in the world, but the "ideological" or "philosophical" issues are critical.

As we have seen, the role of self-interest in the market is central to the debate. Economists have long felt that the moralist's assessment of self-interest has suffered from an inadequate understanding of the good done regularly by the relatively free play of individuals in the market.[52] Novak has performed a needed service in his elaboration of the ways in which the pursuit of one's own interests can be and indeed often is accompanied by more socially directed motives. Of course, even some structures of authority and order within the Catholic church in the United States have evolved to allow for a greater role of individual initiative; for example, diocesan priests now regularly seek out particular pastoral appointments rather than wait for assignments. Until Catholic moral theology deals more creatively with the positive dimensions of self-interest among people of roughly equal power and opportunity, the church's contribution to the ideological debate will fall short.

It is also important for Catholic social teaching to identify at least roughly the range of alternatives that are defensible within the tradition and to focus more attention on those economic structures that fall within that range. While papal documents from *Rerum Novarum* to *Octogesima Adveniens* to *Laborem Exercens* have exhibited a sequential improvement in the former, Catholics will likely have to look to national bishops' conferences for the latter. For all the assistance that Novak has provided in his defense of democratic capitalism, even in his recent *Freedom and Justice*, he continues to deny much importance to the differences between democratic capitalism and democratic socialism.[53] In doing so, he overlooks the very differences which span approximately ninety-eight percent of the opinion in the country. If such differences are too small in principle to be dealt with, what assistance can be provided to the narrower differences between, say, Republican and Democratic plans for welfare reform, taxation, or any of a host of other critical issues facing the nation today? We need a greater and not a smaller contribution of Christianity to the ideological debates raging daily.[54]

3. Consequentialist Analysis and Moral Public Policy.

As I have argued, church leaders have a good deal to learn from the cost-benefit analysis employed so pervasively in public policy circles today. Too often have church statements proposed a moral goal without assessing the detrimental side effects that will accompany its achievement. Ethical responsibility requires a courageous identification of both the good and the bad effects of even morally superior policies. The economic options before us as a nation are laced with hard choices, and only the foolish or the disingenuous ignore them.

Of course, consequentialist analysis is the backbone of mainstream economic analysis. It has also come to be the basis for the defense of democratic capitalism against charges that it ignores responsibilities to the poor. As such, this consequentialist argument has two elements: an empirical and a normative one. Empirically, defenders of the market system like Novak argue that the capitalist system has proven itself to be the most productive in the world and has lifted the poor out of age-old poverty. And it is true that most of the poor in this country have a refrigerator and television, unheard of luxuries among the poor of the rest of the world. Normatively, Novak and others assert that *because* this economic system will produce more wealth in the future than any other and *because* the poor will benefit more thereby, the morally correct judgment is to allow the market to function without much initiative-deadening government interference. The unstated cost, however, is that many currently needy people may not receive the basic assistance today that a different vision of the economy would allow. Additionally, this analysis takes more credit than is due. It overlooks the critical role that political effort (inspired by both moral values and the self-interest of the suffering) played in humanizing the economy against the resistance of generations of the powerful who opposed such steps with many of the same arguments Novak advances today.

4. The Defense of Social Justice.   At the same time that the church must learn from the insights of consequentialist moral analysis, it must remain staunch in its defense of the standards of social justice. The nature of social justice has been treated elsewhere,[55] but it must be noted that the most dominant theme in the Judeo-Christian tradition on economic life is the commitment to justice, especially for the weakest: the widow, the orphan, the poor, and the stranger in the land.

The instinct in the British and American liberal tradition has often been to restrict the term "justice" to individual justice. Some, like Friedrich von Hayek, have rejected the term "social justice" altogether. In the theological defense of democratic capitalism provided by Novak, the term is retained as a respectable part of the Catholic tradition, but its meaning is restricted. Novak argues that "since the foundation of social justice is the dignity of the human person, its first principle is freedom, in which that dignity resides." One wonders what obligations are entailed in social justice, whether for oneself toward others or on the part of others toward the self. Referring to John XXIII in the next sentence, Novak lists the rights such freedom encompasses: the right to life, to liberty, to choose one's own destiny, to the pursuit of happiness, and to choose the meaning of life.[56] Again one wonders what happened to other rights that appear in the standard papal and conciliar listings: the right to food, clothing, shelter, employment, and even at the time of John XXIII, to a just wage. Time and again, standards which the Catholic tradition has taken as obligatory are referred to only as "humane" or "commendable" or "virtuous."[57]

The defense of social justice through economic structures ought not entail a strictly "deontological" ethical stand, which would entail no concern for the negative consequences which such a standard might effect. However, it cannot be strictly consequentialist either, since we face a moral obligation that arises from elements other than the good or bad effects caused. Rather, the Catholic tradition must employ what Charles Curran has termed "a middle position" or "a mixed consequentialism."[58] Curran's own applications tend not to occur in the realm of economic life, but the relevance of this construal of the Catholic position is clear. Church leaders must simultaneously seek efficient solutions to economic problems and still insist on the standards of justice, even if this will restrain productivity.[59]

Among the critical issues facing the church in the defense of social justice are the role of "participation" in the economy and the church's "option for the poor." Greater participation can range from more consultation of workers by managers, to worker representation on company boards of directors (termed "codetermination," a requirement for large firms in much of Western Europe[60]), to the ownership of whole firms by the workers. The extent to which these forms of participation will become more solidly a part of Catholic social teaching and staunchly advocated in policy is yet to be seen. The "option for the poor," arising energetically within liberation theology, has come to be appropriated by the U.S. bishops as a fundamental element of the quest for justice in socioeconomic life. However, the reasoning behind it for the American episcopate is rooted clearly in the natural law tradition. The church defends the human dignity of all persons, but it is the dignity of the poor which is least respected in our society.[61] Some have objected to the bishops "taking sides"; others resonate with Robert McAfee Brown's description of the Latin American bishops: "They're not taking sides," he quipped, "they're changing sides." The U.S. bishops themselves must clarify the meaning of their option for the poor for the American church in their commitments and activities in the coming years.

CONCLUSION

Gaudium et Spes was clearly an unusual document, and arguably the most forward-looking of Vatican II. It marked a significant shift in the methodology of Catholic moral theology and social ethics at the same time as it continued the clear development of Catholic social teaching on socioeconomic life over the past century. The celebration of the *Pastoral Constitution on the Church in the Modern World* constituted by this volume of essays is both tribute to the vision of the document and an act of faith that its creative influence can be magnified over the next twenty years. God willing, its fortieth anniversary may bear witness to a vibrant church in a better world embarking on a new century.

NOTES

1. The only reference to this problem within *Gaudium et Spes* is a minimal one, in the footnote to the title of the document: "In part two [the section treating 'the problems of special urgency'] the subject matter which is viewed in the light of doctrinal principles is made up of diverse elements. Some elements have a permanent value; others, only a transitory one." No attempt is made to identify these explicitly.

2. Pius XII, "Address to the International Union of Institutes of Archeology, History and History of Art," March 9, 1956: *A.A.S.* 48 (1956), 212. Quoted in *Gaudium et Spes*, no. 42.

3. See, for example, Francis Schussler Fiorenza, "The Church's Religious Identity and Its Social and Political Mission," *Theological Studies* 43 (June 1982): 197–225.

4. Pope John XXIII, *Mater et Magistra*, no. 220 as found in Joseph Gremillion: *The Gospel of Peace and Justice* (Maryknoll, N.Y.: Orbis Press, 1976).

5. Pope John XXIII, *Pacem in Terris*, no. 9 (in Gremillion).

6. *Pacem in Terris*, no. 20.

7. Cf. *Mater et Magistra*, nos. 109 and 116. It was not always so; certain confusions concerning socialism contributed to the problem. Once subsequent popes recognized the inadequacy of Leo XIII's misreading of socialist views of private property (he argued they were endeavoring to destroy it altogether), the issue became more clearly whether private ownership *of the means of production* was morally justifiable. See Leo XIII, *Rerum Novarum*, in Gerald C. Tracey, S.J., ed., *Five Great Encyclicals* (New York: Paulist Press, 1939), 2.

8. For a very helpful discussion of the methodological shifts inherent in a shifting anthropology, see Charles E. Curran, *Directions in Catholic Social Ethics* (Notre Dame, Indiana: University of Notre Dame Press, 1985), chap. 1, "The Changing Anthropological Bases of Catholic Social Ethics," 5–42.

9. *Rerum Novarum*, in *Five Great Encyclicals*, 22.

10. *Quadregesimo Anno*, in *Five Great Encyclicals*, 145.

11. *Mater et Magistra*, no. 71.

12. National Conference of Catholic Bishops, *Pastoral Letter on Catholic Social Teaching and the U.S. Economy*, second draft (Washington, D.C.: United States Catholic Conference, October 7, 1985), nos. 135–68.

13. Donnella H. Meadows et al., *The Limits to Growth: A Report for the Club of Rome's Project on the Predicament of Mankind* (New York: Universe Books, 1972).

14. M. Mesarovic and E. Pestel improved the quality of the earlier studies in *Mankind at the Turning Point* (New York: Dutton/Readers' Digest, 1974). The debate over energy in the United States is illustrative of the broader issues. Cf. Ford Foundation Energy Policy Project, final report, *A Time to Choose: America's Energy Future* (Cambridge, Mass.: Ballinger, 1974).

15. See Fred Hirsch, *Social Limits to Growth* (Cambridge, Mass.: Harvard University Press, 1976).

16. For a discussion of the term, see Charles M. Murphy, "Action for Justice as Constitutive of Preaching of the Gospel: What Did the 1971 Synod Mean?" *Theological Studies* 44 (June 1983): 298-311.

17. For an overview of liberation theology, see José Miguez-Bonino, *Doing Theology in a Revolutionary Situation* (Philadelphia: Fortress Press, 1975); Robert McAfee Brown, *Theology in a New Key: Responding to Liberation Themes* (Philadelphia: Westminster Press, 1978); Roger Haight, S.J., *An Alternative Vision: An Interpretation of Liberation Theology* (New York: Paulist Press, 1985).

18. J. Philip Wogaman, *The Great Economic Debate: An Ethical Analysis* (Philadelphia: Westminster Press, 1977).

19. Cf. Paul VI's statement, "Is there need to stress the possible ambiguity of every social ideology?.... The Christian faith is above and sometimes opposed to the ideologies.... ", *Octogesima Adveniens*, no. 27 (in Gremillion).

20. Robert Benne, *The Ethic of Democratic Capitalism* (Philadelphia: Fortress Press, 1981), 229.

21. Michael Novak, *The Spirit of Democratic Capitalism* (New York: American Enterprise Institute/Simon and Schuster, 1982), 333-60.

22. Arthur F. McGovern, *Marxism: An American Christian Perspective* (Maryknoll, N.Y.: Orbis Books, 1980).

23. Joe Holland, *The American Journey: A Theology in the Americas Working Paper* (New York: IDOC, 1976).

24. John W. Houck and Oliver F. Williams, C.S.C., *Catholic Social Teaching and the United States Economy* (Washington, D.C.: University Press of America, 1984).

25. Prentiss L. Pemberton and Daniel Rush Finn, *Toward a Christian Economic Ethic: Stewardship and Social Power* (Minneapolis: Winston Press, 1985).

26. Adam Smith, *An Inquiry into the Nature and Causes of the Wealth of Nations* (New York: Modern Library Edition, 1937), 3.

27. Standing behind this assertion is the economic analysis of supply and demand in microeconomics. When technological change increases efficiency, goods can be produced with fewer inputs and can be sold at a lower price. Our brief survey of the discipline does not leave us time to develop these ideas here.

28. People today don't often experience prices as falling, largely because of the inflation which we have become accustomed to over the last fifteen years or

so. Incomes do not automatically rise in proportion to inflation, but when they do, or when they nearly do, high rates of inflation can mask reductions in "real" (i.e. "inflation adjusted") prices, which actually may be causing a rise in the standard of living. Similarly, the rise in the prices of many goods may be attributable to an increase in their "quality" (e.g. new features in automobiles or televisions), and the increase in consumers' wealth caused by greater productivity in the manufacture of these goods may go unnoticed simply because the overall price is higher. The United States in the first half of the 1980s has experienced a period when the standard of living of most Americans fell or at best remained stable. Looking back over the last two centuries, however, the greater productivity which Smith analyzed did, in fact, result in rising standards of living during most of that period.

29. National Catholic Welfare Conference, *Organized Social Justice: An Economic Program for the United States Applying Pius XI's Great Encyclical on Social Life* (New York: Paulist Press, 1935), cited in Aaron I. Abell, ed., *American Catholic Thought on Social Questions* (Indianapolis: Bobbs-Merrill, 1968), 379.

30. Smith, 59.

31. *Summa Theologica*, II-II, q. 77, a. 1.

32. Ibid. The key here is that "the advantage accruing to the buyer is not due to the seller, but to a circumstance affecting the buyer." While one may charge for the loss to be suffered (due to no longer being able to use the thing *oneself*), "no man should sell what is not his," that is, no seller should charge for an advantage that only a prospective buyer (and not the seller) could derive (ibid.). In the example of a famine, no well-fed seller (who doesn't need to consume an additional pound of rice) should charge more than usual for rice even though the grain is worth far more to hungry people who would be willing, under stress of hunger, to pay far more than usual for it.

33. See Odd Langholm, *Price and Value in the Aristotelian Tradition* (Bergen: Universitetsforlaget, 1979). Franz H. Mueller goes so far as to argue that as late as 1940, official U.S. Catholic documents presume that "the just wage [a special case of the just price] is basically the economically correct wage and vice versa." *The Church and the Social Question* (Washington: American Enterprise Institute, 1984), 153.

34. There was the actual cost of production of this particular object, but that may have been lower or higher than the average cost of production of other identical objects produced by other firms or even by the same firm at other times. If one carpenter works harder and faster but just as carefully as all the others and is able to produce a chair at a lower cost (due to the use of less labor time), is the chair so produced "worth less" than all the other identical chairs produced by others? We should note that Marxian economists who defend the labor theory of value have argued that it is the average cost of production (given the prevailing technology and skills in the industry) that is used as the measure. See Ernest Mandel, *An Introduction to Marxian Economic Theory* (New York: Pathfinder Press, 1939).

35. Cf. Charles Curran, *Directions in Catholic Social Ethics* (Notre Dame, Ind.: University of Notre Dame Press, 1985). See especially chaps. 1 and 2 on the philosophical and theological shifts, respectively.

36. See Joseph Gremillion, *The Gospel of Peace and Justice* esp. 7–13; and Curran, *Directions*, chap. 2.

37. This analysis contended that the "value" of a thing is equivalent to the labor "contained" in it, which is to say, to the labor power necessary to produce it. To be more precise, this measure must include the labor power necessary to produce that portion of the tools, machines, and other inputs that get used up in the production of that particular object. Convoluted as it may seem to the novice, this leads to the conclusion that the value of labor itself is the labor power it takes to produce the laborers. For a more recent and straightforward Marxian articulation of the labor theory of value, see Ernest Mandel, *An Introduction to Marxist Economic Theory* (New York: Pathfinder Press, 1970), 7–28.

38. This is *not* to say that only someone holding the labor theory of value can consistently hold to the idea of a just wage. However, the just wage has a clear correlation with the economic analysis of classical political economy (the economics of Smith and Ricardo) and thus could enjoy a greater respectability among economists than it does today.

39. *Rerum Novarum*, in *Five Greater Encyclicals*, 21.

40. Even the second draft of the U.S. Bishops' pastoral on the economy, generally more careful than previous statements, needs to develop this question of tradeoffs more thoroughly. For instance, the bishops note that "Workers must use their collective power to contribute to the well-being of the whole community and should avoid pressing demands whose fulfillment would damage the rights of more vulnerable members of society" (no. 105) without indicating some of the negative effects which might result from such a stance. With only a few exceptions, when employers have to pay higher real wages to a large group of workers, those employers will reduce the number of jobs they offer. The question is not *whether* there will be an impact on those who are nonunionized but *how great* it will be. This does *not* say that unions shouldn't press for higher wages, but it does say that moral support for the right of workers to organize and bargain collectively (which the bishops *should* give) entails a morally significant tradeoff.

41. This all-too-brief definition overlooks many important distinctions within utilitarianism but it will suffice for our purposes. For a more complete and highly readable treatment of the types of utilitarianism (from an "act-utilitarian" point of view), see J.J.C. Smart's essay, "An Outline of a System of Utilitarian Ethics" in J.J.C. Smart and Bernard Williams, *Utilitarianism: For and Against* (London: Cambridge University Press, 1973) 3–74.

42. Again, see Curran, *Directions in Catholic Social Ethics*, ibid.

43. See, for example, Richard B. McKenzie and Gordon Tullock, *The New World of Economics: Explorations into the Human Experience*, 3rd ed. (Homewood, Ill.: Richard D. Irwin, 1981).

44. There are groups within the nation that wish to weaken such current legislation, and in some areas there is need for reform. Still, these statutes are now considered among the "givens" within which economic policy is made.

45. *Catholic Social Teaching and the U.S. Economy*, no. 161.

46. National Conference of Catholic Bishops, *Catholic Social Teaching and the U.S. Economy*, first draft, *Origins* 14 (November 15, 1984): 337–83.

47. Lay Commission on Catholic Social Teaching and the U.S. Economy, *Toward the Future: Catholic Social Thought and the U.S. Economy: A Lay Letter* (New York: American Catholic Committee, 1984), 6.

48. Ibid.

49. Ibid., 58–59.

50. *The Spirit of Democratic Capitalism*, esp., chap. 9.

51. For a discussion of "the dilemma of political relevance without partisanship," see John A. Coleman, *An American Strategic Theology* (New York: Paulist Press, 1982), 259–61.

52. See Pemberton and Finn, 88–92.

53. Michael Novak, *Freedom with Justice: Catholic Social Thought and Liberal Institutions* (San Francisco: Harper and Row, 1984), 37–38. See also *The Spirit of Democratic Capitalism*, 26.

54. Among the hopeful signs in this regard is the rising interest in the history of Catholic participation in political movements and in the history of the social teaching of the church. See, for example, Gregory Baum, *Catholics and Canadian Socialism: Political Thought in the Thirties and Forties* (New York: Paulist Press, 1980); and Franz H. Mueller, *The Church and the Social Question* (Washington: American Enterprise Institute, 1984). See also Novak, *Freedom with Justice*.

55. See, for example, Daniel C. Maguire, *A New American Justice* (Minneapolis: Winston Press, 1980), especially chap. 4, "The Nature of Justice." See also Pemberton and Finn, chap. 7, "Social Justice and Economic Efficiency."

56. Novak, *Freedom with Justice*, 209. While he mentions John XXIII, no particular citation of any text is given as the source of this particular list of human rights.

57. For example, after noting that action of the developed nations may have "a sometimes devastating, sometimes disproportionately beneficial, impact on the less developed," he says, "concern to avoid harmful effects would certainly be humane and commendable on the part of the stronger party. What cannot be concluded, however, is that trade should be halted" (*Freedom with Justice*, 138).

58. Curran, *Directions in Catholic Social Ethics*, chap. 6, "Utilitarianism, Consequentialism, and Moral Theology."

59. I have here and throughout this essay not questioned the assertions of the defenders of democratic capitalism that it is more productive than alternative economic systems and that interventions in the market will generally increase inefficiency and reduce productivity. The latter in particular is open to debate, since at least the morale of the nation's workforce is critical to national productivity. However, taking these assertions to be true sets up the harder case for the Christian view of ethics in the economic realm, and this will make my presuppositions clearer, even if not more palatable.

60. See Robert J. Kuhne, *Co-Determination in Business: Workers Representation in the Boardroom* (New York: Praeger, 1980).

61. NCCB, *Catholic Social Teaching and the U.S. Economy*, second draft; see, for instance, nos. 20, 28, 67.

Manuel Velasquez

"Gaudium et Spes" and the Development of Catholic Social-Economic Teaching

The socioeconomic doctrines in Chapter III of *Gaudium et Spes* are fascinating. They contain a distillation of the best of the prior seventy-five years of traditional church teaching on economic issues as well as, in embryo, the foundational ideas that emerged as major new themes during the two decades following Vatican II.

A nice example of this ability to draw from the past while setting the foundations for the future is provided by the core ethical value to which the *Constitution on the Church in the Modern World* continually appeals: the "dignity" of the human person which implies that everyone must be enabled to act "according to a knowing and free choice . . . personally motivated and prompted from within" (*GS*, no. 17).[1] This notion of human dignity as self-determination has a long history in Catholic social teaching, and *Gaudium et Spes* accurately reflects the essential outlines of this teaching.[2] But the document goes beyond this tradition when it uses the notion as the basis for critiquing in a radical way the systemic economic structures that characterize much of the world: "Whatever insults human dignity, such as . . . disgraceful working conditions, where men are treated as mere tools for profit, rather than as free and responsible persons; all these things and others of their like are infamies indeed" (*GS*, no. 27). *Gaudium et Spes* does not develop this criticism, which suggests a radical critique of the role that labor must play in market-oriented economies. But the suggestion is taken up by later church documents such as the pastoral letter on justice issued by the bishops of Latin America meeting in Medellín, Colombia in 1968, which stated that laborers must be liberated from their "dependence on inhuman economic systems and institutions: a situation which, for many, borders on slavery" (J, no. 11). Thus, although *Gaudium et Spes* appeals to a very traditional understanding of human dignity, it does so in a manner that opens the way for much more radical future applications. It both summarizes the past and contains the foundations for the future.

My aim in this essay is to examine the extent to which the chapter on socioeconomic issues. The Council, they said, will provide an church's traditional teachings on social-economic matters, and to analyze the extent to which it contains the embyronic ideas that later synods and encyclicals have developed into major church doctrines. My focus throughout is on the normative economic doctrines discussed in *Gaudium et Spes*. That is, I focus on doctrines concerning how society should control decisions about the material goods it will produce, how they should be produced, who should bear the burdens of producing them, and who should enjoy the benefits of their production. Before turning to this task, however, I provide a brief description of how the socioeconomic sections of *Gaudium et Spes* came to be written.

The genesis of the socioeconomic doctrines of *Gaudium et Spes* is to be found in the surprise opening message "to all mankind" issued by the bishops assembled in Rome during the heady first days of Vatican II.[3] In an unusually short document, the world's bishops on October 20, 1962 prophetically announced the major themes of *Gaudium et Spes*. Their short and astonishingly forward-looking statement outlines, in fact, the central concerns that will dominate all future church teachings on socioeconomic issues. The council, they said, will provide an impetus for the "advancement of human dignity." Its first concern henceforth will be for the humble, the poor, the weak ... the many who suffer hunger, misery and ignorance ... those who, lacking the help they need, have not yet achieved a way of life worthy of human beings." For their sake, the bishops of Vatican II wrote, the Council's special concern will be "first of all, peace among peoples," and "secondly ... social justice ... to denounce injustices and shameful inequalities and to restore the rightful order of property and economics so that, based on the principles of the gospel, the life of man may become more worthy of man." This opening message of the Council was critical. Without it, *Gaudium et Spes* would not have been written. Not only did the message commit the bishops to the major themes of *Gaudium et Spes*—the advancement of human dignity and social justice—but it also served as an assertion of the fundamental openness to the modern world that would characterize all the work of the Council, but especially *Gaudium et Spes*. That openness would allow the bishops to insert into *Gaudium et Spes* several important modifications of traditional church doctrines as well as several new ideas destined to become the basis of future Catholic social teaching.

Oddly, after this dramatically prophetic opening declaration, the Council for the next three years gave precious little public attention to the issues of "peace" and "social justice." Instead, its attention remained almost wholly riveted on internal church matters: debates over the liturgy, the role of bishops, marriage law, the renewal of religious life, the function of the Bible, and the issue of religious freedom. External social, political, and economic questions were omitted almost entirely from its public agenda.

Nevertheless, behind the scenes, work on the document that eventually became *Gaudium et Spes* was begun. The decision to address the church's relation to the external socioeconomic world in a document tentatively entitled "The Church in the Modern World" was made on December 4, 1962 in the closing days of the Council's first session. By January 1963 the general outline of the socioeconomic topics to be treated in the document on the church in the modern world was set, and the following month a commission began the long process of drafting and revising what emerged as *Gaudium et Spes* three years later in December 1965.[4]

"GAUDIUM ET SPES" AND TRADITIONAL SOCIOECONOMIC CHURCH TEACHINGS

The chapter of *Gaudium et Spes* that is devoted to socioeconomic matters is filled with an extraordinarily confident optimism concerning Western economic institutions, an optimism that sounds strangely naive to our modern ears. The document applauds industrial development and the "advances" of technology; it rejoices in the Western orientation toward growth; it urges the global expansion of Western culture; it sees progress as the inevitable result of industrialization and assumes that the development of the Third World can be accomplished without major adjustments of the world economy; everywhere it sees signs of "collaboration" and "cooperation." Thus, *Gaudium et Spes* is for the most part oblivious to the problems of pollution, urbanization, inflation, and mass unemployment. And it is oddly blind to the political realities of power conflicts in the international economic arena.[5] Nevertheless, *Gaudium et Spes* was not utterly uncritical. It pointed out that "political, social, economic, racial and ideological disputes still continue bitterly, and with them the peril of a war which would reduce everything to ashes" (*GS*, no. 4). It scolded the individualistic ethic of the West (*GS*, no. 9), and noted that the remarkable prosperity of the industrialized West was associated with gaping inequalities (*GS*, nos. 29, 66). But in its broad orientation, *Gaudium et Spes* accepts with open arms the liberal economic tradition that characterized the West during the sixties.

Although the document has been criticized for its easy embrace of economic attitudes that would later be questioned, this open acceptance of contemporary views perhaps more than anything else enabled it to introduce subtle but important changes into the church's tradition of socioeconomic teachings. That tradition in its modern form began in 1891 with the promulgation of Pope Leo XIII's encyclical *Rerum Novarum*.[6] It was updated first in Pope Pius XI's 1931 encyclical *Quadragesimo Anno*, and again in Pope John XXIII's 1961 encyclical *Mater et Magistra*, published as Vatican II was about to convene. In order to understand the extent to which *Gaudium et Spes* both summarized and modified this tradition of church teaching, it is necessary to review the development of some of the major themes in that teaching, and contrast these with the treatment of the same themes in *Gaudium et Spes*. The differences are striking and instructive. In order to understand better what the writers of *Gaudium et Spes* accomplished, I propose to examine three elements of that teaching: (1) the church's traditional teaching on ownership and control of economically productive assets, (2) its traditional response to economic inequality and poverty, and (3) its traditional position on economic ideologies. The church's teachings on these three important economic issues evolved considerably over the decades.

1. Ownership in Catholic Social Teaching.   Debates on the nature of private property are essentially debates on the legitimacy of economic power. Although couched in terms of "ownership," they are, in fact, debates on the most basic of all economic questions: how should society's productive economic assets be controlled and whose interests may they serve? Answers to this question have traditionally fallen into two categories. The first is the "socialist" response that productive property should be controlled or "owned" in common by society as a whole and that it should serve the common interests of society. The second is the "capitalist" position that productive property should be controlled or owned by individuals who have a right to use it to serve their own private interests.

The position of *Gaudium et Spes* on the nature of property is flexible and open. It holds that "forms of ownership" should be "adapted to the legitimate institutions of people according to diverse and changeable circumstances" (*GS*, no. 69). In themselves, the private property institutions of capitalism thus have no greater moral legitimacy than the common ownership mechanisms of socialism. Moreover, the Council ratifies the view that the "communal purpose" of using earthly goods to meet the needs of all humanity takes priority over any private ownership claims that a nation's property institutions might give to individuals: "Attention must always be paid to the universal purpose for which created goods are meant. In using them, therefore, a man should regard his lawful possessions not merely as his own but also as common property in the sense that they should accrue to the benefit of not only himself but of others" (*GS*, no. 69). The document then goes on to describe with approval several welfare programs by which the state rightly uses property to meet social needs.

These positions on property appear ordinary enough and are entirely consistent with the doctrines of the patristic and medieval church, as the writers of *Gaudium et Spes* are at pains to point out. [7] Yet they contrast sharply with the church's traditional teaching since the late nineteenth century. In *Rerum Novarum* (1891), the first of the great modern social encyclicals, Pope Leo XIII had asserted that property is legitimately controlled only by private individuals who have a right to use it for their private aims. Leo argued for this position by importing into Catholic teaching the startling doctrine of John Locke that private property is a "natural right."[8] "Every man," the pope wrote, "has by nature the right to possess property as his own" (*RN*, no. 5). Leo tempered Locke's position on private property by mentioning in a single passing sentence the older Thomistic tradition which distinguishes between owning property privately and using it to serve social needs.[9] In this earlier Thomistic tradition, rights of private ownership were subordinated to and derived from the social needs of the community—the so-called "common good."[10] But Leo XIII held that the duty to use property to meet social needs was only a duty of charity, not of justice, and was therefore subordinate to the moral rights of private ownership. In fact, the pope wrote, it is wrong for society to enact laws that would require individuals to use their "superfluous" wealth to meet social needs: "But when [family] necessity has been supplied, and one's [social] position has been fairly provided for, it is a duty to give to the indigent out of that which is left over ... a duty not of justice, but of Christian charity—a duty which is not enforced by human law" (*RN*, no. 19).[11]

Leo's encyclical, written in the aftermath of Europe's industrial revolution, was extremely significant as a church response to the poverty and wretched working conditions that the industrialization of Europe had spawned. In several respects *Rerum Novarum* was a radical document. It aligned the church with the poor and exploited class of workers; it definitively established the view that religion must concern itself with socioeconomic matters; and it set the social-economic agenda that future church teaching would have to address. Nevertheless, in its approach to the issues, *Rerum Novarum* was fundamentally conservative insofar as it accepted some of the Lockean premises that underlay the very laissez-faire institutions which had created the social problems it protested. This acceptance of a conservative Lockean approach to property set a problematic with which later popes would have to deal.

The second great social encyclical, *Quadragesimo Anno* (1931), was written by Pope Pius XI to celebrate the fortieth anniversary of *Rerum Novarum* and to "interpret" its teachings in the changed conditions of the early twentieth century. Indeed, a great deal had changed since Pope Leo. The world's economies were still being wracked by the international Great Depression which spread the tragedy of mass unemployment and poverty throughout the world. Businessmen everywhere were using the force of law and the police to destroy the unions through which workers were trying to secure a better life. Capitalism, with its basis in private property, and market competition could no longer be viewed as optimistically as in the time of Leo XIII.

Cognizant of the changed conditions in which he wrote, Pius XI—with some embarrassment, perhaps—began the difficult process of modifying the strange Lockean doctrines of Leo XIII. In *Quadragesimo Anno* Pius subtly deemphasized the private rights of ownership and emphasized instead the "social character" of property. All property, Pius wrote, must be used to provide for "the common good" *as well as* for the individual (*QA*, nos. 47, 49).[12] Thus, the social purposes of property must not be subordinated to the private rights that a system of private property creates. Pius also noted another embarrassment, namely, Leo's view that the duty to use property for the common good was not to be legally enforced. Nevertheless, he rejected this view and held that "the public authority, in view of the common good, may specify what is licit and what is illicit for property owners in the use of their possessions ... [and may] adjust ownership to meet the needs of the public good" (*QA*, no. 49).

In his 1961 encyclical *Mater et Magistra*, Pope John XXIII moved the church further away from the odd doctrines of Leo with the frank recognition that the ownership of productive resources—land, factories, machinery, and other forms of capital—need not be private: "What we have said does not preclude ownership of goods pertaining to production of wealth by states and public agencies" (*MM*, no. 116). Thus, Pope John silently abandoned the Leonine arguments against the socialist programs of state ownership of the means of production.[13] Simultaneously, he emphatically subordinated the private and individualistic aspects of property to its social purposes: "in the wisdom of God the creator, the over-all supply of goods is assigned first of all, that all men may lead a decent life" (*MM*, no. 119). He concludes that property owners may legally be made to put their property at the service of the community's needs, since "in the right of private property there is rooted a social responsibility" (*MM*, no. 119).

Thus, the views embodied in *Gaudium et Spes* nicely summarize the gradual shift in Catholic social teaching away from the Lockean views of Leo XIII, and back toward the more socially oriented Thomistic tradition that gave communal needs a priority over private property rights. Although rights of private ownership are legitimate, they must be subordinated to the social needs of the community, even to the point of giving way to legally mandated social programs that transfer the benefits of wealth to the poor. While the private property institutions of capitalism are legitimate, so too are the common ownership institutions of socialism.

But *Gaudium et Spes* moved beyond the traditional teaching on property in two important respects. First, the Council overturns the traditional Thomistic view that owners of private property are obligated to put only their "superfluous" wealth (i.e., what is not needed to maintain one's social position) at the service of the needy, a view that legitimized the right of the wealthy to hoard their wealth. Instead, the Council declares, "men are obliged to come to the relief of the poor and to do so not merely out of their superfluous goods" (*GS*, no. 69). Second, the Council states that private property institutions must always give way to the more fundamental human right to basic necessities: "If a person is in extreme necessity, he has the right to take from the riches of others what he himself needs" (*GS*, no. 69).

The implications of these two additions are obviously not conservative. In the sentence immediately following the declaration that the hungry have "the right to take from the riches" of the wealthy, the bishops point out that "there are many people in this world afflicted with hunger." The implication is that these hungry masses may legitimately take the goods of the wealthy classes to meet their basic needs. Quoting Gratian, the bishops issue a stern warning that individuals and governments must "feed the man dying of hunger, because if you have not fed him, you have killed him." They leave unmentioned the obvious but radical (and utterly foreign to the teachings of Leo XIII) alternative: or the poor might take from you what is rightfully theirs.

2. The Response to Economic Inequality and Poverty. The issue of inequality is essentially a distributive issue: how legitimate is the manner in which society distributes economic benefits and burdens among its members? This is a question which in turn raises several fundamental questions: (1) Are economic inequalities morally legitimate or is there a limit to the moral acceptability of inequality? (2) How should inequalities be dealt with? (3) Who are those who are most disadvantaged by inequality and what should be our attitude toward them? What position does *Gaudium et Spes* take on these issues?

In its very first sentence, *Gaudium et Spes* announces that its special concern is "those who are poor." From that point on, the document repeatedly contrasts the plight of the poor with the abundance of the wealthy: "While an enormous mass of people still lack the absolute necessities of life, some, even in less advanced countries, live sumptuously or squander wealth" (*GS*, no. 63). *Gaudium et Spes* unabashedly condemns these national and international inequalities, holding that since all men are "created in God's likeness and all have been redeemed by Christ, the basic equality of all must receive increasingly greater recognition" (*GS*, no. 29). Although some degree of inequality is inevitable, nevertheless "the equal dignity of persons demands . . . a more humane and just" distribution of wealth than presently exists (*GS*, no. 29). The persistence of inequalities is unjustifiable in view of the fact that the economic potential which the modern world enjoys can correct this unjust state of affairs (*GS*, no. 63). The document draws the only conclusion possible: structural "reforms are needed at the socio-economic level"(*GS*, no. 63). In particular, it recommends programs of agricultural and industrial "development" (*GS*, no. 64) as well as a number of redistributive mechanisms. In underdeveloped nations, "insufficiently cultivated estates should be distributed to those who can make these lands fruitful" (*GS*, no. 71). (*Gaudium et Spes*, in a much-debated sentence, goes so far as to approve the "expropriation" as long as "equitable compensation" appropriate to the circumstances is provided!) In developed nations, on the other hand, the "body of social institutions dealing with insurance and security . . . and social services" (*GS*, no. 69) that characterizes the modern welfare state should be used to alleviate inequality. Moreover, "public authorities" should ensure that "the distribution of goods [is] directed toward providing employment and sufficient income for the people of today and of the future" (*GS*, no. 70).

These liberal—even radical—views contrast sharply with the conservative tradition of the earliest social encyclicals. Although the central concern of *Rerum Novarum*, for example, is "the misery and wretchedness pressing so unjustly on the majority of the working class" (*RN*, no. 2), it emphatically rejects the view that economic inequalities are in themselves unjust. "Unequal fortune," Leo wrote, "is a necessary result of inequality in condition. Such inequality is far from being disadvantageous" (*RN*, no. 14). Leo was too much of a realist not to see the deep gaps that existed between the rich and the poor. In a passage oddly similar to Marxist writings, he wrote: "Society has been divided into two widely different castes. On the one side there is the party which holds the power because it holds the wealth; . . . which manipulates for its own benefit and its own purposes all the sources of supply, and which is powerfully represented in the councils of the state itself; on the other side there is the needy and powerless multitude, sore and suffering, always ready for disturbance" (*RN*, no. 35). Nevertheless, Leo does not advocate any structural changes to eradicate these conditions. Instead, he merely exhorts wealthy individuals to share their "superfluous" goods with the poor out of "charity" and "generosity" (*RN*, nos. 18-19), and calls on the poor to be content with their lot in "tranquil resignation" (*RN*, nos. 20-21).

Pius XI in *Quadragesimo Anno* moved away from the impotent hand wringing of Leo XIII. Industrialization had by his time spread out beyond Europe into Asia and the New World, where it had brought with it the benefits and blights of capitalism, including periodic, deeply wrenching depressions. Scandals had regularly rocked the financial centers of the world as large trusts and combines of speculators profiteered from the largely unregulated financial and stock markets. And everywhere the world saw the rise of the large corporation, in which massive amounts of power and capital were concentrated in the hands of a few.

In response to these conditions, Pius XI introduced into the encyclical tradition for the first time a specific principle of economic distribution that took into account the rights of the poor laboring classes. Economic production, he wrote, requires the contribution of both the capital of the owner and the labor of the worker. Consequently, both must share equitably in the economic benefits of production: "Wealth must be so distributed among the various individuals and classes of society that the common good of all is thereby promoted" (*QA*, no. 57). In a ringing condemnation, Pius declared that this fundamental principle of distribution is violated by the current distribution of wealth in the industrialized nations of Europe: "The immense number of propertyless wage-earners on the one hand, and the superabundant riches of the fortunate few on the other hand, is an unanswerable argument that the earthly goods so abundantly produced in this age of industrialism are far from being rightly distributed and equitably shared among the various classes of men" (*QA*, no. 60).

The solution Pius proposes for eradicating these unjust inequalities is the "just wage": the worker must be paid a salary sufficient to enable him to acquire some property for himself and to support his family (*QA*, nos. 63-65, 71). In fact, Pius writes in a remarkably modern proposal, it is "advisable" that employees should make workers "sharers of some sort in the ownership, or the management, or the profits" of the firm (*QA*, no. 65). Wage policies should not only take into account the health of the employer's business but should also be set at levels that will not generate unemployment but will "offer the greatest number of opportunities of employment and of securing a suitable livelihood for workers" (*QA*, no. 74). Thus Pius, unlike Leo, recognized that specific structural changes were required by justice and did not merely urge that the wealthy help the powerless out of "charity" while the poor should pray for patience. Nevertheless, he pointedly refrained from suggesting that redistributive programs were morally legitimate.

It was John XXIII in *Mater et Magistra* who first explicitly and directly addressed the moral legitimacy of dealing with inequality through a legally mandated redistribution of wealth. Like earlier popes, John recognized the terrible inequalities that pervaded much of the world: "In some nations, the wealth and conspicuous consumption of a few stand out, and are in open and bold contrast with the lot of the needy" (*MM*, no. 69; see also no. 68). The eradication of such inequalities, his encyclical holds, is a critically important task—more important than increasing productivity, since "the economic prosperity of any people is to be assessed not so much from the sum total of goods and wealth possessed as from the distribution of goods according to norms of justice" (*MM*, no. 74). Like Pius XI, Pope John advocated enforcement of a "just wage," arguing that wages should not be set by the "unregulated competition" of markets where "the more powerful" can impose their arbitrary will (*MM*, no. 71). But John then went on to advocate government redistribution of wealth. The encyclical is clear and emphatic on this point: "It often happens that citizens of the same country enjoy different degrees of wealth and social advancement ... where such is the case, justice and equity demand that the government make efforts either to remove or to minimize imbalances of this sort"(*MM*, no. 150). The encyclical proposes, furthermore, that inequalities can be tempered by the government through social welfare programs: "Since social security and insurance can help appreciably in distributing national income among the citizens according to justice and equity, these systems can be regarded as means whereby inequalities among various classes of citizens are reduced" (*MM*, no. 136). Thus, in a radical departure from previous encyclicals, *Mater et Magistra* advocated that government, not the "charity" of private individuals, should serve as the primary vehicle for dealing with problems of poverty and inequality.

In another important departure from traditional teaching, *Mater et Magistra* dealt with a newly recognized aspect of inequality. Previous social encyclicals had addressed poverty only as it occurred among citizens of the same country. Pope John XXIII forced the church to face the phenomenon of international poverty: the growing gap between the very rich nations and the very poor ones. This issue, he declared, was the "most pressing question of our day" (*MM*, no. 157). In line with the optimistic view of industrialization that characterizes the encyclical as a whole, Pope John claimed that "the underlying causes of poverty and hunger . . . are to be found in the primitive state of the economy" (*MM*, no. 163). Thus, in another significant departure from earlier popes, John XXIII does not blame industrialization for the problem of poverty; instead, he sees it as the solution to the problem. The lack of industrialization in developing countries meant that the richer nations had a "duty to aid poorer countries" by providing them with development aid that was "calculated to increase production" (*MM*, no. 165).

Thus, too, on the subject of inequality *Gaudium et Spes* summarizes the final stages of the church's evolutionary drift away from the view of Leo XIII that inequalities are "not disadvantageous" and toward the view that under certain conditions inequalities are unjust. Economic inequalities are unjust when large numbers of people lack the basic necessities of life while others squander their wealth. Such inequalities should be dealt with through economic development and through redistributive mechanisms enforced by the legal authority of government. *Gaudium et Spes* also states the fundamental stance the church has gradually adopted toward the poor: it must have special concern for the economically poorest groups, especially for the destitute members of the underdeveloped parts of the world, a concern which must go beyond paternalistic pleas to the rich to the extent of demanding a greater empowerment of the poor.

3. Economic Ideologies. An economic ideology is a set of normative beliefs concerning the value of one "economic system" versus another. Modern economic ideologies are thus primarily concerned with the appropriate functions of the two major institutions that constitute contemporary economies: markets and government. Traditionally, economic ideologies are categorized as "socialist" when they limit the role of markets and enlarge that of government by advocating government control of the means of production, government regulation of economic transactions, and government provision of social services. Ideologies are classified as "capitalist" or "laissez-faire" (or, in European nations, as "liberal") when they limit the role of government and enlarge that of markets by urging private ownership of the means of production, government exclusion from all economic exchanges, and the limitation of government to protecting citizens and their property from injury. What kind of an economic ideology does *Gaudium et Spes* advocate?

Gaudium et Spes is pragmatically open to both socialist and capitalist forms of economic arrangements, implying only that a mixed economy embodying socialist institutions—such as "public ownership" of the means of production (*GS*, no. 71) and various social programs (*GS*, no. 69)—as well as more traditional capitalist institutions, would be acceptable. The economy should not be abandoned wholly to "follow a kind of automatic course resulting from the economic activity of individuals," as would be true in a pure capitalism, "nor must it be entrusted solely to the authority of government," as pure socialism would advocate (*GS*, no. 65). *Gaudium et Spes* thus rejects both pure capitalist ideologies which "obstruct necessary reform in the name of a false liberty" and pure socialist ideologies "which subordinate the basic rights of individual persons and groups to the collective organization of production" (*GS*, no. 65).

Earlier church teachings on economic ideologies were not so pragmatic as *Gaudium et Spes*. Pope Leo XIII's *Rerum Novarum*, in particular, is quite antagonistic to socialist views and much more comfortable with capitalism. Socialism is explicitly rejected on two grounds: because it does away with the "natural right" of private ownership and because it attempts to eradicate "legitimate inequalities" (*RN*, nos. 12, 14). Moreover, Leo agrees with the position of John Locke that (as Leo puts it) "the chief thing to be secured [by government] is the safeguarding, by legal enactment and policy, of private property" (*RN*, no. 30).[14] This laissez-faire view of government, of course, implies that government has no business engaging in activities that redistribute wealth or that eradicate inequalities. Nevertheless, Leo cautiously suggests expanding the economic role of government in one crucial direction. He proposes that government might regulate employment and work contracts to ensure that workers are not "ground down with excessive labor" (*RN*, no. 33), to outlaw child labor (*RN*, no. 33), and to ensure that wages are "enough to support the wage-earner in reasonable and frugal comfort" (*RN*, no. 34). However, he cautions, these interventions in the economy should be secured by the activities of unions in order to prevent "undue interference on the part of the State" (*RN*, no. 34). Thus, even in the area of worker protection, the central concern of his encyclical, Leo hesitates to advocate remedies that might smack of a socialist ideology, or which might expand the role of government beyond its "chief" purpose of "safeguarding private property."

Pius XI, forty years later, in his encyclical *Quadragesimo Anno*, was even harsher in his rejection of socialism: "We pronounce as follows:

whether socialism be considered as a doctrine, or as a historical fact, or as a movement, if it really remain socialism, it cannot be brought into harmony with the dogmas of the Catholic Church . . . No one can at the same time be a sincere Catholic and a true socialist" (*QA*, nos. 117, 120). On the other hand, Pius writes that capitalism is "not to be condemned for itself" (*QA*, no. 101).

But Pius recognized two crucial structural inadequacies of capitalism as it had developed by his time. The first is the concentration of power and wealth in the hands of a few, and the second is the unbridled economic competition which created this concentration. "In our days," he wrote, "wealth is accumulated and immense power and despotic economic domination is concentrated in the hands of a few . . . This accumulation of power, the characteristic note of the modern economic order, is a natural result of limitless free competition" (*QA*, nos. 105, 107). In an important theoretical expansion of the economic role of government, Pius declared that government has the duty of imposing limits on market competition and economic concentration (*QA*, no. 110).

In an even more significant expansion of the function of government, Pius advocated government provision of certain social services formerly provided by private organizations. Pius XI agreed with Leo that "It is an injustice for a larger and higher organization to arrogate to itself functions which can be performed efficiently by smaller and lower bodies" (*QA*, no. 79).[15] But he explicitly recognized that industrialization had destroyed many "smaller associations" that formerly could secure various aspects of the common good, now "leaving only individuals and the state." The state must therefore take over many of the functions of smaller associations. In particular, Pius suggested, the state can establish "syndical and corporate organizations" (*QA*, nos. 91-95) of employers and employees, akin to unions to protect workers (*QA*, nos. 82-83). Thus Pius, unlike Leo, was much more willing to recognize the role of government in ameliorating the structural inadequacies of capitalism and the necessity of having the state take over many of the socioeconomic functions formerly carried out by smaller private associations.

Pope John XXIII went much further than Pius in advocating an expansion of the economic role of government along the lines of socialist ideology. In an astonishing departure from every earlier social encyclical, his *Mater et Magistra*, published in 1961, never once condemns socialism.[16] Taken as a whole, in fact, *Mater et Magistra* can be read as a *de facto* approval of the economic programs advocated by moderate socialist ideologues. John's approval of such programs is not surprising since by the time he wrote, Western governments had accepted the tenets of Keynesian economics and had adopted a number of fiscal, budgetary, and regulatory mechanisms that kept unemployment at acceptable levels and moderated the periodic blows dealt by the boom-and-bust cycles of capitalism. As a consequence, the "welfare state," with its moderating panoply of social insurance programs, large systems of public education, and extensive bureaucracies, had become a standard feature of Western societies and had adopted virtually every measure that socialists of an earlier era had advocated.

In keeping with this *de facto* expansion of government, *Mater et Magistra* asserts that it is entirely legitimate for government to take an active role in the economy in regulating what pertains to production as well as to distribution (*MM*, nos. 52-54). Pope John advocates, first, an array of social services, including government support of "highway construction, transport services, marketing facilities, pure drinking water, housing, medical services, elementary, trade, and professional schools" (*MM*, no. 127); regulating "taxes and duties, credit, insurance, prices" (*MM*, no. 131); "the establishment of banks" (*MM*, no. 134); and the provision of "social security and insurance" (*MM*, no. 136). Second, the government is to adopt Keynesian fiscal, budgetary, and monetary policies "to keep fluctuations in the economy within bounds, and to provide effective measures for avoiding mass unemployment" (*MM*, no. 54). Third, the government is to ensure that the economy is not entirely taken over by large enterprises by "fostering" enterprises that are "small and medium-sized" (*MM*, no. 84). Fourth, government ownership of the means of production is to be seen as entirely legitimate (*MM*, no. 116).

In addition to praising the institutions advocated by moderate socialist ideologies, *Mater et Magistra* also proposed two important economic principles. The first is that "Whatever be the economic system, it [must] allow and facilitate for every individual the opportunity to engage in productive activity" (*MM*, no. 55). Here, John in effect advances beyond the paternalism of earlier encyclicals which conceived the poor as passive recipients of the "charity" of the rich. In John's view, economic institutions must enable each person to become active in providing for his own needs.

The second significant economic principle is that "if the organization and structure of economic life be such that the human dignity of workers is compromised, or their sense of responsibility is weakened, or their freedom of action is removed, then we judge such an economic order to be unjust, even though it produces a vast amount of goods [and even though its] distribution conforms to the norms of justice and equity" (*MM*, no. 83). This crucial principle implies, as the encyclical points out, that employees should "have a say in . . . the running and development of the enterprise" in which they work (*MM*, no. 92; see also, no. 91). This is a startling claim. In effect, it states that workers' control of their own work lives is a matter of justice. John in fact later extends the principle to apply also to worker participation in national economic planning (*MM*, no. 99).

Thus, *Gaudium et Spes*, in its pragmatic openness to socialist and capitalist institutions, accurately reflected the development of Catholic economic teaching as it moved away from an ideological tradition that was paternalistic, that tended to advocate free market mechanisms, and that imposed stringent limits on government economic activity. In *Gaudium et Spes*, as in later Catholic social teaching, neither socialism nor capitalism is accepted as an "official" ideology. Instead, both socialist and capitalist institutions are advocated in a pragmatic mix that takes into account the social world created by industrialization and the need to allow workers a real voice in the shaping of economic institutions.

THE INFLUENCE OF "GAUDIUM ET SPES" ON LATER SOCIOECONOMIC CHURCH TEACHINGS

Gaudium et Spes did more than merely encapsulate the best of seventy-five years of an evolving Catholic social-economic tradition. It also contained in embryo some of the fundamental ideas that later church documents would adopt and expand. In the remainder of this essay I sketch in broad strokes some of the major church pronouncements that were influenced directly or indirectly by the ideas and approaches of *Gaudium et Spes*, beginning with what I call the "liberationist" documents written in the first decade after the Council. I then discuss what the recent encyclical *Laborem Exercens* also owes to *Gaudium et Spes*. Finally, in the concluding section, I note the extent to which *Gaudium et Spes* continues to influence contemporary socio-economic documents, examining particularly its influence on the recent letter of the American bishops, *Catholic Social Teaching and the U.S. Economy*.

1. The Liberationist Documents. The most significant contribution of *Gaudium et Spes* was the impetus it gave to the liberationist themes that emerged in church documents during the late sixties and early seventies. Although *Gaudium et Spes* itself cannot be classified as liberationist, it nevertheless contained the foundations for the liberationist themes that emerged in the encyclicals of Pope Paul VI, in the so-called "Medellín" documents of the Latin American bishops, and in the document *Justice in the World*, issued by the 1971 Synod of Bishops.

The "liberationist" approach to economic issues is characterized by its emphasis on the *reform of sinful social structures* rather than on *conversion of the sinful individual.* Perhaps with the exception of the encyclicals of John XXIII, all pre-Vatican II church teaching on economic matters focused almost exclusively on individual virtue and the duties of the individual—what wealthy Christians owe to the poor, for example, or what Christian employers owe their workers. This earlier tradition assumed that the underlying economic and social system should remain unchanged and that so long as individuals fulfill the duties imposed by the system, justice will be served. Justice is thus seen as essentially an individual matter and the religious person is the one who fulfills his or her personal duties within the system.

Although *Gaudium et Spes* continued the tradition of urging individual conversion, it also recognized—cautiously, of course, but to an extent the church had never before articulated—that economic life and economic justice are essentially dependent on the social and economic structures within which individuals live and develop, and that no important changes will take place unless these structures themselves are altered and reformed. *Gaudium et Spes* holds that social structures shape human personalities so that "men are often diverted from doing good and spurred toward evil by the social circumstances in which they live and are immersed from their birth" (*GS*, no. 25). Because the "structure of affairs" is so often "flawed by the consequences of sin" (*GS*, no. 25), the "social order requires constant improvement," a moral requirement that arises from the fact that all social structures are "subordinate" to man "and not contrariwise, as the Lord indicated when he said that the Sabbath was made for man and not man for the Sabbath" (*GS*, no. 26).[17] Edging close to advocating radical structural change, the Council noted that "an improvement in attitudes and widespread changes in society will have to take place" if the "social order" is to achieve its purpose of respecting the dignity and rights of all human beings (*GS*, no. 26). And at one point, as I indicated earlier, the bishops even hint that those who are left hungry by society's property institutions have a "right" to take by force what they need from "the riches" of those who have profited from those institutions (*GS*, no. 69).

This recognition of *social structures* in *Gaudium et Spes*, in spite of its tentative aspects, was crucial for the church. For once it is recognized that social structures themselves—and not merely the selfishness of unvirtuous individuals—can be the cause of injustice, a number of changes must follow. First and most important, working for structural reform will come to be seen as a form of religious activity because such reforms are the work of justice and justice is a constituent of the religiously upright life. Second, the metaphor of "liberation" will emerge as a natural expression of the result of structural reform because unjust structures are typically seen as surrounding constraints which impose burdens. Third, a "preferential option for the poor" will naturally emerge as a fundamental stance of the church because the economically poor constitute the class which by definition is at the lowest levels of the economic system and thus they are seen as the "victims" of the "injustice" of the system. Fourth, a tendency to adopt Marxist analysis and Marxist categories will emerge because Marxism provides the best developed and most sophisticated model for analyzing structural change from a normative point of view. Fifth, and related to the tendency to adopt Marxist analysis, there will emerge a tendency to critique the capitalist elements of the economy and a recognition of the need to assess the possibility of violent revolutionary changes of capitalist structures.

All of these tendencies, in fact, developed and emerged in the church's teaching during the decade following the Council, as the church assimilated the focus on structure that *Gaudium et Spes* initiated and thereby legitimized. The emergence of these themes begins with Pope Paul VI's encyclical *Populorum Progressio*. *Populorum Progressio* focused bluntly on the structural causes that lie at the roots of Third World underdevelopment and of oppressive social structures (*PP*, nos. 7, 57-61). The encyclical calls for radical changes of these structures: "Development demands bold transformations, innovations that go deep" (*PP*, no. 32). So urgent and so deep are the required transformations that "recourse to violence as a means to right these wrongs to human dignity, is a grave temptation" (*PP*, no. 30). Three times Paul VI warns that violent revolutionary change is inevitable if the international economy is not restructured (*PP*, nos. 30, 49, 76). Although revolutionary uprisings in general must be condemned because they usually produce "greater misery" and "injustice" than the situation they would rectify, nevertheless the exception is "where there is manifest, long-standing tyranny which would do great damage to fundamental personal rights and dangerous harm to the common good of the country" (*PP*, no. 31).

Populorum Progressio also issued repeated condemnations of the core aspects of capitalism. In a sweeping statement Paul VI condemns "unchecked liberalism" as a "system" which "considers profit as the key motive for economic progress, competition as the supreme law of economics, and private ownership of the means of production as an absolute right that has no limits and carries no corresponding social obligation" (*PP*, no. 26). In international relations he condemns "the fundamental principle of liberalism" that prices must be set by "free" markets, because "an economy of exchange can no longer be based solely on the law of free competition, a law which, in its turn, too often creates an economic dictatorship" (*PP*, no. 58). He points out that "individual initiative alone and the mere free play of competition could never assure successful development" (*PP*, no. 33) since this risks "increasing still more the wealth of the rich and the dominion of the strong, while leaving the poor in their misery and adding to the servitude of the oppressed" (*PP*, no. 33).

Significantly, *Populorum Progressio* did not condemn collaborating in "social action" with Marxist groups "based upon a materialistic and atheistic philosophy," so long as Christian values can be "safeguarded" (*PP*, no. 39). This was especially significant in view of Paul VI's 1971 encyclical, *Octogesima Adveniens*. There, in a startling reversal of previous papal teaching (particularly *Quadragesimo Anno*), Paul VI declared that Catholicism and socialism were not opposed! Distinguishing between socialism that is based on a worldview that denies God and socialism that remains open to the reality of God, the encyclical acknowledged the possibility of a Christian socialism (*OA*, no. 31). More radically, the encyclical also distinguished various kinds of Marxism: Marxism as a materialist philosophy of history, Marxism as a political regime, and Marxism as a kind of social analysis. This last kind of Marxism, although fraught with risk, is nevertheless not condemned as antithetical to Christianity (*OA*, nos. 32-42).

In 1968 the Conference of Latin American Bishops, meeting in Medellín, Colombia issued four statements on "Justice," "Peace," "Family," and "Poverty in the Church," which carried even further the liberationist themes that had emerged from the incipient structural focus of *Gaudium et Spes*. The Medellín documents forthrightly proclaim the central tenets of the liberationist approach. They argue that faith and justice are essentially related (J, no. 5), that the church must adopt a "preferential option for the poor" (PC, no. 9), and that justice must be sought largely through radical structural reform and not merely through individual conversion (J, no. 3). The Medellín documents, in fact, are the first to use the word "liberation" repeatedly in a favorable sense, asserting that Christ's mission was to "liberate all men from the slavery to which sin has subjected them: hunger, misery, oppression and ignorance, in a word, that injustice and hatred which have their origin in human selfishness" (J, no. 3; see also J, no. 11; PC, nos. 2, 7). Such liberation requires "new and reformed structures" as well as "the conversion of men" (J, no. 3). Workers must be liberated from their "dependence on inhuman economic systems and institutions: a situation which, for many of them, borders on slavery" (J, no. 11). Echoing *Gaudium et Spes*, the Medellín documents held that the situation of rural peasants and Indians must be uplifted through "an authentic and urgent reform of agrarian structures and policies ... [which] goes beyond a simple distribution of land" (J, no. 14). Political authority must be exercised "for the common good" and not to "favor privileged groups" (J, no. 16). In view of "a situation of injustice that can be called institutionalized violence" (P, no. 16), the bishops observe that many now "put their hopes in violence" (P, no. 19). Repeating the views of *Populorum Progressio*, they write: "Revolutionary insurrection can be legitimate in the case of evident and prolonged 'tyranny that seriously works against the fundamental rights of man, and which damages the common good of the country', whether it proceeds from one person or from clearly unjust structures" (P, no. 19). Nevertheless, since armed revolution generally generates greater injustices and evils than it prevents, it must be generally condemned (P, no. 19).

Perhaps, however, the most significant point which the Medellín documents drew from *Gaudium et Spes* is the suggestion that the church must identify with the "hopes, griefs and anxieties ... especially of those who are poor" (*GS*, no. 1). The Medellín documents contain a prolonged discussion of the extent to which the church must adopt a stance that "effectively gives preference to the poorest and most needy sectors" of society (PC, no. 9). The documents do not merely urge their listeners to give aid to the poor. They urge them instead to identify with the poor by adopting their way of looking at the world, by joining them in their struggles against injustice, and by speaking on behalf of the poor: "Solidarity means that we make ours their problems and their struggles, that we know how to speak with them" (PC, no. 10). The church must "share the lot of the poor" by assuming "voluntarily and lovingly the conditions of the needy of this world in order to bear witness to the evil which it represents" (PC, no. 4). The church must ensure that it does not allow itself to become "allied with the rich" (PC, no. 2) and it must "not listen to parties interested in distorting the work" (PC, no. 11) of those who struggle on behalf of the poor.

But by far the most influential of the church's modern statements on structural injustice—and the document that was most heavily influenced by the experience of Vatican II—was *Justice in the World*, issued in 1971 by the Synod of Bishops meeting in Rome from all over the world. Vatican II was fresh in their minds and the bishops were eager to expand on the themes of *Gaudium et Spes*, in particular on the church's role in the socioeconomic world. Taking their lead from *Gaudium et Spes*, the bishops announced in the opening paragraphs that their aim was to discern "the signs of the times" (JW, no. 2) and to listen "to the cry of those who suffer violence and are oppressed by unjust systems and structures" (JW, no. 5). Their basic principles are to be drawn from the church's social teachings, especially from *Gaudium et Spes*, because "as never before, the church has, through the Second Vatican Council's constitution *Gaudium et Spes*, better understood the situation in the modern world, in which the Christian works out his salvation by deeds of justice" (JW, no. 56).

Justice in the World was shot through and through with the liberationist view that injustice is fundamentally a structural issue deriving from a worldwide "network of domination, oppression and abuses . . . unjust systems and structures" (JW, nos. 3, 5). The work of the church is "the liberation of people from every oppressive condition" and action for justice is "a constitutive dimension of the Church's proclamation of the Gospel" (JW, no. 6). Structural injustices, the bishops write, cannot be eradicated by a simple conversion of individuals. For there are "objective obstacles which social structures place in the way of conversion of hearts, or even of the realization of the ideal of charity" (JW, no. 16). Because social structures influence the way in which individuals perceive and deal with the world, they must be changed.

Thus, the structuralist analyses that were incipient in *Gaudium et Spes* had by 1971 developed all of the tendencies that one would have expected from such an approach. Although *Gaudium et Spes* itself was heavily biased toward an older, more individualistic, and Westernized form of liberalism, it contained the foundations of the radical liberationist views that in fact emerged during the late sixties and seventies.

2. Laborem Exercens.   The influence of *Gaudium et Spes* was not limited to the liberationist documents. A careful reading shows that *Gaudium et Spes* also contained the foundations of the main themes of the socioeconomic teachings of Pope John Paul II, as enunciated in his 1981 encyclical *Laborem Exercens*. Because of the contemporary importance of John Paul's encyclical, it is profitable to identify the ideas in *Gaudium et Spes* that play a pivotal role in the argument of *Laborem Exercens*.

Gaudium et Spes urged two basic principles as the foundation of all economic activity. The first is the principle that "labor" is "superior" to "the other elements of economic life," that is, to capital (*GS*, no. 67). For labor is "immediately" related to the person, and it is through labor that the person becomes "a partner in the work of bringing God's creation to perfection" (*GS*, no. 67). Capital assets, on the other hand, "have only the nature of tools" (*GS*, no. 67). Two implications are drawn from this principle of the priority of labor over capital: first, that a just economic system must ensure that every citizen finds "opportunities for adequate employment" with "payment" sufficient for the worker to lead "life worthily ... [with] his dependents" (*GS*, no. 67); and second, that "any way of organizing and directing" labor that makes the worker a "slave" or that does not allow workers to "develop their own abilities and personalities through the work they perform" is likewise wrong and cannot be justified "by so-called economic laws" (*GS*, no. 67).

The second fundamental economic principle urged by *Gaudium et Spes* was the principle that workers must participate in the operation of the economic institutions which affect them. For only such participation respects workers as "free and independent human beings created in the image of God" (*GS*, no. 68). From this principle *Gaudium et Spes* drew three conclusions. First, workers must participate in running their firms and "must have a share also in controlling" the public institutions which affect their economic activities (*GS*, no. 68).[18] Second, workers must be able to form and control unions through which they can secure an effective voice in the economic decisions which affect them (*GS*, no. 68). Third, "the largest number of people" must have an active share in directing a nation's economic development, which must not be left solely to the judgment "of a few men or groups possessing excessive economic power, or of the political community alone, or of certain especially powerful nations" (*GS*, no. 65).

These important principles of *Gaudium et Spes* provided the foundations of Pope John Paul's encyclical *Laborem Exercens*. A fundamental assertion of the encyclical, for example, is the principle of the "priority of labor over capital" (*LE*, no. 12). The encyclical argues that labor should not be treated as a commodity that is bought and sold in markets (*LE*, no. 7). Echoing *Gaudium et Spes*, it asserts that capital is merely "a collection of things" and so it is "only a mere instrument subordinate to human labor" (*LE*, no. 12). Like *Gaudium et Spes*, the encyclical derives from the priority of labor over capital the conclusion that all men and women have a right to work (*LE*, no. 18), to a family wage (*LE*, no. 19), to "rest" (*LE*, no. 19), and to decent working conditions (*LE*, no. 19).

Laborem Exercens also adopts and elaborates the notion drawn from *Gaudium et Spes* that through one's work, a person becomes a "co-creator" with God and helps to bring "creation to perfection" (*GS*, no. 67). Work, according to John Paul, is a process through which man "participates" in God's creativity: "Man, created in the image of God, shares by his work in the activity of the Creator ... , man in a sense continues to develop that activity and perfects it as he advances further and further in the discovery of the resources and values contained in the whole of creation" (*LE*, no. 25). Thus, labor is a participation in God's own activity, the process in which we become like God as we transform the world of nature.

Also fundamental to *Laborem Exercens* is the notion that respect for the dignity and freedom of workers implies that they have a right to participate in the economic decisions that affect them. *Laborem Exercens*, in fact, bases its strong condemnations of capitalism on this idea when it asserts that "the position of 'rigid' capitalism continues to remain unacceptable, namely the position that defends the exclusive right to private ownership of the means of production as an untouchable 'dogma' of economic life" (*LE*, no. 14). The dignity and freedom of workers, the encyclical argues, imply that the means of production must be "socialized" by ensuring that workers become "owners" of their society's capital (*LE*, no. 14). The worker must become a "sharer in responsibility" for the use of capital (*LE*, no. 15).

Laborem Exercens also developed and deepened the structuralist themes of *Gaudium et Spes* by invoking the notion of an "indirect employer." The encyclical defines the "indirect employer" as all those structural elements "other than the [individual] direct employer, that exercise a determining influence on the shaping both of the work contract and, consequently, of just or unjust relationships in the field of human labor" (*LE*, no. 16). These structural elements "determine" the "whole socioeconomic system" and occasion "various forms of exploitation or injustice" because of the influence they have on individuals immersed in the system (*LE*, no. 17). These structural conditions must be reshaped "both on the level of the individual society and state within the whole of the world economic policy and of the systems of international relationships that derive from it," if the objective rights of workers are to be attained (*LE*, no. 17).

CONCLUSION: THE CONTINUING INFLUENCE OF "GAUDIUM ET SPES"

There is no doubt, then, that *Gaudium et Spes* has exerted an important and crucial influence on the shape of Catholic socioeconomic teaching. Its influence still continues to be felt, most recently in the draft of the American Catholic bishops' pastoral letter, *Catholic Social Teaching and the U.S. Economy.*

Gaudium et Spes, as I mentioned, laid down as a basic principle that workers must be able to participate actively in the economic life of the community because only such participation will respect workers as "free and independent human beings created in the image of God" (*GS*, no. 68). This norm of active participation is incorporated into the draft of the American bishops' letter as its fundamental value. The second draft in fact argues that a community is unjust unless it provides "minimum levels of participation in the life of the human community for all persons" (*CST*, no. 81). The letter then links this requirement to another theme of *Gaudium et Spes*: the need to identify with the poor. The American bishops write that a "preferential option for the poor" must serve as a fundamental principle to guide all their discussion: "The fundamental moral criterion for all economic decisions, policies, and institutions is this: They must be at the service of *all people, especially the poor*" (*CST*, no. 28).

The American bishops have also continued to emphasize the structuralist approach that *Gaudium et Spes* brought into the Catholic tradition. In lengthy discussions of American poverty and of the international economy, for example, the bishops focus critically on the economic arrangements that effectively bar the disadvantaged from participating actively in economic life and from sharing in the benefits of society. Interestingly enough, however, the American bishops shy away from advocating radical structural reforms. Instead, they merely urge "reorganizing" reforms *within* the economic systems that are already in place (*CST*, no. 253).

Much more radical in tone was another pastoral document that was also influenced by the notions that *Gaudium et Spes* introduced into Catholic social teaching: the 1983 pastoral letter of the Canadian Catholic Conference of Bishops, entitled *Ethical Reflections on the Current Economic Crisis*. The letter of the Canadian bishops is a radical condemnation of the "moral disorder" inherent in "present economic realities" (*ER*, p. 523). The bishops base their condemnation on two principles, both of which, I have argued, have their modern church roots in *Gaudium et Spes*. The first is "the preferential option for the poor" and the second is the "priority of labor over capital."[19]

But unlike the American bishops, whose draft deliberately refrains from suggesting any need for radical structural reforms, the Canadian bishops claim that the world is presently undergoing a dangerous "structural crisis in the international system of capitalism" (*ER*, p. 524). This structural crisis in turn creates an immoral situation in which the accumulation of capital takes priority over the needs of those who labor and the needs of those who are poor. What is needed is a "fundamental re-ordering of the basic values and priorities of economic development" that will place priority "on the value of human labor and an equitable distribution of wealth and power among people and regions" (*ER*, p. 526). The document calls on people to "develop alternatives to the dominant economic model that governs our society" (*ER*, p. 526) and urges Christians to "identify with the victims of injustice, by analyzing the dominant attitudes and structures that cause human suffering and by actively supporting the poor and oppressed in their struggles to transform society" (*ER*, p. 523). Thus, the Canadian bishops draw truly radical structural conclusions from the two principles that orginate in *Gaudium et Spes*.[20]

The themes that emerged in *Gaudium et Spes*, then, have continued to influence ecclesiastical discussions of economic justice. By comparison, *Gaudium et Spes* appears more radical than some of the progeny it continues to spawn (such as the second draft of the American bishops' letter on the economy), but also seems extremely conservative when compared to other of its progeny (such as the Canadian bishops' letter). This is not surprising, since *Gaudium et Spes* retained intact large portions of traditional church teaching side by side with the new structuralist approaches it embryonically developed. This two-sided approach is at once the greatest strength and the greatest weakness of *Gaudium et Spes*. It is a strength because it enabled the bishops of Vatican II to legitimize their new approaches by embedding them in a document that simultaneously appeals to a more traditional—albeit evolving—understanding of church economic teachings. But it is a weakness because it left unresolved the problem of whether the church would ultimately look back toward the more individualistic teachings of the past—epitomized in the Lockean views of Leo XIII's 1891 *Rerum Novarum*—or forward toward the radical structuralist approaches of the future—most clearly embodied in the approaches of liberation theology. This fundamental ambiguity is the reason why, almost twenty years later, the influence of *Gaudium et Spes* can be discerned in such fundamentally different documents as the more conservative draft of the American bishops' pastoral letter and the more radical letter of the Canadian bishops. And because of this ambiguity, it is difficult to predict the kind of influence *Gaudium et Spes* will have on future church teaching. Indeed, this unresolved tension between conservative and radical approaches to the world lies at the heart of the current crisis that affects all contemporary Catholic theology. It is part of the legacy bequeathed to us by Vatican II.

NOTES

1. All references to church documents are given in the text in abbreviated form, using the numbering—unless otherwise noted below—of the English translation in Joseph Gremillion, ed., *The Gospel of Peace and Justice* (Maryknoll,

N.Y.: Orbis Books, 1976). The following abbreviations are used (listed in the order in which they occur in the text): *GS: Gaudium et Spes;* J: Medellín document on "Justice"; *RN: Rerum Novarum,* in Gerald C. Treacy, ed., *Five Great Encyclicals* (New York: Paulist Press, 1939); *QA: Quadragesimo Anno,* in *Five Great Encyclicals; MM: Mater et Magistra; PP: Populorum Progressio; OA: Octogesima Adveniens;* P: Medellín document on "Peace"; F: Medellín document on "Family"; PC: Medellín document on "Poverty in the Church"; *JW: Justice in the World; LE: Laborem Exercens,* in *Origins,* vol. 11, no. 15 (September 24, 1981): 225-44; *CST: Catholic Social Teaching and the U.S. Economy,* second draft (Washington, D.C.: United States Catholic Conference, 1985); *ER: Ethical Reflections on the Economic Crisis,* published under the title "Alternatives to Present Economic Structures," in *Origins,* vol. 12, no. 33 (January 27, 1983), 521-27.

2. For a brief history of this notion, see David Hollenbach, *Claims in Conflict* (New York: Paulist Press, 1979), especially chapters 2 and 3.

3. "Message of the Fathers of the Council to All Mankind," in Mario Von Galli, ed., *The Council and the Future* (New York: McGraw-Hill, 1966), 109-10.

4. Charles Moeller, "History of the Constitution," in Herbert Vorgrimler, ed., *Commentary on the Documents of Vatican II,* vol. V (New York: Herder and Herder, 1969), 11.

5. This optimistic view, of course, is rooted in the social encyclicals of John XXIII. Not surprisingly, several bishops at the Council objected to the document's orientation, saying that it was "too Western in its approach and talked about urbanization and industrialization while the majority of the world's populations still live in rural areas, and that it speaks only of capitalism in dealing with economic and social life." Floyd Anderson, ed., *Council Daybook,* vol. III (Washington, D.C.: National Catholic Welfare Conference, 1966), 49.

6. That tradition is nicely summarized in Donal Dorr, *Option for the Poor: A Hundred Years of Vatican Social Teaching* (Maryknoll, N.Y.: Orbis Books, 1983).

7. See also Charles Avila, *Ownership: Early Christian Teaching* (Maryknoll, N.Y.: Orbis Books, 1983).

8. The doctrine was startling because it rejected the traditional view of St. Thomas Aquinas that a private property system of control is a social convention that *does not violate* the natural law (Aquinas, *Summa Theologica,* II-II, q. 66, a. ii, obj. 1) but can be justified on grounds of practical expediency (ibid., q. 66, a. ii), and replaces it with John Locke's view that private property is an inherent right that is *required* by the "law of nature" and which arises when a person "annexes" his own labor to what nature provides so that "he hath mixed his labour with, and joined to it something that is his own, and thereby makes it his property" (John Locke, *Two Treatises of Government,* book II, chapter 5, para. 27). Leo XIII adopted this Lockean reasoning in detail, arguing that private property rights are created when a laborer has so "altered and improved" property that his labor "becomes truly a part of it as to be in a great measure indistinguishable, inseparable from it" (*RN,* no. 8). The pope's view originated in the teachings of the Italian Jesuit Luigi Taparelli D'Azeglio, who attempted to graft the Lockean view onto the Scholastic tradition in his major two-volume work, *Saggio Teoretico di Diritto Naturale Appoggiato sul Fatto* (Palermo: 1840-1843). See John Coleman, "Development of Church Social Teaching," *Origins,* vol. 11, no. 3 (June 4, 1981).

Leo's 1891 encyclical based its private property teachings on what amounted to four arguments: man's ability to reason about his future gives him the right to own that which he produces to provide for his future needs; when man "cultivates" nature, it becomes "his" because he impresses his personality on it and makes his labor an "inseparable" part of it (the Lockean argument); private property is necessary to provide for the present and future needs of one's family; and private ownership prevents social "quarrelling, . . . confusion, and disorder," and provides incentives for the individual to "exert his talents or his industry" (*RN*, nos. 5-12).

9. St. Thomas Aquinas, *Summa Theologica*, II-II, q. 66, a. vii.

10. See St. Thomas Aquinas, *Summa Theologica*, II-II, q. 66, a. vii. Note that Aquinas, like Locke after him, distinguishes between two types of ownership. First, there is the general right of ownership over all things, which is conferred on all humanity in common. This right of common ownership is *required* by the natural law (ibid., q. 66, a. i). Second, there are the particular rights of ownership over particular things that a private property system gives to particular individuals. This "division" of humanity's common ownership is "not according to the natural law, but rather arose from human agreement which belongs to positive law" (ibid., II-II, q. 66, a. ii, obj. 1). Although a private property system is not "according to"—i.e., not required by—the natural law, nevertheless, "the ownership of possessions is not contrary to the natural law, but an addition thereto devised by human reason" (ibid.). See James L. Vizzard, S.J., *Who Shall Own the Land* (Des Moines, Iowa: National Catholic Rural Life Conference, n.d.).

11. Leo XIII made a point of deemphasizing the principle that property was to be used for the common good. Donal Dorr points out: "The pope's fear of socialism led him to modify an earlier draft of *Rerum Novarum* in which the right to private property had been subordinated to the wider principle that the goods of the earth are for the common good" (*Option for the Poor*, 48).

12. Leo had not only dismissed the "common use" of property in a single sentence, he had also stipulated that only one's "superfluous goods" had to be used for the good of others, and then only for the good of those "in need" (see *RN*, no. 19).

13. Perhaps to save appearances, however, the encyclical asserts that the "right to private property" still applies to the consumer goods of everyday life: "durable goods, homes, gardens."

14. See John Locke, *Two Treatises of Government*, book II, chapter 9, paras. 123, 124.

15. This is Pius's statement of the so-called "principle of subsidiarity" which future church writings would repeatedly invoke as the "Catholic" principle of limited government.

16. The absence of a condemnation of socialism is given added significance by the fact that two years later, in a remarkable passage in *Pacem in Terris*, Pope John XXIII states that "historical movements that have economic, social, cultural or political ends" and which once "originated . . . and still draw their inspiration" from "false philosophical teachings," could have undergone changes sufficiently "profound" that Catholics now legitimately may "work in

common" with them (nos. 159-60). The phrase "historical movements" here has commonly been interpreted as referring to European socialistic movements, and the passage as a whole as a cautious approval of the "liberalized" forms of socialism that had now entered into the political life of virtually every European nation. Thus, *Pacem in Terris* confirms that *Mater et Magistra* constitutes a clear turning away from the wholesale condemnation of all forms of socialism that was so prominent in earlier papal teaching.

17. The document also indicates the "pressing need to reform economic and social structures" on an international level at *GS*, no. 86.

18. This notion of participation has its roots in *Mater et Magistra* (see especially *MM*, nos. 91 and 92).

19. The Canadian bishops, however, fail to recognize *Gaudium et Spes* as the source of these principles. Instead, they claim that the "preferential option for the poor" has a biblical source, and they cite *Laborem Exercens* as the source of the "priority of labor over capital."

20. The radical nature of the Canadian bishops' proposals is even more obvious in a second document they issued, entitled *Ethical Choices and Political Challenges* (Ottawa, Ontario: Canadian Conference of Catholic Bishops, 1984). This later document was intended to amplify the meaning of the Canadian bishops' original proposals. In the second document, the bishops write that "the basic social contradiction of our times is the structural domination of capital and technology over people, over labor, over communities. What is required is a radical inversion of these structural relationships." Both documents caused considerable controversy among Canadian Catholics.

GORDON C. ZAHN

The Church's "New Attitude toward War"

Any attempt to evaluate or interpret *Gaudium et Spes* and its special contributions to Catholic teachings on war and peace should begin by acknowledging that the document stands in the shadow of Pope John XXIII's great encyclical, *Pacem in Terris*.[1] This is not to diminish its importance in its own right, however. If *Pacem in Terris* is the "breakthrough" or "watershed" document setting forth a new course for the church, *Gaudium et Spes'* contribution was to confirm and extend that document's influence and scope.

Singly and in tandem, both provide a comprehensive review of the challenges posed by modern society, with primary emphasis upon the rights and responsibilities of the person with respect to the political order. And most important of all, they share the objective so easily dismissed as "visionary." They deal with the total elimination of war not only as something necessary but, if Christians would fulfill the mission set before them by their church's Founder, something attainable in time.

The problem, as always, lies in the conditional clause. It is a simple matter to issue a call for practical actions rooted in deepened spiritual commitment. The fact that twenty years after John's successor to the Chair of Peter formally issued the Council's *Pastoral Constitution on the Church in the Modern World* little significant progress has been made toward that goal suggests that not enough has been done to make the message meaningful to those to whom the call was presumably addressed.

The challenge set before "all men of good will" by that holy man and echoed by the Council he brought into being is still there. *Pacem in Terris* begins with the careful development of the essential reciprocality between rights and duties, especially as they relate to the individual citizen, minorities, and the like. It is in Part III and its explanation of the state's responsibilities to other nations in solidarity with the whole of humankind that the discussion centers on issues of war, peace, and disarmament. This section is the heart of the encyclical as it sets forth principles and exhortations which, even today nearly a quarter-century later, carry almost revolutionary implications when taken in the context of more traditional teachings and interpretations. Though there is no indication that John himself departed from the "just war" formulations of Scholastic theology, some of the ideas advanced in this document would lead many to the conclusion that whatever relevance those formulations may once have held had long since vanished.

Basing his demands on justice, right reason and consideration for human dignity and life, he declared that nuclear weapons should be banned, that the arms race should cease, and that balanced and reciprocal steps should be taken to reduce existing stockpiles of destructive weaponry. In a world of jealously sovereign nations committed to maintaining the most favorable balance of power, he proposed a new principle by which peace and security were to be assured, namely, "that the true and solid peace of nations consists not in equality of arms *but in mutual trust alone.*"[2]

As is usually the case, there is a liberal sprinkling of footnote references to statements made by predecessors to demonstrate continuity in papal teaching and practice. The citations to Pius XI and Pius XII notwithstanding, one can be fairly sure that John must have been aware that his encyclical represented a major turning point and, indeed, was intended as such.

Gaudium et Spes, then, builds upon that new foundation and moves the design closer to completion. Its major contribution, perhaps, is the greater binding authority of formal conciliar teachings, but it does not stop at that. It develops themes that were general and abstract in the encyclical and gives them more direct "pastoral" expression. Thus, in echoing the stress placed upon the interdependence and unity of all peoples and nations, it makes more of a point of calling for an openness of political discourse and the avoidance of "narrowness of mind." This does not lessen the obligation to "generous and loyal devotion" to one's country but looks "simultaneously to the welfare of the whole human family, which is tied together by the manifold bonds linking races, peoples, and nations."[3]

Like John before them, the Council Fathers denounce the arms race, calling it a "treacherous trap for humanity"; like the American Roman Catholic bishops in their 1983 pastoral letter,[4] however, they waffle a bit and pull back from an outright rejection of nuclear deterrence as a means of maintaining "peace of a sort."

There is no hesitancy, though, in the Council's condemnation of area warfare, again linking that action with previous papal condemnations of "total war." This, predictably enough, was one of the more sensitive issues to be faced in the deliberations. Certain delegations—most notably, a sizeable number of our own bishops under the leadership of Cardinal Francis Spellman—made a determined stand against those who called for an outright condemnation of nuclear weapons.

As it turned out, the intended "compromise" actually went beyond that, extending the condemnation to *any* act of war "aimed indiscriminately at the destruction of entire cities or of extensive areas along with their population."[5] If some choose to find escape in the "aimed indiscriminately" wording, seeing it as something of a loophole permitting *unintended* indiscriminate destruction, the logic is not all that compelling. From my perspective as a kind of "unofficial *peritus*" for Archbishop T. D. Roberts, S.J.,[6] it was very evident that the Council Fathers were most serious in their deliberations on this issue and not inclined to seek or welcome so devious a solution—certainly not in connection with the only official condemnation they would issue.

Gaudium et Spes echoes John's call for the outlawing of war by international consent. There is, however, a tone of cautious restraint in making that objective contingent upon a "universal public authority" and dismissing unilateral disarmament as an option. As for the "mutual trust alone" principle, it is modified into a statement that "peace must be born of mutual trust between nations rather than imposed on them through fear of one another's weapons."[7] One may assume that these and other changes in emphasis are more a reflection of the deliberative process and not an attempt to weaken or nullify John XXIII's initiative.

THE COUNCIL AND CONSCIENTIOUS OBJECTION

On at least two points of great significance the Council went beyond *Pacem in Terris*. First was the appeal on behalf of "those who for reasons of conscience refuse to bear arms"[8] and second, the equally unprecedented praise for "those who renounce the use of violence in the vindication of their rights."[9] This judgment on my part is undoubtedly colored by my own interests then and since. My service to Archbishop Roberts related most directly to the issue of conscientious objection, and this gave me the opportunity to "lobby" a number of American, Canadian, and English bishops.[10] Though I am sure my efforts had little to do with the final outcome, it was still possible to draw personal gratification from the opportunity.

The conscientious objection provision was particularly important in that it provided a much needed reversal of what many interpreted as a definitive repudiation of that position by Pius XII in his 1956 Christmas Message. In that address Pius had declared that once a nation had determined its rights had been violated and that there was no other recourse short of war, the citizen could not appeal to his own conscience in refusing to perform the services required by law. It was something of an open secret that the statement had been inspired by the political controversy surrounding the reintroduction of conscription in West Germany, but its wording seemed to give it far wider application.

Although one might take the major thrust of *Pacem in Terris* to be a "prudential correction," if not open retraction, of the disputed statement, the closest it gets to addressing the issue directly is the general principle that "if civil authorities pass laws or command anything opposed to the moral order and consequently contrary to the will of God, neither the laws made nor the authorizations granted can be binding on the consciences of the citizens."[11] Coupled with the later assertion (perhaps the most widely debated statement in the entire encyclical) that "in an age such as ours which prides itself upon its atomic energy it is contrary to reason to hold that war is now a suitable way to restore rights which have been violated,"[12] this *could* be read as opening the door Pius had slammed shut. The linkage, however, is admittedly inferential.

Any affirmation of support for conscientious objection, however reluctant, represented a distinct change of course for the official church. Scholars like Stanley Windass, Jean-Michel Hornus, John Cadoux, and others[13] might speak of nonviolence and the rejection of military service as "the only stream of thought" in the early Christian centuries, but that "stream" had been choked off in the post-Constantinian church. The liturgical calendar might still honor young Maximilian (beheaded in A.D. 295 for refusing military service) and a Martin of Tours who, fifty years later, would risk a similar fate by declaring that as a Christian it was "not lawful" for him to fight, but the pacifism of primitive Christianity had been supplanted by the "just war" tradition introduced by Saints Ambrose and Augustine and perfected by Thomas Aquinas and the neo-Scholastics.

Neither *Pacem in Terris* nor *Gaudium et Spes* would depart from that tradition, though the Council did take one extremely important step that is not generally recognized. Whatever value the "just war" tradition might have (and as a pacifist I see it as having little or none), it was effectively negated by the application of the companion principle which gave the "presumption of justice" to legitimate authority in case of doubt. Since it would be difficult to establish the injustice of a ruler's decision in such matters beyond all doubt (not having access to all the facts, as the familiar objection has it), this principle served as something of a blank check for any and all sides in any given war.

Schema 13, the draft of what would become *Gaudium et Spes*, contained an explicit reaffirmation of that dubious principle. That it was dropped from the final version is highly significant for any discussion of the morality of war and peace. Unfortunately, since the schema was not a "public" document, few people are aware of the omission and its implications. The Christian may still take some justification in putting trust in his government, but he is no longer obliged to do so if he has good reason to believe that such government or its actions are unworthy of his trust.

From a situation in which (according to Cadoux) "no Christian ever thought of enlisting in the army after his conversion until the reign of Marcus Aurelius (A.D. 161-180) at the earliest,"[14] the church had moved first to a theory that justified some wars and ultimately to one which held that service in war was not only a virtuous act but one that could, in the event of battlefield death, open the gates of paradise.

In the strictest sense, of course, conscientious objection did not become an issue before the introduction by Napoleon of the "citizen army" and conscription to fill its ranks. This is not to say that previous wars had not found ways of compelling, or impressing, men into the service of the king or lesser nobles. Now, however, the way was opened to a more systematic selection of warriors drawn from the entire population.

The concept was broadened to the "nation in arms" which, in its turn, opened the way to the justification of "total war" (with our own Civil War serving as a kind of pilot project). Here, again, though history from the most ancient times records ghastly tales of the annihilation of the defeated, it took the combination of massive armies, more destructive (and impersonally destructive!) weapons, and a strategy fitting both to bring humankind into the era of "modern" warfare.

That the introduction of compulsory military service created a need to provide for those who because of moral or religious conviction would refuse was not immediately recognized by the war-making authorities. Our own nation, as we well know, received a steady influx of immigrants driven from their homeland on this account. In spite of this experience, our nation's record was not too good. The first sustained experiment in conscription during World War I (the earlier attempt in the Civil War was too spotty and was in part invalidated by the opportunity to "buy out" of military service) made no provision for conscientious objectors. Reaction to the pattern of shameful abuse (long sentences in military prisons, mistreatment sometimes resulting in death, and so forth) led to what appeared to be a more "democratic" arrangement during World War II but one which, in reality, fell far short of that ideal. If the overt injustices of World War I were avoided, they were replaced by a program of alternative service (for those who were recognized as valid conscientious objectors) which was a hidden and subtle, but still effective, suppression of a dissident minority.[15]

This was not, I hasten to add, a matter of concern to the Catholic church. The handful of Catholics who claimed deferment on grounds of conscience—and I was one of that number—knew they were ignored and, in effect, rejected by their spiritual leaders. Draft boards were assured by priests that, sincere though an applicant for such classification might be, he was not entitled to it for the simple reason that "a Catholic cannot be a conscientious objector." In at least one case the FBI investigator assigned to check the man's sincerity reported that he had received such answers from no fewer than *five* priests!

In this context the importance of the Council's cautious legitimation of conscientious objection should need no elaboration. It was not, of course, a "sensational" development; indeed, it is safe to say it went unnoticed by most commentators. *Gaudium et Spes* itself, it is well to note, did not get the attention it clearly deserved. It came toward the end of a long series of Council documents and pronouncements which had become, if not commonplace, familiar, and what notice it did receive understandably focused on the portions dealing with its concerns about the nature of modern war and its increasingly destructive weaponry. Had the Council Fathers made what should have been the logical link between those concerns and the possibility of Christians' refusing to participate in modern war and use those weapons, more attention might have been paid.

To Archbishop Roberts, the schema's recommendation that governments should positively favor the rights of conscience in making their laws (substantially what was included in the document finally approved) was "lamentably weak and insufficient." In an intervention prepared for presentation to the Council, he focused on the witness of Franz Jaegerstaetter, an Austrian peasant beheaded in 1943 for refusing to serve in the military forces of the Third Reich. "What we must do here," he declared, "is to give clear testimony that the Church affirms the right of the individual conscience to refuse unjust military service, and assure those of the Faithful who bear such witness that they will always have her fullest support." Pleading with his peers to accept this man's sacrifice as a source of inspiration, the archbishop saw it as "perhaps the major scandal of Christianity" that over the course of centuries "almost every national hierarchy in almost every war has allowed itself to become the moral arm of its own government, even in wars later recognized as palpably unjust."[16]

The Council's modest statement certainly did not represent the "break with this tragic past" called for in the Roberts intervention and was far from his desired "clear and unambiguous affirmation of the right and the obligation of each Christian to obey the voice of his informed conscience before and during a time of war." Even so, it created an atmosphere in which the issue could be discussed, by implying, if not directly affirming, the legitimacy of that stand as an option for Catholics.

If nothing else, it reduced (though it did not eliminate) the influence of the Pius XII Christmas message as a decisive factor in such discussions. As already noted, that message was issued at the time the resumption of conscription was being debated in West Germany. A particularly contested feature of that debate was the section dealing with the issue of conscientious objection as it might, or might not, apply to Catholics. Only two prominent theologians were willing to support that possibility publicly. After the pope's Christmas message, however, one of them felt obliged to remain silent on the issue in deference to papal opinion, even though he considered it wrong. The Council's "corrective" action came too late to contribute to the German debate (which, incidentally, was resolved in favor of would-be Catholic objectors), but it made it less likely that similar obstructions might apply elsewhere as the result of mistakenly attributed papal infallibility.

There is no way, of course, of measuring the extent to which *The Church in the Modern World's* opening inspired, or even contributed to, the great increase in the number of Catholics claiming recognition as conscientious objectors in the Vietnam war. Most likely, whatever influence it had was indirect; once something previously regarded as "radical" and possibly "heretical" becomes a matter open to discussion and consideration, one can expect a certain number will be attracted to it. In this case, of course, the nature of the war itself must be taken into account and, possibly the strongest influence of all, the dramatic growth of a recognizably Catholic antiwar movement. With priests and nuns going to jail for actively protesting against the war, it became a more reasonable option for draft-eligible Catholics to refuse to accept orders to military service.

Inspiration or not, the statement was helpful to many in establishing the legitimacy of their claims. There may still have been priests (and draft boards) willing to declare that Catholics could not be conscientious objectors, but it was difficult to maintain that position when it came to actual classification procedures or (as was still necessary in far too many instances) appeals from unfavorable decisions at the local level.

THE EMERGENCE OF SELECTIVE CONSCIENTIOUS OBJECTION

The Council's affirmation has been superseded, of course, by subsequent and stronger statements from bishops, whether speaking individually or in national conferences, and even in papal allocutions.

The church has moved on to a posture somewhat similar to that called for by Archbishop Roberts, and the 1983 pastoral letter of the United States hierarchy gives promise that, given the escalating danger of a war that is clearly forbidden, endorsement of conscientious objection as the *preferred* option for the Catholic is not out of the question. That possibility is already foreshadowed in the pastoral's declaration that "no Christian can rightfully carry out orders or policies deliberately aimed at killing noncombatants."[17] With the development and deployment of area-destroying weapons, it is becoming ever more obvious that the direct killing of noncombatants can no longer be avoided, whatever the declared intention might be.

The traditional linkage of conscientious objection and pacifism no longer holds. It is obvious that the total rejection of war as incompatible with the Christian message and mission imposes the obligation to refuse to serve in war—and this, one suspects, is the kind of objection the Council Fathers had in mind. Today the issue has broadened to one of *selective* conscientious objection as a logical consequence of the church's traditional "just war" teachings.

Already in the period before the Second World War moralists had recognized (though not all were ready to draw the necessary conclusions) that modern war could no longer meet the carefully delineated "conditions" of the presumably "just" war. The German Dominican, Fr. Franziskus Stratmann, was perhaps the best known of those who developed the position, but there were many others as well. In this country, Msgr. Paul Hanly Furfey and the noted Trappist, Thomas Merton, shunned the classification of "pacifist" but recognized the impossibility of any modern war meeting the Thomistic conditions.

Furfey and Merton followed through by endorsing the conscientious objection position and provided support and encouragement to those who took it. (Indeed, Merton had seriously considered doing so himself before his decision to enter the Gethsemane monastery.) It is not all that clear that Stratmann—and certainly not the thousands of German Catholics who joined the *Friedensbund* he helped organize—gave much thought to the behavorial implications of his writings. German military traditions left no place for conscientious objection, and once Hitler came to power the refusal to serve was made a capital crime. The new German draft, as noted above, does make provision for such exemption and there is evidence that many Catholics have taken advantage of it.

But the problem of "selectivity" remains for them as it does for us. *Gaudium et Spes* makes no reference to the distinction, quite possibly because it was locked into the expectation that this was the only version likely to affect Catholic behavior. Since Vatican II, of course, there has been a resurrection of a more thoroughgoing pacifism among Catholics, and the refusal to serve in a war which did not meet the conditions of a "just war" has now been joined by a position which holds that it is wrong for the Christian to serve in any war at all.

BEYOND VATICAN II: "THE CHALLENGE OF PEACE"

If *Gaudium et Spes* were written today, there would have to be much more than a suggestion seemingly made "in passing" that governments make some provision for conscientious objection. The American bishops' pastoral takes it as a starting-point, but credits the Council with an emphasis which may go beyond what was intended at the time. It speaks of "the stress it placed on the requirement for proper formation of conscience" as "a dominant characteristic" of the Council's evaluation of modern warfare. True, that characteristic was present and dominant, but it was not as directly linked to the conscientious objection issue as that reference would suggest. And when the bishops elaborate upon the implications they see ("Moral principles are effective restraints on power only when policies reflect them and individuals practice them. The relationship of the authority of the state and the conscience of the individual on matters of war and peace takes a new urgency in the face of the destructive nature of modern war"),[18] they come much closer to the real issue that was not so obvious then but would probably have to be the central point of debate today.

Weapons designed for committing (or at least threatening to commit) that "offense against God and man himself" have increased in number, in potency, and in efficiency of delivery over the past two decades. The Fathers of the Council must have anticipated some development but they cannot be blamed for not anticipating its full extent and the danger of total annihilation it now presents. As they looked at the whole problem of nuclear deterrence they saw it almost exclusively in terms of *possession*. Some of those "lobbyists for peace" tried to present the issue in the perspective of *preparation* instead, but without much success.[19]

Had the effort succeeded, the conscientious objection provisions would have been (or should have had to be) quite different. It is not just that such weapons exist, not even that they are at hand for possible use; what is important and deserved much more attention than it was given then (or has received since) is that *individuals, many of them Christians, are actually preparing to put them to their forbidden use under command.*

In our own country today, Catholics are serving and being trained to serve on Trident submarines carrying missiles already targeted to do what *Gaudium et Spes* condemns; Strategic Air Command bombers are "on the ready" around the clock, loaded with warheads infinitely more powerful than the bombs which destroyed Hiroshima and Nagasaki; missile silos, with Catholics and other Christians set to turn the key or press the button that will "take out" several population centers, already await the "Peacemakers"[20] designed to multiply the destructive potential those silos already contain.

Nor should we focus our concern on nuclear weapons exclusively. The current administration is most persistent in its efforts to resume research and manufacture of poison gas and the exploration of other categories of chemical and bacteriological weapons. The justification offered stresses the fact that potential enemies are doing these things and that it is essential to "national security" that this nation not fall behind. The moral strictures set forth in *Gaudium et Spes* (and echoed in the American Roman Catholic bishops' 1983 pastoral) are, in effect, irrelevant and do not enter into the policy-and-planning equation at all.

In this context, that incidental reference to the legitimacy of conscientious objection takes on a significance far beyond anything the Council realized. If the issue were to be reopened today, one suspects the debate would not be whether governments should make provision for such a stand but, instead, whether the church should declare that stand the most, perhaps the *only*, appropriate stand for the responsible Christian to take.

EVALUATING WAR WITH AN ENTIRELY NEW ATTITUDE

One cannot say how that debate would be resolved, but *Gaudium et Spes* can take credit for providing the starting-point, "lamentably weak and insufficient" though it may have been. Unfortunately, there is little to indicate that, even if those far-reaching implications were taken seriously, the church would be prepared to translate them into the specifics of required, or even recommended, practice.

The "evaluation of war with an entirely new attitude" that the Council Fathers claimed they were forced to make stopped short of what was needed and has not been completed even yet. If the situation has changed from what they described, the changes have been in the wrong direction. As they saw it then, "The men of our time must realize that they will have to give a somber reckoning for their deeds of war. For the course of the future will depend largely on the decisions they make today."[21]

Those decisions, in their turn, depend to a great extent upon how we who claim to be Christian react to the policies and politics which have brought us to the brink of annihilation. And how we, especially we who are Catholic, react will depend upon the direction and the quality of leadership provided by the church.

Gaudium et Spes took up the challenge presented by *Pacem in Terris*. It is significant that the "entirely new attitude" passage carries a footnote reference to the encyclical. If it failed to meet the challenge completely, it is because its response was an attitude that was not *entirely* "new." Instead, by holding on to the "just war" tradition—discredited though it already was by the experience of two world wars and, even more, by the dread promise of even greater excesses certain to be experienced in any future war—the Council Fathers effectively blocked any serious consideration of what should have been seen as a possible alternative, the return to the absolute commitment to the pacifism and nonviolence that characterized the earliest Christian centuries.

From the time of Pius XII, the official leadership of the Catholic church has recognized the dangers we face and has made a consistently commendable effort to call attention to the moral dimensions of the problem. At the same time, however, it has been reluctant to divorce itself from pragmatic political considerations. The result, all too often, is a bizarre combination of outright denunciation of evil and toleration of the instrumentalities of evil. When the choice had to be made, it was most likely to be prudence over prophecy.

If, in the words of John Paul II, "the scale and the horror of modern warfare—whether nuclear or not—makes it totally unacceptable as a means of settling differences between nations,"[22] one would look for that statement to be coupled with one defining *participation in war* as behavior "totally unacceptable" for the Christian. Such, alas, has not been forthcoming. It is not enough to say that war should be relegated "to the tragic past, to history," or that "it should find no place on humanity's agenda for the future,"[23] without calling upon the Catholic faithful to make certain that they have no part in it.

The fervent appeals for balanced disarmament and for an international world order capable of achieving peace through justice deserve the fullest support. The contributions made by *Gaudium et Spes* (and by *Pacem in Terris* before it) in giving emphasis to these as objectives of highest priority should not be minimized. But whether they are achieved or not has little bearing upon the issue of whether the followers of Christ can ever be permitted to turn to violence to gain even such praiseworthy goals.

To do him justice, there are times when Pope John Paul II comes close to making such a declaration. At Drogheda, for instance, he proclaimed the following:

> ... with the conviction of my faith in Christ and with an awareness of my mission, that violence is evil, that violence is unacceptable as a solution to problems, that violence is unworthy of man. Violence is a lie, for it goes against the truth of our faith, the truth of our humanity. Violence destroys what it claims to defend: the dignity, the life, the freedom of human beings. Violence is a crime against humanity, for it destroys the very fabric of society.[24]

It is fairly obvious that he was thinking of the violence that has disrupted life in Ireland for generations. Even so, the generality of his denunciation is such that it becomes applicable (or one would be quite justified in thinking so) to war, the ultimate expression of violence. In that same discourse he addressed young people and pleaded with them not to speak the language of hatred, revenge, and retaliation, not to follow leaders who would train them in the ways of inflicting death. And in what seems a direct reversal of a familiar platitude (without justice there is no real peace) often employed as a reluctant justification of war, he continued, "Do not think that courage and strength are proved by killing and destruction. The true courage lies in working for peace ... *Violence is the enemy of justice. Only peace can lead the way to justice.*"[25]

Whether so intended or not, such statements can be read as a fuller exposition of the brief reference to the renunciation of violence in vindication of rights in *Gaudium et Spes*. That reference, however, included what some might see as a crucial escape clause: "provided that this can be done without injury to the rights and duties of others or of the community itself."[26] It is, therefore, one of the truly significant contributions of the 1983 pastoral that it presents a case for nonviolence as a feasible and potentially effective form of "popular defense."[27] No less important is its emphasis on the need for study and research to develop the training programs and organized support such alternatives to war would require.

To the extent this appeal is heard and acted upon, it is possible that *Gaudium et Spes'* seemingly innocuous references to conscientious objection and nonviolence may prove to be the key to that "entirely new attitude" proposed by Vatican II. In reality, of course, if the pacifist interpretation possesses the validity I would claim for it, that attitude is not "entirely *new*." Instead it would represent a belated return to the *old*, the original attitude of the Christian.

The American Roman Catholic bishops seem to sense this too. In what may be the most inspiring, even prophetic, passage in their pastoral. *The Challenge of Peace*, they declare: "To be a Christian, according to the New Testament, is not simply to believe with one's mind, but also to become a doer of the word, a wayfarer with and a witness to Jesus. This means, of course, that we never expect complete success within history and that we must regard as normal even the path of persecution and the possibility of martyrdom."[28]

Wayfarer and witness! What does this mean? One who understood the meaning of those terms and who would have welcomed the bishops' reminder was Thomas Merton. Years before, in one of his essays, he had written:

> The Christian is and must be by his very adoption as a son of God, in Christ, a peacemaker. (Matthew 5:9). He is bound to imitate the Savior who, instead of defending Himself with twelve legions of angels (Matthew 26:53) allowed Himself to be nailed to the Cross and died praying for His executioners. The Christian is one whose life has sprung from a particular spiritual seed: the blood of the martyrs who, without offering forcible resistance, laid down their lives rather than submit to the unjust laws that demanded an official religious cult of the Emperor as God. That is to say, the Christian is bound, like the martyrs, to obey God rather than the state whenever the state tries to usurp powers that do not and cannot belong to it. We have repeatedly seen Christians in our time fulfilling this obligation in a heroic manner by their resistance to dictatorships that strove to interfere with the rights of their conscience and of their religion.

Unfortunately, as he goes on to say, "We are no longer living in a Christian world."[29]

It is perhaps not accidental that the paragraph in which the American Roman Catholic bishops define the meaning of *Christian* opens with a similar observation. They say, "It is clear today, perhaps more than in previous generations, that convinced Christians are a minority in nearly every country of the world—including nominally Christian and Catholic nations."[30] It remains to be seen whether the bishops' words will receive the serious and prayerful hearing they deserve. If they do, there is reason to hope we may yet find our way back and that our response to what the bishops set forth as "the challenge of peace" may save humanity from the "global suicide" freely chosen which, in Merton's words, would be "a moral evil second only to the Crucifixion."[31]

If we succeed, part of the credit will belong to those two generally unnoticed (and where noticed, usually ignored) passages in *Gaudium et Spes*. And we will succeed if, as Christians, we are prepared to commit ourselves to the renunciation of violence with the same confidence in the love and power of God that inspired the earliest followers of Christ.

This twentieth anniversary of the Council's great work is also the fortieth anniversary of the bombings of Hiroshima and Nagasaki, the events described by Paul VI as "butchery of untold magnitude."[32] It is appropriate, then, to recall the words of his successor, the present Holy Father, on the occasion of his visit to the scene of that butchery.

"War," he declared, "is the work of man. War is destruction of human life. War is death." The entire address was an appeal for the renunciation of war and for everyone to recognize the obligation to work toward its elimination. "To remember Hiroshima is to commit oneself to peace. To remember what the people of this city suffered is to renew our faith in man, in his capacity to do what is good, in freedom to choose what is right, in his determination to turn disaster into a new beginning. In the face of the man-made calamity that every war is, one must affirm and reaffirm, again and again, that the waging of war is not inevitable or unchangeable. Humanity is not destined to self-destruction."[33]

The most effective way of affirming something, we must remember, is by action—or, as in the case of conscientious objection, refusing to perform actions contrary to the values and truths one seeks to affirm. If we are to overcome war and the threat of war, all of us—popes, bishops, and ordinary people in the pews—must begin to practice what we preach. Perhaps we must go even deeper. The problem may be that we do not really believe what we preach or, the most troubling possibility of all, do not actually believe what we *believe* we believe. Today, in this nation with its seemingly total commitment to an escalating arms race, those brief references to conscientious objection and nonviolence in *Gaudium et Spes* might provide us with a revealing test of how many of us who claim to be Christian are ready to affirm the Church's repudiation of war by their actions.

NOTES

1. John XXIII, *Pacem in Terris*, issued April 11, 1963. The text citations are taken from David J. O'Brien and Thomas A. Shannon, eds., *Renewing the Earth: Catholic Documents on Peace, Justice, and Liberation* (New York: Image Books, 1977). Further citations will be indicated by the letters *PT*.

2. *PT*, no. 113. Italics mine.

3. *Pastoral Constitution on the Church in the Modern World* (*Gaudium et Spes*), document of the Second Vatican Council issued by Pope Paul VI on December 7, 1965. Text citations are from O'Brien and Shannon, *Renewing the Earth*. Further citations will be indicated by the letters *GS*. This reference is from no. 75.

4. National Conference of Catholic Bishops, *The Challenge of Peace: God's Promise and Our Response* (Washington, D.C.: United States Catholic Conference, 1983), especially nos. 167-99.

5. *GS*, no. 80.

6. *Periti* were the officially designated advisors to the bishops attending the Council. As a "titular" archbishop (he had resigned some years before as the Archbishop of Bombay), Roberts was not provided with such *peritus* privileges. To make up for this, Richard Carbray, an old friend of the archbishop, and I volunteered our assistance—Carbray as Latinist for the full duration of the Council and I as a short-term advisor on the question of conscientious objection, one of the archbishop's special interests.

7. *GS*, no. 82.

8. *GS*, no. 79.

9. *GS*, no. 78.

10. "Lobbyist" may be too imposing a term. A number of American Catholics took it upon themselves to travel to Rome to deliver personal and group petitions in support of issues they believed crucial to the causes of peace and justice. For instance, a number of women (led by Dorothy Day, Eileen Egan, and others involved in peace activities and service to the poor) engaged in a prayer vigil and fast while Schema 13, the draft of what became *Gaudium et Spes*, was being discussed. At one point, their presence and action were brought to the (favorable) attention of the Council. The proceedings were surprisingly open. The actual sessions, of course, were closed (except for the presence of official *periti*), but otherwise the bishops were generally disposed to meet with outsiders, even to the point of accepting their help. James Douglass, for example, has been credited with participating in the preparation of several interventions given by bishops at the Council. In my own case, I had the opportunity to speak with the combined English hierarchy at one of their luncheon gatherings and conferred with a few of the U.S. bishops, in addition to advising Archbishop Roberts on the intervention he wished to submit.

11. *PT*, no. 51.

12. *PT*, no. 127.

13. Perhaps the best known (and most often cited) resource in this area is R.H. Bainton, *Christian Attitudes toward War* (Nashville: Abingdon Press, 1966). Stanley Windass, *Christianity versus Violence* (London: Sheed and Ward, 1964) is unfortunately out of print. C. John Cadoux, *The Early Christian Attitude to War* (New York: Winston Press, 1982) and Jean-Michel Hornus, *It Is Not Lawful for Me to Fight* (Scottsdale, Penna.: Herald Press, 1980), are other valuable resources, the latter especially so because of its comprehensive footnotes.

14. Cadoux, *The Early Christian Attitude to War*, 256.

15. Gordon C. Zahn, *Another Part of the War: The Camp Simon Story* (Amherst: University of Massachusetts Press, 1979) is a semi-autobiographical

account of the brief history of the only Catholic Civilian Public Service camp for conscientious objectors to World War II. Several chapters are devoted to the CPS program and its shortcomings in this respect.

16. Although the text of the Roberts intervention is part of the published record of the Council, he did not have the opportunity to make an oral presentation in the *aula*. The debate schedule for the section dealing with conscientious objection was shortened; although he had been definitely scheduled and his speaking privilege strengthened by a petition with the required number of signatures, he was not called. Though it probably had no bearing on this disappointing development, Roberts was widely regarded as something of a maverick— not only for his strong endorsement of conscientious objection but, even more, for his willingness to support the possibility that the contraceptive "pill" could ultimately be approved under church teachings. An interesting sidelight to all this was the comment made to me shortly before the opening of the first session of the Council. The Jesuit director of the Creighton University Peace Institute excused his early departure from a conference we were attending by explaining he was on his way to Rome to protest the participation of "a pinko archbishop from Bombay" in the Council deliberations! Fortunately, he did not succeed in that purpose.

17. *The Challenge of Peace,* no. 148.

18. Ibid., no. 231.

19. James Douglass was particularly effective in promoting this distinction in his discussions with bishops during the Council. Though he succeeded in convincing some, the approved version of *Gaudium et Spes* failed to make the distinction.

20. President Reagan's insistence upon using this name for the hotly contested MX missile which the U.S. Catholic Conference (and Cardinals Bernardin and O'Connor in separate statements) criticized as a dangerously destabilizing weapons system is an example of the "crisis of language" described by Thomas Merton. "The illness of political language—which is almost universal and is a symptom of a Plague of Power that is common to China and America, Russia and Western Europe—is characterized everywhere by the same sort of double-talk, tautology, ambiguous cliché, self-righteous and doctrinaire pomposity, and pseudoscientific jargon that mask a total callousness and moral insensitivity, indeed a basic contempt for man." The complete essay is well worth reading and can be found in the collection of Merton's writings on peace, *The Nonviolent Alternative* (New York: Farrar, Straus, and Giroux, 1980).

21. *GS,* no. 80.

22. John Paul II, homily at Bagington Airport, Coventry, England, May 30, 1982.

23. Ibid.

24. John Paul II, homily at Drogheda, Republic of Ireland, September 29, 1979.

25. Ibid. Italics mine.

26. *GS,* no. 78.

27. *The Challenge of Peace,* see especially nos. 221-30.

28. Ibid., no. 276.

29. Thomas Merton, "Peace: Christian Duties and Perspectives" (in *The Nonviolent Alternative*). This was a favorite paragraph for Merton, repeated in at least two other essays in that collection.

30. *The Challenge of Peace,* no. 276.

31. Merton, "Peace: A Religious Responsibility," 124.

32. Paul VI, World Day of Peace Message, 1976.

33. John Paul II, speech at Peace Memorial Park, Hiroshima, Japan, February 25, 1981.

JUDITH A. DWYER, S.S.J.

Beyond Vatican II: The American Catholic Hierarchy and Modern Warfare

This chapter assesses the significance of the teaching of *Gaudium et Spes* on modern warfare by investigating the impact of the conciliar document on subsequent American Roman Catholic hierarchical statements and by indicating where the American Catholic hierarchy now presses beyond conciliar thought.[1] Although American Protestant churches have issued important statements regarding modern warfare, as have Catholic episcopal conferences in Europe and the British Isles,[2] I limit the scope of this chapter to the American Catholic hierarchical situation for two reasons. First, the recent American Catholic bishops' pastoral letter, *The Challenge of Peace: God's Promise and Our Response*, continues to generate much debate, particularly within the academic community.[3] Second, being "Catholic" and yet living in superpower "America" is an experience that provides its own unique set of problems, a situation documented by numerous American Catholic historians and theologians and explicitly recognized by the bishops is their letter.[4] This chapter, therefore, inspects the significance of Vatican II from the lens of the American Roman Catholic church—an American church which both draws from the richness of the universal church and contributes to that richness; an American church situated in a superpower country whose political/military decisions have global ramifications.

"GAUDIUM ET SPES" ON MODERN WARFARE

How does Vatican II clarify and advance church teaching regarding the morality of modern warfare?[5] A first important point is that the Council continues to recognize the legitimacy of certain types of warfare and does so without amending *Pacem in Terris*, the 1963 encyclical issued by Pope John XXIII.[6] This conciliar affirmation of the traditional right of a nation to engage in legitimate defense once every means of peaceful settlement had been exhausted (no. 79), clarifies the controversy over *Pacem in Terris* and the interpretation that John XXIII had refuted the possibility of just war in modern times.[7] The Council, however, is also cautious; it distinguishes just defense from the desire to subjugate other nations; it recognizes the fact that not every military or political use of war potential is lawful (no. 79).

Second, although *Gaudium et Spes* does not explicitly situate its treatment of war under the more general "just war tradition," this tradition certainly permeates the document.[8] *Jus ad bellum* criteria are evident in several ways. Having admitted the possibility of a just war in modern times, *Gaudium et Spes* further stipulates that this war must be *defensive in nature* and must be declared only after every means of peaceful settlement has been exhausted (*last resort*). Likewise, the document affirms the role of *legitimate authority* with its awesome responsibilities in this complex era and its duty to protect the people entrusted to its care.

Gaudium et Spes unambiguously denounces any act of war (conventional or nuclear) aimed indiscriminately at cities and their populations (no. 80). Implicit in this teaching is the traditional *jus in bello* principle of discrimination, although the document does not explicitly use such phrases as "noncombatant immunity" or "direct attack against the innocent." The Council, therefore, does not elaborate on why indiscriminate warfare (with either conventional or nuclear weapons) is morally wrong, although one may presume that such massive and direct killing of innocent persons is what constitutes that crime against God and humanity about which the Council speaks. Indeed, in the paragraph preceding this condemnation (no. 79), the Council opens its entire discussion of war by recalling the "permanent binding force of universal natural law and its all-embracing principles" and declaring that "actions which deliberately conflict with these principles, as well as orders commanding such actions are criminal." This appeal to the natural law and its proscription against the direct killing of innocent human life surely provides the underpinning for the document's subsequent condemnation of indiscriminate bombing.

Gaudium et Spes does not explicitly invoke the *jus in bello* principle of proportionality, but its teaching that "massive and indiscriminate destruction far exceeds the bounds of legitimate defense" touches on this principle of proportionality and is implicit in the Council's proscription against "total war" (no. 80).

While all these components of just war theory are present in *Gaudium et Spes*, the document does not, however, sufficiently make this evident. A more explicit situation of the entire topic under the general umbrella of "just war tradition" would have more clearly indicated both the reasoning behind conciliar teaching and the indispensability of the theory itself when undertaking an ethical evaluation of modern warfare.

The Council's failure to condemn the use of nuclear weapons as *malum in se* (evil in itself) constitutes a third significant aspect of *Gaudium et Spes*. While condemning total warfare and indiscriminate warfare, that is, certain acts of war, the Council refrains from an outright proscription against the use of nuclear weapons, a particular weapon of war.[9]

A fourth important point in conciliar teaching surrounds the issue of deterrence. To its credit, Vatican II evidences a sensitivity to the precarious balance of power in the international community and to the nuclear deterrent which is integral to that balance. In contrast to Pius XII and John XXIII, who actually said very little about deterrence,[10] *Gaudium et Spes* at least attempts to address the problem and does so by situating the debate. The Council acknowledges that weapons are not amassed solely for war and notes that many contend that the deterrent has maintained a peace of a sort. The Council does not embrace this reasoning but simply admits the argument as indicative of a school of thought. *Gaudium et Spes* quickly adds that this balance is not a safe way to preserve a steady peace and that the causes of war threaten to grow gradually stronger. But the Council stops short of condemning deterrence.

Several questions, however, plague *Gaudium et Spes'* treatment of the issue. Implicit in the Council's statement is that an "amassment of weapons" constitutes the deterrent. The Council does not elaborate or delineate on the "type" of deterrent used in the early 1960s, namely, a "mutual assured destruction" deterrent and its threat to enemy populations. This omission is significant since the Council clearly condemns the indiscriminate bombing of cities but fails to address the fact that the deterrent rests upon the threat to attack Soviet cities (values) directly, should the deterrent fail. The Council therefore does not venture into important distinctions within deterrent theory and thus neglects to distinguish between countercity (value) deterrence and flexible counterforce deterrence. Likewise, the "intention" behind possessing such massive nuclear weapons is not analyzed. Is there a distinction, as some theorists hold, between "intention to deter" with nuclear weapons and "intention to use" nuclear weapons?[11] The Council, therefore, does not attempt to answer all the moral questions involved in deterrence and instead chooses to remain vague about certain implications of the amassment of weapons which maintains a "peace of a sort." While it is appropriate that the Council not attempt to provide easy answers to this most complicated issue, the decision not to probe more deeply into the question of deterrence indicates why subsequent study of the issue by hierarchy and theorists had to confront so many fundamental questions.

·A fifth important conciliar development is *Gaudium et Spes'* assessment of the arms race. Building on earlier pronouncements by John XXIII,[12] the document denounces the arms race as "an utterly treacherous trap for humanity" which injures the poor "to an intolerable degree" (no. 81). The Council then predicts that if the arms race persists, "it will eventually spawn all the lethal ruin whose path it is now making ready." Without elaboration, Vatican II calls for "new approaches" initiated by "reformed attitudes" in order to remove this trap and to emancipate the world from its "crushing anxiety." The Council encourages humanity to make use of the "interlude" to find means for resolving disputes in a manner more "worthy of man" than "the slavery of war"; the document also calls upon everyone to labor for the end of the arms race and for the time when all war can be completely outlawed by international consent.

The call to establish some "universal, public authority," acknowledged by all as such and endowed with effective power, constitutes a sixth aspect of *Gaudium et Spes'* treatment of this particular problem of special urgency (no. 82). Toward that end, the Council calls on international centers to devote themselves vigorously to the pursuit of peace—a peace born of mutual trust and not imposed by fear of another's weapons.

The document advances a seventh important aspect of its teaching when it calls for a disarmament process which proceeds at "an equal pace according to agreement and backed up by authentic and workable safeguards" (no. 82). The Council explicitly notes that it does not endorse unilateral disarmament but rather a program that would dismantle the armaments bilaterally. However, no concrete proposals for agreements or suggestions for "workable safeguards" are forthcoming.

An eighth and final important aspect of conciliar thought on modern warfare is its recognition of the need to undertake an evaluation of war with "an entirely new attitude" (no. 80). Hints of this new attitude appear when the Council, immediately after this call for a new attitude, notes that contemporary persons "must realize that they will have to give a somber reckoning for their deeds of war." Indeed, "the course of the future will depend largely on the decisions they make today." Then follows the condemnation of total war and indiscriminate acts of war against civilian populations. While the document refers to *Pacem in Terris* in its proscription against total war, its clear denouncement of both total warfare, and especially indiscriminate bombing of cities, is significant in hierarchical teaching. Pius XII had warned against weapons which "escape control," and John XXIII had denounced weapons of massive destruction,[13] but the specific condemnation of the use of weapons (conventional or nuclear) against an urban population makes the principle of discrimination very concrete for this contemporary era.

The Council's support of conscientious objection against specific acts of war which violate natural law (no.79) is an additional indication of the "new attitude" about which Vatican II speaks. For the first time, Catholic hierarchical teaching hails as courageous the right to refuse an unjust command by a military commander. Likewise, the Council's support for those who object to warfare in general, and who therefore practice nonviolence, represents a highly significant, tradition-breaking step in Catholic thought. This conciliar position, which refutes the earlier teaching of Pius XII on the matter,[14] recognizes the stance of those who, in conscience, believe all warfare to be immoral.

Although the Council left many unanswered questions regarding modern warfare, its teaching nevertheless became foundational for future Catholic analysis of this particular problem of special urgency. Development of conciliar thought, however, especially its call for an entirely new attitude toward warfare, came gradually and painstakingly, as witnessed by the evolution of thought which occurred within American Catholic hierarchical statements.

AMERICAN ROMAN CATHOLIC HIERARCHICAL TEACHING

The Challenge of Peace: God's Promise and Our Response, the most significant American Catholic episcopal letter to date on the morality of modern warfare, owes its ecclesial foundation and the starting-point for its moral arguments regarding modern warfare to *Gaudium et Spes*, a point clearly acknowledged in the letter's first section (nos. 5-26).[15]. Like the pastoral constitution itself, *Challenge of Peace* does not hesitate to address pressing contemporary issues. Note the bishops:

> Building peace within and among nations is the work of many individuals and institutions; it is the fruit of ideas and decisions taken in the political, cultural, economic, social, military and legal sectors of life. We believe that the Church, as a community of faith and social institution, has a proper, necessary and distinctive part to play in the pursuit of peace (no. 21).

Essential to the building of peace about which the bishops speak is an evaluation of a stark reality: the presence of 50,000 nuclear weapons scattered throughout the globe. It is this complicated subject matter which is the focus of the specific moral analysis found within the letter.

While I have written about *Challenge of Peace*'s analysis of the morality of using nuclear weapons elsewhere,[16] it may be helpful for our purposes here to summarize briefly the particular points in the 1983 letter which either reiterate Vatican II or press beyond conciliar teaching regarding the use of modern weapons.

Aware of the various strategies for fighting nuclear war, the bishops explicitly delineate their position in light of just-war principles, an attempt which improves upon the conciliar analysis of modern warfare and represents a fresh approach for American Catholic episcopal statements as well. Earlier pastoral letters, *Human Life in Our Day* (1968), *To Live in Christ Jesus: A Pastoral Reflection on the Moral Life* (1976), and John Cardinal Krol's congressional testimony in behalf of the United States Catholic Conference (1979) [hereafter cited as USCC], while important developments in American Catholic analysis of modern warfare, neglected to situate their investigations explicitly within the framework of traditional just-war theory.[17]

Challenge of Peace explicitly reiterates *Gaudium et Spes'* position when it unequivocally condemns counterpopulation warfare, whether conventional or nuclear (nos. 147-49). This conciliar condemnation, picked up in American Catholic episcopal documents *Human Life in Our Day* and *To Live in Christ Jesus*, as well as in Krol's 1979 congressional testimony, is now, however, more sharply cited as a violation of the traditional principle of discrimination. *Challenge of Peace*, moreover, specifically names certain groups within the human community who retain the right of immunity from direct military attack—"schoolchildren, hospital patients, the elderly, the ill, the average industrial worker producing goods not directly related to military purposes, farmers, and many others" (no. 108).

Challenge of Peace goes beyond Vatican II and any previous American Catholic episcopal statement when it condemns "first use" of nuclear weapons. The bishops "do not perceive any situation in which the deliberate initiation of nuclear warfare, on however restricted a scale, can be morally justified. Nonnuclear attacks by another state must be resisted by other than nuclear means" (no. 150). The rationale for this position is the bishops' "extreme skepticism" about the prospects of controlling nuclear exchange. The risk of escalation, rooted in human sinfulness and made readily accessible by the technology of the weapons systems, is so great that it leads the bishops to condemn initiating nuclear war (nos. 151-53). Implicit in this judgment is the assessment that the proximate danger of escalation outweighs any good which might be accomplished by first use of nuclear weapons. Initiation of nuclear warfare is therefore disproportionate.

The 1983 pastoral letter breaks additional new ground in moral analysis of modern warfare when it examines a third possible use of nuclear weapons—retaliatory, limited, counterforce exchange (nos. 157-61). In contrast to counterpopulation warfare, counterforce strategies target missiles directly against the enemy's combatant forces, military bases, and defense-related industries. The bishops question the real possibility of a "limited nuclear exchange" against the theoretical possibility and raise a series of questions which challenge the actual meaning of "limited." Once again, the bishops make a prudential judgment on the morality of "limited nuclear warfare" as they implicitly apply the principle of proportionality to the concrete situation. They reiterate their great skepticism that a limited nuclear exchange would remain limited for very long; they question whether such an exchange could hold a "reasonable hope of success" for bringing about justice and peace; they argue that "the burden of proof remains on those who assert that meaningful limitation is possible." Explicitly citing the principle of proportionality, the bishops reject any type of counterforce combat which would take place in heavily populated areas where massive civilian casualties would occur. Such a strike, while not intentionally indiscriminate, violates the just-war principle of proportionality.

The bishops, however, stop short of condemning every possible use of nuclear weapons as evil; like the conciliar document, they condemn certain actions of war rather than use of a specific weapon of war. I believe that the bishops refrain from an outright condemnation of any use of a nuclear weapon because of the dilemma of deterrence. Should the bishops unequivocally condemn any use of nuclear weapons, then deterrence becomes ineffective, an empty bluff, since the deterrent is credible only insofar as the enemy believes that some nuclear weapons will be used, should deterrence fail. Reflecting Vatican II's teaching and subsequent papal thought, *Challenge of Peace* neither condemns deterrence nor calls for unilateral disarmament (nos. 186, 205). Logically, then, the bishops must leave open the question of any use of nuclear weapons. They do not explicitly oppose every use of nuclear weapons; neither do they list any cases in which use would be considered moral. Capturing the paradox of the nuclear issue, that nuclear weapons are maintained in order to prevent use, the bishops deliberately leave a note of ambiguity regarding the moral licitness of any use of nuclear weapons.

Challenge of Peace's treatment of deterrence, the most complicated aspect of nuclear ethics, addresses some of the questions left unanswered in *Gaudium et Spes* and somewhat clarifies the American

Catholic episcopal position on this question. While a detailed analysis of the history of American episcopal teaching regarding deterrence goes beyond the scope of this chapter, it is important to note that previous positions ranged from an erroneous interpretation of Vatican II by Archbishop Peter Gerety who, during 1976 Congressional testimony on behalf of USCC, claimed that *Gaudium et Spes* had "tolerated" deterrence; to an unwitting (I believe) condemnation of deterrence in *To Live in Christ Jesus*, where the bishops proscribed not only the use of strategic weapons but *the threat to use them*; to Krol's 1979 testimony, which tried to blunt the earlier *To Live in Christ Jesus* condemnation. Here Krol interprets the 1976 pastoral letter as condemning the *declared intent to use* strategic nuclear weapons against civilian populations; Krol contends, however, that the church is willing to tolerate possession of nuclear weapons as the lesser of two evils, while disarmament negotiations proceed.[18]

Challenge of Peace renders a "strictly conditioned moral acceptance" of deterrence, a position which indicates the strong influence of Pope John Paul II's 1982 message to a special session of the United Nations (nos. 173-75),[19] since such terminology does not appear in earlier papal, conciliar, or American Catholic episcopal statements. The bishops' endeavor to apply John Paul's statement regarding the moral acceptability of deterrence to specific United States strategy, however, marks a significant advance in the moral analysis of deterrence by church hierarchy (no. 177). John Paul's teaching regarding deterrence, like the earlier conciliar position, remains rather general. Neither John Paul II nor *Gaudium et Spes* analyzes the type of deterrence strategy at work; likewise, they do not investigate the intention which lies behind the threat of deterrence. Similarly, previous American Catholic episcopal statements, although proscribing the threat to use strategic weapons against enemy populations (*To Live in Christ Jesus*, 1976) and the declared intent to use such weapons against civilians (Krol, 1979), did not apply this teaching to either traditional just-war theory or specific United States strategy. In *Challenge of Peace*, the bishops explicitly investigate counterpopulation and counterforce deterrent strategies in light of just-war principles of discrimination and proportionality; they also examine current government policies regarding deterrence.

Although the bishops give "a strictly conditioned moral acceptance" to deterrence, they clearly condemn any deterrent strategy which intends to kill the innocent directly (no. 178). Here they draw from the traditional principle of Catholic theology which holds that one ought not to do or intend to do that which is immoral. The intention to kill the innocent as part of a strategy of deterrence violates the just-war principle of discrimination. The bishops indicate, however, that government officials have assured them that it is not United States policy to target the Soviet civilian population as such or to use nuclear weapons deliberately for the purpose of destroying population centers (no. 179).

While such assurance honors the principle of discrimination, deterrence strategies must also adhere to the equally important *jus in bello* principle of proportionality. The bishops, therefore, question whether or not certain attacks on military targets or militarily significant industrial targets would involve "indirect" (that is, not directly intended) but massive civilian casualties. Citing the fact that the U.S. strategic nuclear targeting plan has identified sixty "military" targets within the city of Moscow and that 40,000 "military" targets for nuclear weapons have been identified in the whole of the Soviet Union, the bishops warn that such attacks, although not intentionally indiscriminate, could involve such massive civilian casualties that "in our judgment such a strike would be deemed morally disproportionate" (nos. 180-82). They also warn that counterforce targeting is often joined with a declaratory policy which conveys the notion that nuclear war is subject to precise, rational control—an argument about which the bishops have serious doubts (no. 184).

Despite these warnings, however, the bishops render a "strictly conditioned moral acceptance of deterrence," although they do not consider this strategy to be "adequate for a long-term basis for peace" (no. 186). The "conditioned" aspect of their acceptance is highly important and includes such factors as a rejection of the notion of nuclear "superiority"; support for an immediate, bilateral, verifiable halt to the arms race; a call for negotiated bilateral deep cuts in the present arsenals of the superpowers (nos. 187-91).

Although *Challenge of Peace* pushes far beyond both Vatican II's rather minimal assessment of deterrence and John Paul II's more general teaching on the matter, the American Catholic bishops still leave many aspects of the morality of deterrence unresolved. This fact is not lost on the bishops, who raise a series of questions in the document which remain unanswered:

> May a nation threaten what it may never do? May it possess what it may never use? Who is involved in the threat each superpower makes: government officials? or military personnel? or the citizenry in whose defense the threat is made (no. 137)?

The bishops recognize that threat is integral to the effectiveness of deterrence; they do not, however, explore the legitimacy of such a threat, a topic which Catholic theorists consistently address. Choosing not to entangle themselves in such analysis, the bishops assume that threat is necessary for credible deterrence and that this threat is explicit. The bishops do not judge who is involved in the threat which each superpower makes, but simply raise some possibilities: government officials, military personnel, the citizenry in whose defense the threat is made.

Beneath the query, "May it [a nation] possess what it may never use?," lies the complicated ethical dilemma surrounding the intention behind deterrence, as well as the suggestion of the nuclear bluff. Beyond their condemnation of the intention to use the missiles directly against innocent persons and their warning against any intention which would entail disproportionate damage, the bishops can say little more. It is impossible, despite the "declaratory policy" of the United States government, to know the actual intention which lies behind the threat of deterrence, since the actual planning and targeting policies to be followed in a nuclear attack remain classified information. Possession and threatened use of nuclear weapons do not necessarily mean that the United States intends to use the weapons in the manner publicly threatened. Preparations "to retaliate in a massive way if necessary" do not necessarily translate into the intention to use the weapons in such a fashion. Ambiguity, therefore, is the soul of deterrence, a strategy whose effectiveness is dependent upon whether or not the enemy perceives the threat to be credible.[20] The bishops state that *if* the intention behind deterrent strategy is either indiscriminate or disproportionate, then deterrence is immoral; *that* such is the case, the bishops do not and cannot know.

The bishops do not explicitly address the possibility that even if higher levels in the military/political structures do not intend to use the weapons indiscriminately or disproportionately, there still remains the "chain of command" and the distinct possibility that somewhere down that chain, the personnel who keep ready and who train with the weapons must intend to use them as the United States has threatened to use them. The bishops also do not take up the question of whether or not there can actually be a specific subject involved in deterrence, that is, one who can have subjective intentions, since the problem rests with the body politic and not with a concrete individual subject whose intention can be known to that subject and to God. In this case, one must rely on official public acts in order to determine intentionality, a reliance which forces the investigator back to the "declaratory policy" of the United States.[21] Since moral clarity on these issues is so difficult to achieve and since theorists are divided about moral resolutions to the dilemma of deterrence, the bishops choose not to probe these questions inherent in the paradox of deterrence.

In the end, have the American Catholic bishops embraced a nuclear bluff, as some theorists contend?[22] Such a strategy possesses nuclear weapons and threatens to use them, but in reality, does not intend to use them. Theoretically, the bishops do not advance a nuclear bluff because *Challenge of Peace* refrains from condemning every possible use of nuclear weapons as intrinsically evil. The letter leaves a "centimeter of doubt" about the morality of use.[23] In reality, however, the bishops cite no example of "use" which they deem to be moral. If in theory the bishops have not advanced a strategy of "nuclear bluff," it could be argued that for all practical purposes, they have embraced the bluff, given their assessment of current weapons technology. The bishops, however, deliberately shy away from being any more explicit regarding deterrence. They neither condemn the strategy nor call for unilateral disarmament, an action which could destabilize the international balance and provoke aggression. Logically, then, they issue a "strictly conditioned moral acceptance" of deterrence and refrain from explicitly declaring all uses of nuclear weapons to be intrinsically evil.

A final question prompted by the bishops' position on nuclear deterrence centers on their "strictly conditioned" moral acceptance. What happens if the conditions set down by the bishops, such as their opposition to first-strike weapons systems, remain unfulfilled? Recently, President Ronald Reagan won a significant congressional victory regarding the deployment of the MX missile—a system which several experts in strategic theory would place in the category of a "first-strike" weapons system.[24] In addition, efforts to develop Reagan's proposed "Strategic Defense Initiative" (or "Star Wars") program also continue, despite the fact that many American scientists have criticized the effort as a wasteful expense of federal funds and scientific talent that would have little chance of technical success.[25] Do such developments alter the bishops' "moral acceptance" of nuclear deterrence? *Challenge of Peace* is silent on this matter; the letter simply states "we cannot consider it [deterrence] adequate as a long term basis for peace."

In summary, the depth of analysis of deterrence found in *Challenge of Peace* far surpasses the rather meager treatment of the issue found in *Gaudium et Spes*—a development one would expect after a period of twenty years. Yet, the bishops' decision to issue a "strictly conditioned moral acceptance" of nuclear deterrence leaves certain key questions unresolved. It remains for subsequent hierarchical statements and further analysis by theorists to address these more complicated aspects of the dilemma of deterrence.

Challenge of Peace, in addition to deepening ethical analysis of nuclear warfare and deterrence, also reiterates Vatican II's endorsement of pacifism. The American Catholic bishops clearly distinguish pacifism as an option for individuals from the moral obligation incumbent upon public authority to protect the citizens entrusted to its care; a government threatened by armed aggression *must* defend its people and this defense includes the use of armed force, if necessary. This reasoning, based on just-war theory (a construct which evolved, in part, because of the Church's awareness of the sinfulness of humanity and the eschatological tension within which the church lives), precludes the Catholic Church from embracing nonviolence as its sole position.[26]

Finally, one could argue that *Challenge of Peace* itself is a direct outgrowth of Vatican II's mandate to evaluate war "with an entirely new attitude," but the 1983 letter's frequently mentioned call to develop a "theology of peace" more specifically reflects this conciliar hope. Section One of the letter describes some of the necessary components for such a theology:

> A theology of peace should ground the task of peacemaking solidly in the biblical vision of the kingdom of God, then place it centrally in the ministry of the Church. It should specify the obstacles in the way of peace, as these are understood theologically and in the social and political sciences. It should both identify the specific contributions a community of faith can make to the work of peace and relate these to the wider work of peace pursued by other groups and institutions in society. Finally, a theology of peace must include a message of hope (no. 25).

Seeds of a theology of peace are also present in Section Three of the 1983 document which suggests, among other things, the investigation of nonviolent means of conflict resolution, the need for unilateral initiatives on the part of the United States, and the formulation of international policy which will support the already present state of global interdependence (nos. 200-73). It is also in this section of the letter that the bishops, while acknowledging the current disordered world in which the superpowers exist, nonetheless call for new international structures of cooperation—structures required by the growing interdependence of the nations and people of the world, as well as the extragovernmental presence of multinational corporations.

Similarly, when specifying obstacles in the way of peace, an emerging theology must seriously consider *Challenge of Peace*'s concern regarding nuclear proliferation (no. 208), as well as the letter's call for prohibitions outlawing the production and use of chemical and biological weapons (no. 210). The document also expresses concern over the alarming increase in the production and sale of conventional weapons throughout the world (nos. 211-13) and calls for a balanced reduction of conventional forces (no. 218).

Finally, the development of a theology of peace and the ability to evaluate war with an entirely new attitude will be impossible without the type of prayer, penance, and education described in the fourth section of the pastoral letter. Conversion and a deeper sense of dependency on God, as well as a critical awareness of the complexity of these issues, are essential elements to shaping new attitudes which, in turn, reflect renewed hearts and minds.

CONCLUSION

The Second Vatican Council called upon the church to enter into dialogue with the modern world and to address the serious problems which confront the contemporary human community, one of which is the question of modern warfare. This conciliar vision sparked the American Roman Catholic bishops, who, up to that point, had said very little about the problem of modern warfare, despite their situation in a superpower country. Patriotism and support of government policies had tended to be the bishops' approach as a largely immigrant church struggled to be both "Catholic" and "American."[27] Gradually, however, through *Human Life in Our Day, To Live in Christ Jesus,* and the 1979 congressional testimony of John Cardinal Krol, there emerged certain pieces of teaching which both reflected the Council and indicated the growth of a critical episcopal spirit regarding certain policies of the United States government. *Challenge of Peace,* a sophisticated and subtle document, represents the most significant American Catholic episcopal statement to date on the problem of modern warfare; it also reflects a hierarchy which has "come of age" and which no longer hesitates to confront the United States government, when the bishops deem this, on principle, to be necessary. The 1983 pastoral letter builds on the eight significant points which *Gaudium et Spes* makes regarding modern warfare; it also pushes beyond the Council, for instance, in its analysis of first use and retaliatory counterforce use of nuclear weapons, and in its investigation of deterrence.

Ongoing ethical analysis of the complex topic of modern warfare must continue, however, in order that reasoned judgments may help to fashion political/military policy. The challenge to develop a theology of peace, which would provide the principles by which the church could view warfare with an entirely new attitude, represents a pressing demand now incumbent upon church hierarchy and theorists. "A better world is here for human hands and hearts and minds to make," note the

American Catholic bishops in closing (no. 337). Such a call, reflecting the spirit of Vatican II and the bishops' own hope in a bright future and in a God who wills it for us, awaits response from a church which finds itself, on pilgrimage, in the modern world.

NOTES

1. *Gaudium et Spes* as found in Joseph Gremillion, ed., *The Gospel of Peace and Justice: Catholic Social Teaching since Pope John* (Maryknoll, N.Y.: Orbis Books, 1976), 243-335. Documentation from *Gaudium et Spes*, which appears within the text of my chapter, cites the appropriate section number.

2. For an assessment of statements by various Protestant churches, see my "The Role of the American Churches in the Nuclear Weapons' Debate," in Paul Cole and William Taylor, eds., *The Nuclear Freeze Debate: Arms Control Issues for the 1980s* (Boulder, Colo.: Westview Press, 1983) and David A. Hoekema, "Protestant Statements on Nuclear Disarmament," *Religious Studies Review* 10 (April, 1984): 97-102. For a helpful summary and analysis of perspectives from Europe and the British Isles, see Francis X. Winters, "After Tension, Detente: A Continuing Chronicle of European Episcopal Views on Nuclear Deterrence," *Theological Studies* 45 (June, 1984): 343-51.

3. National Conference of Catholic Bishops, *The Challenge of Peace: God's Promise and Our Response* (Washington, D.C.: United States Catholic Conference, 1983). For examples of the response which the pastoral letter has generated among scholars, see the following works: Judith A. Dwyer, ed., *The Catholic Bishops and Nuclear War: A Critique and Analysis of the Pastoral, The Challenge of Peace* (Washington, D.C.: Georgetown University Press, 1984); Philip J. Murnion, ed., *Catholics and Nuclear War: A Commentary on the Challenge of Peace* (New York: Crossroad, 1983); James E. Dougherty, *The Bishops and Nuclear Weapons: The Catholic Pastoral Letter on War and Peace* (Hamden, Conn.: Archon, 1984).

4. See, for instance, Aaron I. Abell, *American Catholicism and Social Action: A Search for Social Justice* (New York: Doubleday, 1960); Charles E. Curran, *American Catholic Social Ethics: Twentieth Century Approaches* (Notre Dame, Ind.: University of Notre Dame Press, 1982); Dorothy Dohen, *Nationalism and American Catholicism* (New York: Sheed and Ward, 1967); John Tracy Ellis, "American Catholics and Peace: An Historical Sketch," in James S. Rausch, ed., *The Family of Nations* (Huntington, Ind.: Our Sunday Visitor Press, 1970), 13-39; David J. O'Brien, *American Catholics and Social Reform: The New Deal Years* (New York: Oxford University Press, 1968); *The Renewal of American Catholicism* (New York: Paulist Press, 1971). See also sections 2 and 4, United States Catholic Conference edition of *The Challenge of Peace*, where the American Catholic bishops specifically recognize the significance of their presence in a superpower nation.

5. For a more detailed analysis of this section, see my doctoral dissertation, "An Analysis of Nuclear Warfare in Light of the Traditional Just-War Theology:

An American Roman Catholic Perspective, 1945-1981" (Ph.D. dissertation, The Catholic University of America, 1983).

6. *Pacem in Terris,* as found in Joseph Gremillion, *The Gospel of Peace and Justice: Catholic Social Teaching since Pope John* (Maryknoll, N.Y.: Orbis Books, 1976), 201-41.

7. An erroneous English translation of the encyclical stated that "it is hardly possible to imagine that in the atomic era war could be used as an instrument of justice." A better translation reads, "Thus in this age which boasts of its atomic power, it no longer makes sense to maintain that war is a fit instrument with which to repair the violation of justice." *Pacem in Terris,* no. 127.

8. For a similar assessment, see J. Bryan Hehir, "The Just-War Ethic and Catholic Theology: Dynamics of Change and Continuity," in Thomas A Shannon, ed., *War or Peace? The Search for New Answers* (Maryknoll, N.Y.: Orbis Books, 1980), 15-39.

9. The first draft of Schema 13 (the section of *Gaudium et Spes* concerned with peace/war) actually read " . . . nevertheless, the use of arms, especially nuclear weapons, whose effects are greater than can be imagined and therefore cannot be reasonably regulated by men, exceeds all just proportion and therefore must be judged before God and man as most wicked," a statement which led most to believe that the Council had condemned the use of nuclear weapons. See John Connery, "War, Conscience, and the Law: the State of the Question," *Theological Studies* 31 (June, 1970): 290-91. The final version of the document, however, backs away from this outright condemnation, partly as a result of pressure exerted by a group of American Catholics. For an account of this, see Patricia F. McNeal, *The American Catholic Peace Movement: 1928-1972* (New York: Arno Press, 1978).

10. Pius XII's remarks regarding nuclear weapons focused on the question of use, especially given the weapons' immense power for destruction. John XXIII's statements distinguished "coexistence" from living together, recognized the deterrent, noted the economic ramifications of the enormous stocks of armaments and deplored the fact that the human community had to live in constant fear, since a conflagration might be set off by some uncontrollable and unexpected chance; they included, however, no substantial analysis of deterrence as such. See my "Analysis of Nuclear Warfare in Light of Traditional Just-War Theory," chap. 2, for an assessment of the teaching on modern warfare by both pontiffs.

11. See Robert A. Gessert and J. Bryan Hehir, *The New Nuclear Debate* (New York: The Council on Religion and International Affairs, 1976) for an elaboration of Hehir's distinction between intention to use and intention to deter. See also David Hollenbach, *Nuclear Ethics: A Christian Moral Argument* (New York: Paulist Press, 1983) for similar reasoning.

12. See John XXIII's *Mater et Magistra* and *Pacem in Terris,* as found in Gremillion, *The Gospel of Peace and Justice,* 143-241.

13. Pius XII, "Address to Delegates of the Eighth Congress of the World Medical Association," September 30, 1954 and found in *Acta Apostolicae Sedis* 46 (1954): 589; John XXIII, *Pacem in Terris,* no. 127.

236   *Judith A. Dwyer, S.S.J.*

14. Pius XII, "The Contradiction of Our Age: The Christmas Message of Pope Pius XII to the Whole World," December 23, 1956 in *The Pope Speaks* 3 (Spring, 1957): 331-46, with the specific reference at 343.

15. Documentation cites, within the text of this chapter, the relevant paragraphs from the United States Catholic Conference edition of *The Challenge of Peace*.

See also essays by David Hollenbach, "*The Challenge of Peace* in the Context of Recent Church Teachings," and J. Bryan Hehir, "From the Pastoral Constitution of Vatican II to *The Challenge of Peace*," both of which appear in the Murnion collection, *Catholics and Nuclear War*.

16. See my "*The Challenge of Peace* and the Morality of Using Nuclear Weapons," in Judith A. Dwyer, ed., *The Catholic Bishops and Nuclear War*, 3-21.

17. National Conference of Catholic Bishops, *Human Life in Our Day* (Washington, D.C.: United States Catholic Conference, 1968); *To Live in Christ Jesus: A Pastoral Reflection on the Moral Life* (Washington, D.C.: United States Catholic Conference, 1976); John Cardinal Krol, "SALT II: Statement of Support," *Origins* 9 (September, 1979): 195-99.

18. Peter Gerety, "The Ethics of International Relations," testimony before the Senate Foreign Relations Committee, January 21, 1976 in *Origins* 5 (February 5, 1976): 520-28; *To Live in Christ Jesus*, 34; John Cardinal Krol, "SALT II: Statement of Support," 16.

19. John Paul II, "Message, U.N. Special Session 1982," no. 3.

20. John Cardinal Krol once asked, "Is not deterrence to a large extent in the eye of the beholder?" See his "The Churches and Nuclear War," *Origins* 9 (September 27, 1979): 235-36.

21. One may argue that Ronald Reagan, as President of the United States, is the subject and that even though he threatens to use nuclear weapons against the Soviet Union, he may have no intention to do so. However, Reagan does not speak as an individual but as the highest official elected by the citizens of the United States, that is, as a representative of a political body. Therefore, one is again forced to the official government position on the matter, since no "subject" in the personal sense of the word exists.

22. See William V. O'Brien, "The Challenge of War: A Christian Realist Perspective," in Judith A. Dwyer, ed., *The Catholic Bishops and Nuclear War*, 37-63; "Proportion and Discrimination in Nuclear Deterrence and Defense," *Thought* 59 (March, 1984): 42-52, for an example of this thinking.

23. The phrases, "centimeter of doubt" and "centimeter of ambiguity" are those of J. Bryan Hehir, staff person to the National Conference of Catholic Bishops. He described the letter as leaving a "centimeter of doubt" on an NBC special, "The Bishops and the Bomb," May 15, 1983; see Tom Bethell, "The Bishops' Brain," *The American Spectator* (July, 1983): 3 for the phrase, "centimeter of ambiguity."

24. The American Catholic bishops, faithful to the position articulated in *Challenge of Peace*, urged Congress to reject the MX missile system. See "U.S. Bishops Urge Rejection of MX Missile," *Origins* 14 (March 28, 1985): 667, 669-70. See, for instance, Herbert Scoville, *MX: Prescription for Disaster* (Cambridge, Mass.: MIT Press, 1981) for an assessment of the MX as a first-strike system.

25. On the question of the Strategic Defense Initiative, see Kim McDonald, "Thousands of U.S. and Canadian Scientists Signal Their Opposition to 'Star Wars' Plan," *The Chronicle of Higher Education* 30 (June 12, 1985): 7, 10; Charles L. Glaser, "Star Wars Bad Even If It Works," *Bulletin of the Atomic Scientists* 41 (March, 1985): 13-16; Robert Jastrow, "The War against 'Star Wars'," *Commentary* 78 (December, 1984): 19-25, with responses in "Letters from Readers," *Commentary* 79 (March, 1985): 4-23; McGeorge Bundy, George F. Kennan, Robert S. McNamara, and Gerard Smith, "The President's Choice: Star Wars or Arms Control," *Foreign Affairs* 63(Winter 1984/85): 264-78. For a favorable assessment of the idea, see Zbigniew Brzezinski, Robert Jastrow, and Max M. Kampelman, "Defense in Space Is Not 'Star Wars'," *The New York Times Magazine*, January 27, 1985, 28ff. For an ethical analysis, see Gregory S. Kavka, "Space War Ethics," *Ethics* 95 (April, 1985): 673-91.

26. See Francis X. Meehan, "Nonviolence and the Bishops' Pastoral: A Case for the Development of Doctrine," in Judith A. Dwyer, ed., *The Catholic Bishops and Nuclear War*, 89-107, for an attempt to move beyond the complementary relationship between just-war teaching and nonviolence as it is articulated in *Challenge of Peace*. Notes Meehan, "The central thesis of this chapter is that the Church is moving, and I believe, must move to such a realistic evaluation of modern warfare that for all practical purposes it will become a Church of nonviolence" (p. 91). See Charles E. Curran, "Roman Catholic Teaching on Peace and War within a Broader Theological Context," *Journal of Religious Ethics* 12 (1984): 61-81, for a position similar to my own regarding pacifism and the broader church.

27. See Avery Dulles, "Vatican II and the American Experience of Church," in Gerald M. Fagin, ed., *Vatican II: Open Questions and New Horizons* (Wilmington, Del.: Michael Glazier, 1984), 38-57, for an informative study on the American Catholic experience before and after the Council. See also note 4 for documentation regarding the "Catholic" and "American" dilemma.

Contributors

James Gaffney, Ph.D. is Professor of Ethics at Loyola University in New Orleans. He is the author of many articles and of seven books, the latest of which is *Sin Reconsidered*. He is married and the father of two children.

William E. May, Ph.D. is Professor of Moral Theology at The Catholic University of America. A married layman, he and his wife are the parents of seven children, ranging in age from 14 to 26. He has written extensively on marriage, sexual ethics, and the natural law. He is the author of *Becoming Human: An Invitation to Christian Ethics; Human Existence, Medicine, and Ethics;* and most recently, *Catholic Sexual Ethics,* which he coauthored with Ronald Lawler, O.F.M.Cap. and Joseph Boyle, Jr.

James McGinnis, Ph.D. and **Kathleen McGinnis,** M.A. are the parents of three children and have done extensive work in the area of the social mission of the Christian family. Their publications include *Educating for Peace and Justice,* a three-volume manual for teachers, and *Parenting for Peace and Justice*. Both currently work at The Institute for Peace and Justice, St. Louis, and serve as peace education consultants for schools, seminaries, and religious communities.

Anne E. Patrick, S.N.J.M., Ph.D. is Assistant Professor of Religion at Carleton College, Northfield, Minn. She is the author of numerous articles on women and religion and is currently completing a book on the ethical and religious dimensions of George Eliot's fiction. She was founding president of the Washington Council of Women Religious (1971-73), and later chaired the Committee on Women in Church and Society of the National Assembly of Women Religious (1973-75). A Ph.D. graduate of the University of Chicago, she currently serves on the board of directors of the Catholic Theological Society of America.

Richard A. McCormick, S.J., S.T.D. is Rose F. Kennedy Professor of Christian Ethics at the Kennedy Institute of Ethics, Georgetown

University, and Research Associate at the Woodstock Theological Center. He is the author of numerous books and articles on ethical questions, including *How Brave a New World?*, *Ambiguity in Moral Choice*, and *Health and Medicine in the Catholic Tradition*. A past president of the Catholic Theological Society of America, he received the Society's Cardinal Spellman Award in 1969 as "Outstanding Theologian of the Year."

John Langan, S.J., Ph.D. is Research Fellow at Woodstock Theological Center, Washington, D.C. He coedited, with Alfred Hennelly, S.J., the Georgetown University Press volume, *Human Rights in the Americas: The Struggle for Consensus* and has written and lectured extensively on questions related to human rights and the history and current expressions of just war theory. In 1983, Langan was Visiting Assistant Professor of Social Ethics at Yale Divinity School; he currently serves as a consultant to Chemical Bank of New York and its training program in ethics for its executives.

Patrick J. Leahy, Vermont's junior senator, was first elected to the Senate in 1974—the only Democrat in the state's history to attain that office—and was reelected to a second term in 1980. He holds a law degree from Georgetown University Law Center, and is a member of four major Senate committees: Appropriations, Agriculture, Judiciary, and Intelligence. He has a strong interest in government efficiency and economy, agriculture, the environment, and control of nuclear weapons.

Daniel Rush Finn, Ph.D. is Dean of the School of Theology, Saint John's University, Collegeville, Minn., and President of the Midwest Association of Theological Schools. He is co-author, with Prentiss L. Pemberton, of *Toward a Christian Economic Ethic* and has contributed to the *Annual of the Society of Christian Ethics*, *Review of Social Economy*, and *New Catholic World*.

Manuel Velasquez, Ph.D. is Associate Professor of Philosophy at the University of Santa Clara. Publications include *Business Ethics: Concepts and Cases* and *Ethics: Theory and Practice*, coedited with C. Rostankowski, and essays in *Academy of Management Review* and *New Catholic World*. He is a frequent lecturer on business ethics and other problems related to the socioeconomic sphere.

Gordon C. Zahn, Ph.D. is National Director of the Pax Christi U.S.A. Center on Conscience and War, and professor emeritus at the

University of Massachusetts-Boston. Best known for his *In Solitary Witness: The Life and Death of Franz Jaegerstaetter,* he has also published *German Catholics and Hitler's Wars; War, Conscience and Dissent;* and *The Camp Simon Story.* Awards and honors include an honorary doctorate from LaSalle University, the Pax Christi Award from St. John's College, Collegeville, Minn., and the Distinguished Service Award from the Washington Theological Union.

Judith A. Dwyer, S.S.J., Ph.D. currently teaches at Weston School of Theology. Her publications include editing and contributing to the Georgetown University Press volume, *The Catholic Bishops and Nuclear War,* and essays in *Harvard Educational Review, Religious Studies Review,* and *New Catholic World.* She has lectured nationally on questions related to social ethics, particularly on the problem of nuclear warfare and deterrence.